The Political Anthropology of Internationalized Politics

The Political Anthropology of Internationalized Politics

Edited by
Sarah Biecker and Klaus Schlichte

ROWMAN & LITTLEFIELD
Lanham • Boulder • New York • London

Published by Rowman & Littlefield
An imprint of The Rowman & Littlefield Publishing Group, Inc.
4501 Forbes Boulevard, Suite 200, Lanham, Maryland 20706
www.rowman.com

6 Tinworth Street, London SE11 5AL, United Kingdom

British Library Cataloguing in Publication Data

A catalogue record for this book is available from the British Library

ISBN: HB 978-1-5381-4950-8
eBook 978-1-5381-4951-5

Library of Congress Control Number: 2020947573

ISBN 978-1-5381-4950-8 (cloth)
ISBN 978-1-5381-4992-8 (pbk)
ISBN 978-1-5381-4951-5 (electronic)

Contents

Acknowledgments

Political anthropology, and in particular its alleged "method" ethnography, have attracted some attention in the discipline of International Relations (IR) over the last ten years. But this has not yet let to a consolidation of what political anthropology would mean for the study of international politics.

We consider this volume to be an attempt of such a consolidation, and we see the realm of internationalized politics as the main field for which such an opening of mainstream IR is not only possible, but indeed necessary. In the fields of development, security, global health, and finance we observe more and more imbrications, layers, concatenations of actors, agendas, policies, and reactions that the still dominant institutionalist perspective of IR, even if enlarged by a perspective on non-state actors, is less and less apt to grasp. The dominant perspective, to aim for "global governance" with its functionalist teleology, denouncing any obstacle in its way as a pathology, has steadily lost plausibility over the last ten years. Political anthropology, we argue, can help the discipline to build new paradigms, but this time not as deduction from grand schemes but by closer looks on how the world is actually ruled and how forms, aims, and means of internationalized politics have already become.

The authors that have contributed to this book are all convinced, as a result of their research experience, that "going there" is not only a necessary step, but that there are many interesting lessons from political anthropology that IR scholars can benefit from when they study subjects in which "international" means layers and layers of symbolic codes, contradictory patterns of interaction, and, of course, a lot of political conflict. The theoretical results of these insights, we would argue, are not preordained. In fact, the encounter with political anthropology opens ways to new forms of empirical evidence and new ways of thinking, often beyond the well-trodden paths of IR theories.

This book would not have been possible without the means that both editors benefited from in the framework of the Priority Programme 1664 "Creativity and Adaptation in Africa," funded by the German Federal Government through the German Research Foundation (Deutsche Forschungsgemeinschaft, DFG). It was in our subproject on "Policing Africa" that we not only learned on the ground how complex internationalized politics are. We also got acquainted with a host of anthropologists with which we had regular meetings and often steamy debates. We do hope they benefited as much from our contradictions as we did from theirs.

We used means from this project for an international call, and the authors assembled in this volume have met twice in Bremen for discussing the topic, single drafts, and general ideas. We are grateful to the DFG for funding these meetings as well as our research, to the Hanse-Wissenschaftskolleg at Delmenhorst for hosting our group, and for all those that helped us to put this book together, in particular to Jude Kagoro, Marie Kübler, Claudia Herold, and Nino Manizhasvili.

Bremen and Berlin, in November 2020

Chapter 1

For an Extended Experience

The Political Anthropology of Internationalized Politics

Sarah Biecker and Klaus Schlichte

Do we need political anthropology for the study of international politics? We think, yes. Yet, while ontological and epistemological differences have become a favorite subject in International Relations (IR), we do not intend to add a further round of self-reflection and self-critical introspections on alleged "turns" to the discipline. Instead, we intend to summarize and outline steps, achievements, and promises of an encounter with another academic discipline that itself has undergone a lot of self-reflection and internal quarrels: *Ethnologie*, as it is called in German and French, social and political anthropology in English.

We do so because we are convinced that in times of ever more internationalized politics, IR has something to gain from this neighboring social science, as a number of contributions have shown (cf. Autesserre 2014; Devin and Hastings 2018; Franke Roos 2013; Feldman 2012; Sande Lie 2015). But it is also a result of our own discoveries, dealing with a—at first sight—rather marginal research subject, namely Uganda's police force. It turned out to be telling, we found, for what is at stake in internationalized politics.

The first discovery was about history: the Ugandan police is a colonial creation. This historicity matters enormously if we want to understand the symbols, the forms, and a number of practices of the Ugandan police still today. And this history is an international one: police forces in the British Empire were replete with officers who have worked on two or three, sometimes four different continents. The penal code that still is a core legal basis for policing in Uganda is itself a product of a long-standing foreign rule, first in Ireland, then in India, and later in British East Africa. The Ugandan police force thus has an international history, right from its colonial inception (Kagoro and Biecker 2014; Biecker and Schlichte 2015).

Our second discovery was about contemporary internationalization: how can we explain that the contemporary Ugandan police are so internationalized on various levels? Their official language is English, and a number of British police institutions have been conserved within it, at least formally. But furthermore, there is an endless row of teaching, education, and exchange going on between Ugandan and other police forces, ranging from the United States, Ireland, Belgium to North Korea, just to mention a few. Practices of policing, textbooks, teaching personnel of police forces have seemingly been traveling across the globe for decades.

Our third observation concerned the simultaneous "globality" and particularity of policing in Uganda: there is a global police culture at work that stirs the imagination of Ugandan police officers and the Ugandan public about what it means to be a police officer. Ugandan police officers don't like drunk drivers, they think pot smokers are criminals, and they conceive themselves as guardians of order. Their ethos is partly a globalized ethos of policing, their statistics use globalized categories, and even their budget is in part funded by international budget support to the Ugandan government.

Our fourth observation is perhaps the most important for the subject of this book: we discovered how little political science and international relations have to offer for the study of such highly internationalized fields. Police, like the military, are considered to be a natural reservation of national, that is, state politics. Our first three observations are nowhere neither mirrored in theories of IR nor does the discipline offer much as analytical tools to study such highly internationalized political fields.

It seems to us that the standard distinctions of IR like between non-state actors, states, and international organizations are unable to cover what we saw in our research. But what would be an appropriate language to think of these internationalized—and yet seemingly specific—forms and practices? If the vocabulary of IR is not enough to cover the historicity, the connections, overlaps, adaptations, the everyday, and reinterpretations that we see at work, what other academic fields would be of avail?

Anthropology proved to be the most helpful here. Anthropology as "generous, open-ended, comparative, and yet critical inquiry into the conditions and possibilities of human life in the one world we all inhabit" (Ingold 2017, 22) enables political scientists to reach paths beyond classical IR perspectives. It is anthropology, or more specifically its overall ethnographic approach, which offers to see, observe, investigate, and analyze dimensions of internationalization, globality, and particularity, or the everyday. It is anthropology, which is particularly apt to "see the general in the particular" (Evans-Pritchard 1961, 3).

As we will discuss later, it is no coincidence that IR scholars working on Africa are perhaps more prone to be drawn into the circuits of anthropology.

How internationalized politics are might become much quicker apparent in African politics than elsewhere, and due to the colonial past, anthropology was the social science on the continent, not sociology or political science. But we argue that anthropology generally should be considered a natural ally of IR like history and geography. In fact, no other discipline has had such a deep and long-standing encounter with people from different political contexts, with conflict and cooperation across oceans and continents. The strength of anthropology is that it does not only "furnish us with knowledge *about* the world . . . it rather educates our *perception* of the world, and opens our eyes and minds to other possibilities of being" (Ingold 2008, 82 emphasis in original). Both characteristics are as much as important for IR as they are for anthropology. Moreover, ethnography, the core methodology of anthropology, is helpful to check a number of commonly held assumptions of mainstream IR theories and methodologies. It furthermore is an alley for engaging into critical self-reflection that has gained traction in recent years, in particular with regard to its "globality" (cf. Acharya 2014).

Hitherto, though, there has not been a serious exchange between the two disciplines. While anthropology has already made some inroads into comparative political science,[1] its encounter with IR is at the same time very old and very recent. It was the work of classical political anthropology about "stateless" societies that were attractive for theorizing the "anarchical society" of world politics (cf. Bull 2002: 61). This direct encounter seemingly soon came to a halt, and it is now quite indirectly that anthropological literature is perceived in IR. Pierre Bourdieu's work can serve as an example here (cf. Adler-Nissen 2012).

Over the last ten years, it was rather the term "ethnography" that appeared as an import of anthropology in IR. Some authors already wrote about an "ethnographic turn" in IR (Sande Lie 2013). This might be an exaggerated view, since participant observation, a core element of ethnography, is still absent in the methods books of political science, even if some authors ask for the study of "the everyday international" (Guillaume 2011; Hobson and Seabrooke 2014). Doctoral students have many obstacles to overcome if they want to do fieldwork for several months in allegedly dangerous or any other places; and in opposition to linguistics, philosophy, sociology, or even geography, classical authors of anthropology are very rarely quoted or referred to in IR discussions (cf. Kapiszewski et al. 2015, 3).

In our view, the understanding of ethnography in IR often seems to be rather selective and instrumental. Conducting some semi-structured interviews in places other than home are classified as "ethnographic," day visits to organizations or institutions are described as "fieldwork." As Vrasti (2008) has argued, and as we hope to show in the contributions of this volume, ethnography is rather a methodological attitude than a technique: it means to reflect constantly about research practices and representations, to conduct research not only *about* but also *with* people, to accept fieldwork as a necessary compliment to desk work, to take real-life experiences as data and to take first-person narratives or creative writing styles as serious as the usual political science language because both can be theoretical and intellectual, valid and astute.

In opposition to the empirical standard procedures in political science and IR, namely to draw on published sources, on official productions of state agencies or international organizations, ethnography is furthermore a reflexive process of primary data production. And finally, it is an attitude that tries to take the positionality of the author into account and does not hide differences between observers and the observed in a depersonalized language. One could well interpret it as an antidote to an ever more aggregated world of "data" that forms the empirical basis of standard IR. Statistics of international organizations, Non-Governmental Organization (NGO) reports, and press reporting seem to constitute the bulk of empirical references in IR. Apart from critical discourse analysis there is little done in order to find alternative access to "the world out there" so that standard IR undergoes the risk of reproducing official representations of the world instead of assessing them critically.

With this volume we want to show that the encounter with anthropology and ethnography offers interesting and valuable ideas for developing critical and alternative ways of studying internationalized politics. For this endeavor we can in fact already draw on a number of convergences between the two disciplines that we find particularly prolific and mutually enriching. This concerns more general tendencies like practice theoretical approaches in IR and critical security studies.

But there is also more concrete research, for example, on the study of the state, works on bureaucracy, and finally the study of development and intervention politics and policies.[2] Development policy is a classic case of "internationalized politics"; we will use it here as a—in our view—precursor of what we assume will emerge in many other fields as well in the near future in so far as more and more policy fields will be shaped by actions, schemes, adaptations, reiterations of what has been designed elsewhere, embroiling an ever increasing number of actors. The usual threefold distinction between international organizations, states, and domestic actors that dominates IR and political science will not suffice to come to terms with these dynamics.

The postcolonial world, as we argue, seems to be a forerunner to what we assume will take place in all parts of the world or is already doing so. We are convinced that the analysis of such internationalized politics in any context can only benefit from the experiences, models, thoughts, and theories of anthropology. That is why we think IR scholars should engage with this neighboring discipline. Anthropology would help IR to leave the armchair, approach the everyday, familiarize the foreign, explain the familiar from different perspectives, and start to see that "any study *of* human beings must also be a study *with* them" (Ingold 2008, 83, emphasis in original). It would also allow to have a critical look at the endeavor of IR as well as "the radical promise of ethnography lies in its ability to expose IR as culturally and historically specific account of modern man and his political place in the world" (Vrasti 2008, 310). In that vein, this volume consists of suggestions about how anthropology could enrich the research process and methodological discussions in IR, in particular with regard to such internationalized fields like the ones presented in this volume. As we want to show in the following section of this introduction, there are already three fields of cross-disciplinary debates in which much more mutual recognition has emerged between IR and political science on the one hand, and political anthropology on the other. The then following sections will address six lessons that we think can be concluded from the encounter of anthropology and IR. They concern the relevance of everyday life, the perspective of "politics from below," methodical and theoretical openness, the merit of open research designs, the extension of what counts as empirical experience, and finally the relevance of authorship and subjectivity. Finally, we will present what each contribution of this volume has to add on the argument.

EXCHANGING GLANCES: STATES, BUREAUCRACIES, AND DEVELOPMENT

It is probably not a coincidence but for particular reasons that it is the study of African states, where we find one of the closest and most established encounter between anthropology and political science. Even this volume still mirrors this situation that has its roots in the historical division of labor in the social sciences. The common interest in the state or the regulation of seemingly stateless societies might have been an early point of convergence of both disciplines. Anthropology was part of a colonial governmentality; it was supported to establish knowledge about the colonial subjects so that they could be ruled more effectively, as critical anthropologists argued later (cf. Lewis 1973). Despite this, the early output of these endeavors, like Meyer Fortes and Edward Evans-Pritchard's comparison of "stateless" African societies (1940), received recognition far beyond disciplinary boundaries.

Politics in Africa has remained one of the subjects on which political science and anthropology have met and entered a transdisciplinary debate. Anthropological studies of politics and states on the African continent since the late 1980s have in fact become main references in current debates. James Ferguson's *The Anti-politics Machine* (1990) or works in political science on states in Africa, like Jean-François Bayart's *Politics of the Belly* (1993), draw extensively on anthropological literature. This relation seems no longer to be a one-way road. In recent years anthropologists have taken up political science contributions. This applies to the "image of the state" (Migdal and Schlichte 2005) adopted by Bierschenk and Oliver de Sardan (2014), the "governance" paradigm adopted by Förster and Koechlin (2015), or the attempts to synthesize political science work for a "stategraphy" by anthropologists (Thelen et al. 2018).

That this dialogue has set in only so late seems to have at least two reasons. First, the African continent and its political life has been a challenge for political science as few of its established conceptual distinctions apply. As a consequence, ex-negativo categorizations of "failed" or "weak" or "limited" states in Africa predominate in political science literature. The study of "political systems" in Africa usually reproduces this image of overall deficiencies and the malfunctioning of states measured with ideal-typical notions. Concepts like rent-seeking and neopatrimonialism should explain everything.[3] The great variety of politics in Africa has rather been studied by anthropologists, and it was only slowly acknowledged that there is something to learn from political anthropology for political science too (cf. Hagmann and Péclard 2010). With this volume, we want to intensify this encounter by opening a new field of research and inviting for its theorization—internationalized politics.

The other reason for dialogue appearing so late might reside in the history of social sciences in Africa: the precarious situation of African academia and the established traditions in social sciences have led to a sociological void in the African studies. While anywhere else the sociology of contemporary societies builds a bridge between the two disciplines, there is no sociology of African societies to speak of. Anthropology has filled this gap only partly; the bridging effect of sociology between political science and political anthropology was absent. The absence of a real sociology of African contexts meant that the traditional bridge between nomothetic and more ideographic social sciences did not exist.

The main lesson of the anthropology of the state, namely do disaggregate the state (see also Migdal and Schlichte 2005), has still to lead an uphill battle in most parts of the discipline that sees governments and their agencies as unitary actors, even if embroiled in "two-level-games" (Putnam 1988) or "multilevel governance" (Hooghe and Marks 2001). As the situation of scholarship on African states shows, it is thus still a considerable challenge to bring anthropological work and IR studies together (cf. Hansen and Stepputat 2001). But two other fields have already progressed in this endeavor, namely the study of international organizations as bureaucracies, and the study of development both as a policy field and a field of practices and theories "at work." We will briefly outline where we see major accomplishments in both research areas in order to build a bridge to the next section, dealing with lessons to learn for IR scholars or political scientists more generally for the study of internationalized politics.

Seen from the Inside: The Anthropology of Bureaucracies

In IR the insight that international organizations are after all bureaucracies too, came rather late (Barnett/Finnemore 2004). Precursors on the bureaucratic character of foreign policy making (cf. Allison 1971) had in the meantime fallen into oblivion. The old Weberian understanding that "every domination both expresses itself and functions through administration" (Weber 1978; 1922, 948) has been revived since and has, in conjunction with Foucauldian inspirations, led to a new and flourishing field of empirical studies on the forms of knowledge and on the practices of the very personnel and administrative apparatuses of international politics. Some of them are in fact ethnographic in character and cast doubts on the heroic version of international politics according to which either institutions or the decisions of statesmen and women as presidents or cabinet members are the core of international politics. Iver B. Neumann (2012) in his participant observation in Norwegian diplomacy, for example, has shown the mostly mundane and nitty-gritty work of "state-folks." In critical security studies, the analysis of apparatuses and single institutions (e.g., Bigo 2002) has come close to the anthropological studies' findings on the forms of knowledge that rule in the guarding of state boundaries and the global regimes of migration (cf. Feldman 2012). Work on police forces in political science as well as in social anthropology has revealed how deeply internationalized this bureaucratic core is that we find even in African police forces (cf. Biecker and Schlichte 2015; Beek et al. 2017).

Studies on bureaucracies also promise to shed light on forms of knowledge that are both a prerequisite and a product of forms of rule. It shows, for example, that in international politics, knowledge forms seemingly correspond to organizational requirements. Ethnographies of international organizations have shown that knowledge regimes in such organizations are rather based on their governmental aspiration than on empirical knowledge about the spaces they attempt to govern (Sande Lie 2015). These are highly relevant insights for political scientists and IR scholars generally still waiting to be recognized and discussed as they may have major impacts on future research directions.

Both in sociology and political anthropology, bureaucratic practices and bureaucratic forms of knowledge have been at the core of studying state dynamics for quite a while. Both political sociology and social anthropology have stressed this point repeatedly. One can think here of Timothy Mitchell's seminal contribution on the "state effect" (1999) as well as of

Pierre Bourdieu's characterization of the state as "a producer of principles of classification" (2012, 263). These insights, which have in both authors' cases been generated through constant comparative analysis of "Western" and "non-Western" contexts, stand in clear contradiction to the reification of states as cohesive actors that we still observe in most parts of IR.

What we can learn from this still fugacious encounter between anthropology and IR research on bureaucracies is that the study of practices allows us to detect myths and reifications in our image of international politics. More importantly, the analysis of bureaucratic practices and the forms of knowledge produced and maintained by the symbolic forms of which the state consists and that it reproduces could be applied to other agencies and fields of operation as well. What knowledge forms are produced in the "international" sphere? How do international organizations and nongovernmental organizations produce and structure a reality beyond state registers? As the contributions of Eckl and Biecker and Schlichte show, there are new forms of knowledge and knowledge production in internationalized politics that cannot easily be ascribed to either international organizations or state agencies.

Anthropology and "Development" as a Precursor of Internationalized Politics

A field in which the encounter of IR and political anthropology seems to be more advanced than elsewhere—or are at least more visible or more studied—is the field of development policy (cf. Mosse 2011; 2013). This too is a recent development. From the late 1950s up until the 1980s, most political science scholars more or less identified themselves with the modernization projects of colonies and decolonized states. Economic growth was the ultimate value, and struggle only persisted on the question whether it could best be achieved through capitalist world market integration or through models of "self-reliance" with strong interventionist states. "Development" as such was not questioned in those decades. Since the late 1990s, however, postcolonial studies and the "turns" in IR have led to a new, critical, and analytical angle. Again, anthropology seems to be a bit ahead of what IR scholars have undertaken in this regard.

Anthropologists were late, too: it is probably due to the anti-colonial habitus that developed in anthropology as a result of the discipline's imbrication with colonial politics that the term "development" and the connected field of development policies did not attract much attention for a long time. Instead, development was often considered as "evil twin" of anthropology as James Ferguson (1997) has phrased, himself being an author who produced one of the first critical studies about the power effects of a development project (Ferguson 1987). Over the past fifteen years, however, a growing interest of anthropologists in development policy (cf. Mosse 2011; 2013; Olivier de Sardan 2005) has resulted in a host of research that brought the discipline very close to what IR scholars studied in the age of "humanitarian interventions" (cf. Barnett 2011; Koddenbrock 2016).

The proliferation of actors, in particular of IOs and NGOs, has become a standard theme in this debate of IR, like the effects of standardization, the reminiscence of interventions to colonial rule, and the question of the importance of local conditions. Interventions and development policies are the field in which IOs in fact became ruling organizations, even if only as parts of new political arrangements. Refugee camps, monetary regimes, free-trade zones, tax havens, and the sites of multilateral military interventions became the most visible expressions of internationalized politics that attracted both IR scholars' and anthropologists' attention. The outsourcing of state functions in semiprivate organizations (cf. Hibou 2004) that accompanies the transformation to the "managerial state" (Genschel and Zangl 2014) adds to the impression that the old state-centered understanding of how the world is ruled would not fit anymore.

The ethnography of fields of internationalized politics that we suggest in this volume will thus be helpful in order to grasp the conflicts that ensue from this spread of overlapping competences, and the proliferation of actors, schemes, and standards. As Julian Eckl's contribution on the WHO shows, there is no reason to believe that a growing role of IOs would lead to a higher rationality of organizations. And Tomas Martin's chapter on politics in the Ugandan prison sector suggests that there is not simple diffusion going on, but rather processes of vernacularization of norms, which are quite difficult to foretell.

With the merging of development and security (see Duffield 2001) the most pertinent field in that regard is the study of multilateral interventions. In IR, the age of "humanitarian intervention," starting with the intervention of NATO into remnants of the Yugoslav Federation 1999, has triggered an intense debate in which more and more scholars have taken recourse to more or less ethnographic methods.[4] This field has attracted attention partly because the respective milieus, UN agencies and international non-governmental organizations (INGOs), were very close to the lifeworlds especially of younger scholars who also at times had gathered personal professional experience in this field, be it as "humanitarians" (Autesserre 2014), consultants (Koddenbrock 2016), or military officers (Münch 2015). In our view, research on intervention that included anthropological perspectives has been particularly prolific as it produced new insights and perspectives on how international politics actually work, beyond the official narratives and rationalizations of great powers and international organizations.

Two findings from this recent research field might be mentioned that show what becomes visible with a perspective inspired by anthropological traditions. First, the politics of intervention is replete with subcultures, different temporalities, and institutional self-referentiality, even when multilateralism seems to indicate agreement and cooperation (cf. Stepputat and Larsen 2015). And second, these new forms of internationalized domination create new niches and opportunities for new actors, in particular intermediaries (cf. Münch and Veit 2017), whose strategies and limits we only have begun to understand. Their particular power seems to be based on their ability to translate between the globalized sphere of politics and the contextual conditions, which often remain opaque for the intervening organizations.

If we consider multilateral interventions as "avant-garde" of internationalized politics, these and other findings might open new avenues for future research in policy fields that show similar tendencies of internationalization. Global health is certainly such a field, but the history of technology or of global legal studies might follow suit. In the last section of this introduction, we want therefore to outline what we think is the promise and the challenge of pursuing the encounter that we suggest to promote.

WHAT IR CAN GAIN FROM POLITICAL ANTHROPOLOGY

In political science, politics are still mostly conceived in their juridical, institutional form. But this usually means to study politics with concepts and along statutes that are invoked by governmental actors. From its inception, political science has thus had this bias of prioritizing the rule over the exception, the rulers over the ruled. The recent "turns" of the IR mentioned above indicate that this standard form of researching the official needs to be complemented, though, by the study of practices, of routines, of narratives, and the use of artifacts involved in the carrying out of policies or single decisions, by looking at what people do and how they behave, no matter whether they are part of the "government" or not. Ethnography, in the sense as, for example, an early author like Marcel Mauss (2013 [1967]) described it, has done all this for decades. It is however less clear how we could translate what anthropologists say about their work, describing it as a sequence of direct and continuous contact of experience, integrated methodical design, and writing as the turning of data into text (cf. Breidenstein et al. 2013, 31f.). In this section, we would like to present a few ideas of what the encounter between the disciplines could mean for the development of IR in terms of methods and theory building. We thus follow a reminder Wanda Vrasti has made quite early in the debate: ethnography is more than a method, but "an exercise in being truthful about the distance we travel from research questions to finished manuscript" (Vrasti 2008, 79). Taking this "exercise" seriously also means to rewrite IR and abandon "the strange idea that reality has an idiom in which it prefers to be described" (Geertz 1988, 140).

A first particular strength of ethnography is certainly the analysis of *the everyday*. While other disciplines like history have as well undertaken efforts to connect mundane micro-arenas to bigger theories, political science and IR have so far not paid much attention to the everyday action and interaction that could with good reasons be named "real politics." Studies on local political arenas, parliament debates and press conferences or the work of Bayart/ Mbembe/Toulabor (2008) on "politics from below" certainly come close to what political anthropologists like Marc Abélès (1991) have in mind when they give extensive descriptions of what politicians or state agents actually *do* on a regular work day. One can in fact argue that "the everyday life" of politics is in fact the "actual" (*das Eigentliche*) of politics (cf. Rhodes et al. 2007; Rhodes 2011).

In such an ethnographic perspective the familiar becomes estranged, its taken-for-grantedness is taken away. As Abélès argues, anthropology, due to its long encounter with irritation, has a particular advantage as the irritation caused by the encounter with "foreign" sets of rules has as a consequence to question the familiar order of things. With its traditional perspective to "look from below" (*vue d'en bas*), it is much more attentive for the multitude of technologies, symbols, and rituals that conceals power and domination in modern democracies (Abélès 2012, 142).

In standard political science, this taken-for-grantedness that is usually not questioned, although we have all reasons to assume that it is here that the core of rule, of domination, resides: the firm reasons, the anchorage of rule is not to be sought where justifications are challenged in conflict or confirmed by negotiation. It resides rather in those regularities and procedures that go unnoticed because they have become almost invisible routines.

Anthropology, however, is well aware of the fact that here too, things are not as obvious as a nonreflective approach to the social world would think of it. The "everyday" is no exception to the rule that social relations and constellations cannot be reduced to observable behavior. Seemingly simple and mundane actions and interactions need a careful hermeneutical approximation as well, as anthropologists would stress. The usual self-critical reflection of the regarding scholar, of his/her patterns of attention, of sensitivities and blind spots, applies in this field as in the study of any other empirical material.

Another strength of political anthropology seems to be its *methodical openness*: it is probably one of the most important merits of its ethnographic approach that it allows to detect relations and phenomena that often elapse scholarly attention when theoretical and conceptual frameworks and rigid research designs command the research process. Ethnography is perhaps rather to be conceived as a programmed irritation, as an open reiterative process (cf. Swedberg 2014) and not just as the application of a preconceived procedure that has been entirely designed beforehand. It is this controlled openness of the research process that allows for discoveries, which seem to be unknown to political science proper.

Quite often, this openness leads to surprising insights: while IR scholars would address the Dublin rule in European asylum policy rather study as an intergovernmental process or, in a more critical perspective, as a "securitization," ethnographic studies have revealed by following the trajectories of asylum seekers and through participant observation in state agencies that behind the screen of clear-cut policies and allegedly rational bureaucracies actual practices are rather contradictory, undecided, and arbitrary (cf. Agier 2008). In institutionalist political science, if detected at all, these phenomena are usually pathologized as "dysfunctional," "unintended consequences," or "slack." But this does not hinder institutionalists to believe in the overall rationality of formal institutions. Reading through anthropological literature, one would rather think of political science as an over-rationalization of government.

This hints to another quality of ethnography: like other forms of empirical research, it is primary data collection. However, it differs from other forms of empirical investigation in at least two regards: first, it usually works with an *open theoretical framework*, and second, it is skeptical about the production of data as "immutable mobiles" (Latour 1988). Like in other social sciences, social anthropology is a field of many theoretical strands, most of which are connected to discussions and usages in other disciplines. Fierce battles about theoretical perspectives are not unknown either. But in research designs, theoretical openness is seen by most anthropologists as a virtue: observations turned into descriptions are certainly not free of theoretical imprints, but the art of interpreting observations and descriptions mainly consists rather in playing with a variety of ideas and theoretical impulses than in a rigid application of a fixed theoretical framework.

While invasive forms of data collection like surveys or structured interviews are also part of repertoire, the central importance of participant observation and the reflexive position of the researcher stand in a tension with the standard idea of data collection in political science or IR. Ethnography has replaced the idea of strong truth claims based on a truth theory of representation: the production of data as "immutable mobiles" has been replaced by an understanding of material that unavoidably has a limited reproductability but is closer to lifeworlds. To admit that the subjectivity of a researcher has an impact on how and what kind of data are produced, does, however, not imply total subjectivism: like in other methodologies, triangulation is a key requirement for ethnography, and arguments about the appropriateness of data production and about interpretations of such collected material are part and parcel in anthropology as in other sciences.

The works referred to above have in our view already shown that we can gain if we open the study of international politics for theoretical and method-ological imports from social and political anthropology. We strongly believe that "this is not yet it." Like any other innovation that takes place at the boundaries of established academic disciplines, it is both promising and risky. The promise certainly consists of an extended experience, as anthropological perspectives direct our scholarly attention to new objects, investigated with techniques that have only recently found their way into IR. To acquire accep-tance in the discipline is still a challenge and will take time.

The actual challenge, however, lies in the subject of study: the "great trans-formation," that we are used to label awkwardly as globalization or interna-tionalization, will lead to new hermeneutical challenges. Politics will become ever more layered, and new hybrid and creole worlds of meanings will develop out of these encounters. How to describe the hermeneutical access to these new worlds is a challenge which both disciplines, IR and anthropology, will have to deal with. How could such an approach look like?

THE PLEA FOR AN EXTENDED EXPERIENCE

The basic operation of any ethnography of internationalized politics would in any case be a personal observation and simple description, just in the tradition of sociological phenomenology. We consider this to be the first data-generating step. Social phenomenology would always start in a concrete lifeworld that should not be imagined to be just the private, mundane setting. The office and the parliament are lifeworlds too, just as a military barrack or a conference room. What counts is to avoid the error that the formal world, what is written by jurists and presented by organizations, is the only world. What we know from anthropological work on international politics already is that behind and beneath the official there are other layers of routines, mean-ing, and practices that we need to understand in order not to gloss over what might be the actual cement of politics. As the contributions in this volume show, this necessitates conceptual creativity.

The promise of anthropology of internationalized politics then is that the basis of this enlarged empirical basis and an enlarged conceptual language would allow for new theoretical growth. It would be based on an enlarged empirical experience (*Erfahrung*) and not just derived from conceptual dis-cussion alone or from theoretical deduction that are then checked against a mass of numerical data. Such a research approach would start out with an enlarged understanding of what can become empirical data, and it would try to interpret it with an enlarged theoretical vocabulary. Therefore, nothing predicates that a given social theory—usually derived from a very restricted historical experience, mostly Europe's or North America's—should be appropriate to understand without modification aimed at grasping the manifold varieties of social life elsewhere.

In order to get this enlarged material, the choice of the first entry point might be arbitrary: the journey of a politician (Abélès 1991), the everyday life of a police officer (Biecker and Schlichte 2013), or the life cycle of documents in an international organization (vgl. Harper 1998) can do this job. All these might be valid starting points. They need to be complemented, of course, by further access roads, and by a variation of materials looked at. The aim of anthropological research is in any case an approximation, a de-exotization of what is foreign, unknown, unfamiliar, without subsuming it under preconceived ideas.

This is basically first a hermeneutical and then an interpretive task. Like in Weber's ideas of an interpretive sociology, an interpretation would start with the hermeneutical reasoning of "subjective meanings" that are part and parcel of any explanation in social sciences beyond what Max Weber called "mere behavior" (*bloßes Sichverhalten*). No subjective meaning can be inferred without context knowledge, embedding in their social environment, since it is the context in which meaning is produced (vgl. Cassirer 1989, 97). The rules of anthropology coincide here with unorthodox research methodology that Richard Swedberg (2014) has suggested for social theory, based on the methodological writings of Max Weber and Charles S. Pierce.

GLOBALIZATION AS HERMENEUTICAL CHALLENGE

Anthropology and those IR scholars that think of qualitative methods as indispensable share this common vantage point: any inquiry must include a hermeneutical effort. Now, in the age of globalization, artifacts and discourse are embedded into an ever more globalized net of mutual references (*Verweisungszusammenhang*). On first sight, this is an advantage in terms of research strategy: as things and utterances relate to each other, the disclosure of the real international politics can be started from any point. Where to start is therefore less important than to get started at all.

But, as a hermeneutical basic rule, in order to understand meaning of any data, we need to have some understanding of the context. The meaning of anything—usually the subjectively referred sense of a social actor, but also the meaning of an artifact—can only be reconstructed through knowledge about the web of messages and meanings that surround and utterance or an artifact. It is here that the promises of an anthropologically enriched IR and of the gains of ethnography are the biggest: it seems to be a way of going established modes of reasoning and to immerse into social contexts and not just in the official representations of published documents, and statistics produced by organizations.

The extension of experience, that affects global subjects as much as their researchers, is at the same time the issue on which most work is needed in methodological reflection: the "layering" of contexts, the acceleration and multiplication of encounters, leads to a new hermeneutical challenge for all social sciences dealing with the present. Globalization and concomitant internationalized politics are a challenge for all social sciences, and while anthropology has a lot to offer to disentangle the layering of meanings, it is by no means a universal recipe. As the contributions of this volume show, the offer of anthropology needs adaptation and reflection to become really fruitful in the study of internationalized politics. Before we summarize this with regard to each chapter's argument in this perspective, we characterize the challenge with regard to core ideas of anthropological methods: participant observation, field notes, the role of the author, and the practice of writing.

Participant observation is one core idea of anthropology to get into the hermeneutics of a context. It is the core method of any ethnography. As such it "aims to describe life as it is lives and experienced, by a people, somewhere, sometime" (Ingold 2017, 21). In this understanding, "being there" (Bradburg 1998) comes closest to the phenomenological idea of Edmund Husserl "epoche," as the immediate nearness of persons, of communication, of actions seems to suggest a particularly true impression. Of course, this argument for participant observation builds on a number of presuppositions like linguistic competence, comprehension, length of presence, and broad forms of documentation. Despite these challenges, under the label of "immersion" (Schatz 2009) these research practices have already gained recognition in fields like comparative politics. Their general value seems unquestioned, despite all doubts about reliability, representativeness, and reproducibility this method might provoke. What comes to the fore in the contributions of this volume is that there are other challenges in investigating internationalized politics. If "the field" is multisited, can it still be investigated by a single person? If not, how does the positionality of authors, so dear to ethnography, relate to a division of labor among researchers? It is these new challenges that our volume wants to address as well.

While field notes based on participant observation are still the primary material of ethnography (cf. Emerson et al. 2011), nobody would nowadays restrict ethnography to it. There are further "techniques d'enquête" (Izard 2000, 470) which have become standard forms of data collection, like interviews of all forms, the collection of documents, or the production of documentation in all kinds of media. Triangulation, the combination of at least two different, mutually independent perspectives on the same subject, and the combination of at least two different kinds of data, seems to be a counter-argument against the critique that field research is an insufficient, often even mystified form of data collection as Christian Bueger argues in his chapter in this volume. The critique has its point, however, as "having been there" does not guarantee a sufficient quality of data. "Restudies," teamwork, and diversification of vantage points are usually named as remedies against the shortcomings of subjectivity. But it seems that unavoidably, ethnographic work remains an individual activity, undergoing the danger of personalization or even romanticization. This raises questions about possible division of labor between researchers as internationalized politics usually take place in several arenas. What are the requirements and the practical advices for the analysis of internationalized politics that can be developed here on the basis of anthropological experience?

An equally open question of an ethnography of IR remains the issue of *authorship and subjectivity*. Only recently has this become a theme of IR at all (Löwenheim 2010). What does it mean to be an author? In how far does our subjectivity play into the work we do as scientists? Is this something we need to control for or something we should exploit? How do we write an academic text? Do the standards we apply do justice to conventions or to the subject under study?

On first sight, these questions seem to affect the reliability of research results that have been produced by ethnographic methodology. If the author is such an important subject for the interpretation of results, does this not imply subjectivism, if not arbitrariness of this form of scholarship? We do not think so and would rather stress the gains we get from such interrogation. What ethnographic writing and the reflection of authorship produce is not a destabilization but an enrichment as it lays open what happens in practice in all methods as well—after all, all data is interpreted by observers. We as scholars, like the people we study, follow routines and take things for granted that are no longer questioned. In fact, no academic text is universally comprehensible. Its writing and its reading require a long socialization into standards and conventions that are probably not fully rationalized but handed down and learned. The question of authorship, of writing as an essential part of the production of knowledge and its hidden presuppositions, helps us to detect the hidden and unuttered presuppositions that create credibility or doubts in academic writing.

Like in any other social science, data is at one point turned into a text. But *writing* is also producing data through writing. Anthropology has been much more attentive to this process than political science: "anthropology talks about showing it, not saying it; about letting the data decide the form of presentation" (Neumann 2012, 187). The practice of writing, the second translation so to say, has so far not attracted the attention of political scientists: "there is no such book title as 'Writing Political Science'" (Neumann 2012, 186). The standard political science methodology reduces this question to that of operationability. Only how a concept is translated into a numerically measurable variable is of interest in standard political science. Then, the numbers and the coefficients, it is claimed, speak for themselves. Seeing what is written in political science and how it is done, we have good reasons to believe that there is much more going on than what is written down. After all, any text is a story that tries to make sense of observations, which are already interpreted, mixed with the speaker's own imagination. In the case of writing on the basis of field notes, it is already a second translation. Writing is thus another vector of "subjectivation" in ethnography in the sense of creating something that is and remains subjective even if it finds the approval of others. It is however the merit of anthropology to hint to this process while other social sciences has remained silent about it (cf. Vrasti 2008). But what practical lessons can we infer for the investigation of internationalized politics here? In the following, we will discuss these questions by going through the contributions one by one. Each chapter, we think, has a message on what political anthropology and ethnography can contribute to a better understanding of internationalized politics.

OVERVIEW OF CHAPTERS

Christian Bueger's contribution to this volume concerns a core question of the encounter between international relations and political anthropology. Based on his consultancy work with governance actors that deal with piracy as a security issue, he questions the applicability of the concept of the "field"—as an often presupposed condition of anthropological work—for the study of internationalized politics. When interaction and communication is not only "multisited" but dispersed in many arenas and happening between them, the idea that dense interaction constitutes an object of study as a "field" might become dubious. This critical argument is important for future conceptualizations, we think, both in terms of methods but also for the theoretical categorization of internationalized politics that increasingly evade simple spatial ascriptions. One might, however, not follow Bueger's suggestion to replace the term of "ethnography" by the term "praxiography" as he sees in the analysis and theorization of practices, the most promising avenue that has been opened in the interdisciplinary "practice turn" in the social sciences (cf. Reckwitz 2003; Pouliot 2008; Bueger and Gadinger 2014). His contribution is also stimulating for the reflection of nearness as an advantage or constraint as his research is based not just on participant observation, but on active involvement in the governance of piracy. What this shows, namely that IR scholars can seemingly in some instances directly link up with what actors do in internationalized politics, is another interesting anthropological observation by him, raising questions about similarities and differences between reflective activities like research and consultancy.

While Bueger's contribution already shows that there is no easy formula for how to import concepts, methods, and core ideas of political anthropology into IR, *Sophia Hoffmann's* chapter adds further specifications on this critical point. In some recent contributions she discerns something like a sacred "halo" around ethnography as an alternative approach, especially in critical security studies. The main message of her chapter, however, is about research conditions as indicators about the subject. Contrasting two research experiences, one on Iraqi migrants in prewar Syria and a later one on security measures of international aid in Jordan after 2011, she discusses the limits of ethnography. It is bound, as we can learn from her contribution, to a number of conditions in order to unfold its full capacities. While it might be worthwhile, often the only approach under conditions of political repression, it requires temporal and spatial flexibility that in other, often more liberal arenas are not easy to arrange. In both cases, as her article shows, the attempt to use the approach as such is already telling about the social and political qualities of the space under investigation.

At first sight, *Julian Eckl's* chapter is the closest to the traditional core of IR in this volume. International organizations have been a prominent subject of the discipline, first under the question of international cooperation as in the "regime" debate (cf. Krasner 1983) and later with regard to the implications of their bureaucratic nature (cf. Barnett and Finnemore 2004). Eckl considers them to be first and foremost "sites," arenas of interaction, and his study of the WHO assemblies shows marvelously how fruitful and innovative an ethnography of IOs can be. His contribution not only shows what else can become empirical material if ethnographic ideas are applied. It also is highly informative about the production process of documents that standard political science would take as given data. His insights raise doubts about the rationality of IO politics, and this in turn opens an entirely new perspective for the theoretical discussion on international organizations. Eckl's chapter conceives them as multisited organizations (cf. Schlichte and Veit 2012), and this opens interesting new avenues for studying internationalized politics beyond taken-for-granted categories that petrify understandings of homogenous and unitary actors.

The next section of this volume suggests that in the policy field of security we can observe an already advanced stage of internationalization, both in the private and in the public domain. *Tessa Diphoorn* delivers a showcase of how international relations and political anthropology can enrich each other in their perspectives in security studies without losing their disciplinary profiles. It is in particular the understanding of every-day security that becomes visible through this encounter. Diphoorn as an anthropologist remains critical, at the same time, toward large concepts like "assemblage" or "securitization" arguing that their analytical value seems to be limited. In her emblematic presentation of her research on security forces in South Africa and Kenya, she shows what the merit of participant observation is in order to dissolve rationalized images of a security situation and alleged cooperation in "public-private partnerships." Like other ethno-graphic contributions in the young field of studies on African police forces (see Beek et al. 2017), her research shows what we miss if we rely only on officialized versions of what agencies are and do. At the same time, as Diphoorn reminds us, ethnographic core practices like following the actors and painstaking writing of field notes are time-consuming in comparison to document analysis or logistical regressions based on official statistics. The fine-grainedness of ethnography comes at a cost.

Tomas Max Martin's chapter on vernacularization of global discourses in Ugandan prison politics is first of all a warning not to buy too easily into "diffusion mechanism" that are so dear to many political scientists (cf. e.g., Börzel and Risse 2012). His text is at the same time a rich micro-study of a forgotten arena of internationalized politics and an enriching reflection upon conceptual strategies in social sciences. The history of the global penitentiary system is still unwritten. But even this single case shows how productive the study of these institutions is. Global discourses matter, but not simply by "dif-fusion." Martin shows that vernacularization as a mid-level concept is much more apt to characterize the ongoing dynamics in the arena he studied. Using the concept of "practical norms" (cf. te Herdt and Olivier de Sardan 2015) stresses the need to employ a vocabulary in ethnographic tradition that allows to sort observations and is also sufficiently open to non-anticipated ones. What becomes visible then is that "the will to improve" (Li 2007) that is at the root of interventions still underestimates the agency of the alleged weak (cf. Bayart 2000). Norms do not just travel, they are moulded, translated, adapted, and not simply adopted.

Jessica Anderson's contribution, based on field research in the informal state of Somaliland, deals with a core subject of political science: the pro-duction of power. Her months-long participant observation in aid agencies' offices has led her to the interpretation of this business as a "knowledge market" in which local intermediaries play the core role. Her findings reso-nate with observations on earlier cases of internationalized politics, namely dense descriptions of colonial rule and its erection (von Trotha 1994; Münch and Veit 2017), but also of multilateral interventions in Afghanistan and the DR Congo. In such cases we see what Anderson highlights: international-ized politics are about real translations going on, and it is performed and carried out by real translators—local employees or brokers who can bridge the gap between the international lingo and local cultural, social, and political contexts. Neither the language, nor the aims, nor the simple purpose of interventions, be they state-led or carried out by international NGOs, is self-explaining. It needs a stratum of knowledgeable go-betweens who master the codes of both worlds. These middlemen, as Anderson argues, are however themselves subject to subjectivation—by adopting the standards, the procedures, the deadlines and the forms, their subjectivity is a product of the mostly asymmetric power relations of international aid.

Using theoretical ideas from political anthropology and exploring fields of internationalized politics with ethnographic methods does not exclude linkages to macro-social arguments. For the field of monetary politics, a long-standing instance of internationalized rule, *Kai Koddenbrock* and *Mario Schmidt* are able to show how biographies in precarious settings in Kenya are embedded into the dynamics of global monetary capitalism. Ethnographic research is not irreconcilable with big statements and global questions. It can indeed offer new perspectives and new questions. Their study opens at least two innovative alleys for research: not only does it invite for comparative studies, it can also be seen as an alternative presentation of what global capitalism and its financialization actually is. Depending on which lifeworld we are talking about, so-called "global" phenomena can take on fairly different guises. Are aggregated numbers and balance sheets its most appropriate representation or is it the lifeworlds and everyday life problems of those who have no leverage on its institutional design?

In our own contribution (Biecker and Schlichte), finally, we try to connect several strands of recent discussions in sociology and social anthropology with IR themes. Science and technology studies (STS) have over the last fifteen years heavily influenced how anthropologists study internationalized settings and global policy fields like health, physical infrastructure, bureaucracy, or development (cf. Latour 1998; Rottenburg 2009; Hull 2012a; b). One result of this turn is a new attention to artifacts and material objects as embodiments and carriers of technologies, understood as connections of imaginations, routines, and physical structure by practices. Our particular interest here lies in the fact that the products of these technologies of rule tend to develop a life of their own by creating a new reality that becomes the only relevant one for government action. We find this understanding helpful as a comprehensive and flexible approach to study questions of political power and domination in internationalized politics in a way that can do without worn-out distinctions as between domestic and international, state and society, public and private. We also argue that our concept of "technologies of government," that we present here, is apt to incorporate traditions of political sociology that have gained more and more adherents in IR over the last fifteen years, as the boom of "International Political Sociology" witnesses. In brief excursions into police work and into fiscal politics in Uganda we try to show that with this approach, we improve the analytics of domination and we have created a conceptual tool that ideally fits for the requirements of investigating internationalized politics.

We suggest that the study of internationalized politics should have conceptual consequences too. Our own ethnographic work on different state agencies in Uganda and on international donors has shown that the usual distinctions between domestic and foreign actors or between African and Western technologies are not supported by what we see in our material. Rather, we see attempts to govern from all sides, and an imbrication of different actors with similar means in what we call "technologies of government." The use of numbers seems to be of particular importance therein, but we also highlight an artifact of globalized bureaucratic rule that has attracted less attention despite its universal career: files, the blood and the backbone of traditional bureaucracies, are at the same time a telling epitomization of what we see at work in internationalized politics, namely the construction of social realities by the practice of writing and translating social realities into representations that then govern the minds of those who claim to govern.

The range of ethnographic elements introduced in this volume for an enlarged study of international politics reaches from participant observation to the analysis of artifacts, from the inspection of lifeworlds to the reflection of on-the-ground research strategies under conditions of political oppression, and to the mundane life of international organizations. With these studies, we do not claim that we have exhausted what is possible or that the ways followed here are the royal roads for any inquiry into international politics. Our suggestion is just to pursue an encounter that all authors in this volume have experienced as enriching and fruitful. We neither preach a gospel nor would deny the usefulness of established approaches altogether. Our aim is rather to hint to alternatives, and in our view necessary complements to what is the gospel of standard political science and IR, in particular in its US-American version (cf. Waever 1998; Schmidt 2011; Levine and Barder 2014). We are convinced that recent discussions about "global IR" (Acharya 2014) announce a sea change in what the study of politics worldwide will necessitate. If this volume is of avail in that endeavor, we would find our mission accomplished.

NOTES

1. See, for example, Aronoff/Kubik 2012; Chabal/Daloze 2006; Kapiszewski/Maclean/Read 2015; Rhodes et al. 2007, Rhodes 2011; Schatz 2009; Weeden 2010.

2. Cf. Bergamaschi 2014; Bliesemann de Guevara/Kostic 2018; Feldman 2012; Goetze 2017; Harper 1998; Sande Lie 2015; Mosse 20011, 2013; Veit 2012.
3. Cf. Médard 1991; Bratton/van de Walle 1994; Engel/Erdmann 2007.
4. The *Journal of Intervention and Statebuilding*, founded in 2003, has become one epicenter of this discussion.

BIBLIOGRAPHY

Abélès, Marc. *Anthropologie de l'Etat*. Paris: Armand Colin, 1991.
Abélès, Marc. *Anthropologie de la globalisation*. Paris: Payot, 2012.
Acharya, Amitav "Global International Relations (IR) and Regional Worlds. A New Agenda for International Studies." *International Studies Quarterly* 58 (2014): 647–59.
Adler-Nissen, Rebecca (ed.). *Bourdieu in International Relations. Rethinking Key Concepts in IR*. New York: Routledge, 2012.
Agier, Michel. *Gérer les indésirables. Des camps de réfugiés au gouvernement humanitaire*. Paris: Flammarion, 2008.
Allison, Graham. *Essence of Decision: Explaining the Cuban Missile Crisis*. Boston, Mass.: Little Brown, 1971.
Aronoff, Myron, and Jan Kubick. *Anthropology and Political Science*. New York: Berghahn, 2012.
Autesserre, Séverine. *Peaceland. Conflict Resolution and the Everyday Politics of International Intervention*. Cambridge, Mass.: Cambridge UP, 2014.
Barnett, Michael. *Empire of Humanity: A History of Humanitarianism*. Ithaca, NY: Cornell UP, 2011.
Barnett, Michael, and Martha Finnemore. *Rules for the World. International Organizations in Global Politics*. Ithaca, NY: Cornell UP, 2004.
Bayart, Jean-François. *The State in Africa. Politics of the Belly*. London: Longman, 1993.
Bayart, Jean-François. "Africa in the World. A History of Extraversion." *African Affairs* 99(2000): 217–67.
Bayart, Jean-François, Achille Mbembe, and Komi Toulabor. *Le politique par le bas*. Paris: Karthala, 2008.
Beek, Jan, Mirco Göpfert, Olly Owen and Johny Steinberg (eds.). *Police Forces in Africa*. Oxford: OUP, 2017.
Bergamaschi, Isaline. "The Fall of a Donor Darling: The Role of Aid in Mali's Crisis." *Journal of Modern African Studies* 52(2014): 347–78.
Biecker, Sarah, and Klaus Schlichte. "Policing Uganda, Policing the World?" *Working Paper 2/2013 of the Priority Programme 1448 of the German Research Foundation Adaptation and Creativity in Africa: Technologies and Significations in the Making of Order and Disorder, Halleand Leipzig*(2013).http://www.spp1 448.de/fileadmin/media/galleries/SPP_Administration/Working_Paper_Series/SP P_1448_WP2_Biecker-Schlichte.pdf, last accessed October 29, 2020.
Biecker, Sarah, and Klaus Schlichte. "Between Governance and Domination—The Everyday Life of Uganda's Police Forces." In *The Politics of Governance: Actors*

and Articulations in Africa and Beyond, edited by Lucy Koechlin, and Till Förster, 93-114. New York: Routledge, 2015.

Bierschenk, Thomas, and Jean-Pierre Olivier de Sardan (eds.). *States at Work. Dynamics of African bureaucracies*. Leiden: Brill, 2014.

Bigo, Didier. *Police en réseaux: l'éxperience europénne*. Paris: Presses de Sciences Po, 2002.

Bliesemann de Guevara, Berit, and Kostic, Roland (eds.). *Knowledge and Expertise in International Interventions. The Politics of Facts, Truth and Authenticity*. London: Routledge, 2018

Börzel, Tanja, Thomas Risse. "From Europeanization to Diffusion: Introduction." *West European Politics* 35 (2012): 1–19.

Bourdieu, Pierre. *Sur l'Etat. Cours au Collège de France 1989–1992*. Paris: Seuil, 2012.

Bradburg, Daniel. *Being There. The Necessity of Fieldwork*. Washington/London: Smithsonian Institution Press, 1998.

Bratton, Michael, and , Nicolas van de Walle. "Neopatrimonial Regimes and Political Transitions in Africa." *World Politics* 46 1994): 453–89.

Breidenstein, Georg, Stefan Hirschauer, / Herbert Kalthoff, and/ Nieswand, Boris Nieswand. *Ethnographie. Die Praxis der Feldforschung*. Konstanz: UVK, 2013.

Bueger, Christian, and Frank Gadinger. *International Practice Theory: New Perspectives*. Basingstoke: Palgrave MacMillan, 2014.

Bull, Hedley. *The Anarchical Society. A Study of Order in World Politics*. (first ed. 1977), Houndmills: Palgrave, 2002.

Cassirer, Ernst. *Zur Logik der Kulturwissenschaften. Fünf Studien*. Darmstadt: Wissenschaftliche Buchgesellschaft, 1989.

Chabal, Patrick, and Jean-Pascal Daloz. *Culture Troubles. Politics and the Interpretation of Meaning*. Chicago, Ill.: Chicago UP, 2006.

Devin, Guillaume, and Michel Hastings (eds.). *10 concepts d'anthropologie en science politique*. Paris: CNRS éditions, 2018.

Duffield, Marc. *Global Governance and the New Wars: The Merging of Development and Security*. London: Zed Books, 2001.

Emerson, Robert M., Rachel I. Fretz, and/ Linda L. Shaw. *Writing Ethnographic Fieldnotes*, 2nd ed.Chicago Ill: Chicago UP, 2011.

Engel, Ulf, and Gero Erdmann. "Neopatrimonialism Reconsidered: Critical Review and Elaboration of an Elusive Concept." *Commonwealth and Comparative Politics* 45 (2007): 95–119.

Evans-Pritchard, Edward Evan. *Anthropology and History*. Manchester: Manchester UP, 1961.

Feldman, Gregory. *The Migration Apparatus. Security, Labor, and Policymaking in the European Union*. Stanford, Cal.: Stanford UP, 2012.

Ferguson, James. "Anthropology and Its Evil Twin: Development in the Constitution of a Discipline." In *Internationale Development and the Social Sciences: Essays on the History and Politics of Knowledge*, edited by Frederick Cooper, and Randall Packerd, 150–75. Berkeley, Cal.: University of California Press, 1997.

Ferguson, James. *The Anti-Politics Machine. "Development," Depoliticization and Bureaucratic Power in Lesotho*. Cambridge: Cambridge UP, 1990.

Fortes, Meyer, and Edward Evans-Pritchard (eds.). *African Political Systems*, Oxford: Oxford UP, 1940

Förster, Till, and Lucy Koechlin (eds.). *The Politics of Governance: Actors and Articulations in Africa and Beyond*. London: Taylor & Francis, 2015.

Franke, Ulrich, and Ulrich Roos (eds.). *Rekonstruktive Methoden der Weltpolitikforschung. Anwendungsbeispiele und Entwicklungstendenzen*. Baden-Baden: Nomos, 2013.

Geertz, Clifford. *Works and Lives, The Anthropologist as Author*, Stanford: Stanford, Cal.: Stanford UP, 1988.

Genschel, Philipp, and Bernhard Zangl. "State Transformation in OECD Countries." *Annual Review of Political Science* 17(2014): 337–54.

Goetze, Catherine. *The Distinction of Peace: A Social Analysis of Peacebuilding*, Ann Arbor. Mich.: University of Michigan Press, 2017.

Guillaume, Xavier (ed.). "The International as an Everyday Practice, Forum Contributions." *International Political Sociology* 5 (2011): 446–62.

Hagman, Tobias and Didier Péclard. "Negotiating Statehood: Dynamics of Power and Domination in Africa." *Development and Change* 41(2010): 539–62.

Hansen, Tomas B, and Finn Stepputat, (eds.). *States of Imagination. Explorations of the Postcolonial State*. Durham, NC: Duke UP, 2001.

Harper, Richard H.R. *Inside the IMF. An Ethnography of Documents, Technology and Organizational Action*. London: Academic Press, 1998.

Hibou, Béatrice (ed.). *Privatizing the State*. New York: Columbia UP, 2004.

Hobson, John, and Leonhard Seabrooke (eds.). *Everyday Politics of the World Economy*. Cambridge: Cambridge UP, 2009.

Hooghe, Liesbet, and Gary Marks. *Multi-Level Governance and European Integration*. Lanham MD: Rowman & Littlefield, 2001.

Hull, Matthew S. : *Government of Paper. The Materiality of Bureaucracy in Urban Pakistan*. Berkeley/Los Angeles/London: University of California Press, 2012a.

Hull, Matthew S. "Documents and Bureaucracy."*Annual Review of Anthropology* 41(2012b): 251–67.

Ingold, Tim. "Anthropology is Not Ethnography." *Proceedings of the British Academy* 154 (2008): 69–91.

Ingold, Tim. "Anthropology Contra Ethnography." *HAU: Journal of Ethnographic Theory* 7 (2017): 21–6.

Izard, Michel. "Méthode ethnographique."In *Dictionnaire de l'ethnologie et de l'anthropologie*, edited by Pierre Bonte, and Michel Izard, 470–74. Paris: Quadrige, 2000.

Kagoro, Jude / Biecker, Sarah 2014: For whom to the police work? The Ugandan police between militarization and everyday duties, Paper presented at the bi-annual meeting of the International Political Science Association (IPSA), Montreal, July 2014.

Kapiszewski, Diana, Lauren M. Maclean, and / Benjamin L. Read. *Field Research in Political Science. Practices and Principles*. Cambridge: Cambridge University Press, 2015.

Koddenbrock, Kai. *The Practice of Humanitarian Intervention. Aid Workers, Agencies and Institutions in the Democratic Republic of the Congo*. New York: Routledge, 2016.

Krasner, Stephen (ed.). *International Regimes.* Ithaca NY: Cornell UP, 1983.

Latour, Bruno. "Drawing Things Together." In *Representation in Scientific Practice*, edited by Michael Lynch and Steven Woolgar, 19-68. Cambridge: MIT Press, 1988.

Levine, Daniel J., and Alexander D. Barder. "The Closing of the American Mind: "American School" International Relations and the State of Grand Theory." *European Journal of International Relations* 20 (2014): 863–888.

Lewis, Diane. "Anthropology and Colonialism." *Current Anthropology* 14, (1973): 581–602.

Li, Tania M. *The Will to Improve. Governmentality, Development and the Practice of Politics.* Durham, NC: Duke UP, 2007.

Löwenheim, Oded. "The "I" in IR: An Autoethnographic Account." *Review of International Studies* 36(2010): 1023–1045.

Mauss, Marcel. *Handbuch der Ethnographie.* Stuttgart: Fink, 2013 [1967].

Médard, Jean-François (ed.). *Etats d'Afrique Noire: Formations, mécanismes et crises.* Paris: Karthala, 1991.

Migdal, Joel S. and Klaus Schlichte. "Rethinking the State." In *The Dynamics of States.The Emergence and Change of State Domination Outsite the OECD,* edited by Klaus Schlichte, 1–40. Aldershot: Ashgate, 2005.

Mitchell, Timothy. "Society, Economy and the State Effect." In *State/Culture: State-Formation After the Cultural Turn,* edited by G. Steinmetz, 76–97. Ithaca, NY: Cornell UP, 1999.

Mosse, David (ed.). *Adventures in Aidland. The Anthropology of Professionals in International Development.* New York: Berghahn Books, 2011.

Mosse, David. "The Anthropology of International Development." *Annual Review of Anthropology* 42 (2013): 227–46.

Münch, Philipp. *Die Bundeswehr in Afghanistan. Militärische Handlungslogik in internationalen Interventionen.* Freiburg: Rombach, 2015.

Münch, Philipp, and Alex Veit. "Intermediaries of Intervention: How Local Power Brokers Shape External Peace- und State-Building in Afghanistan and Congo." *International Peacekeeping* 25 (2017): 266–92.

Neumann, B. Iver. *At Home with Diplomats. Inside a European Foreign Ministry.* Ithaca, London: Cornell UP, 2012.

Olivier de Sardan, Jean-Pierre. *Anthropology and Development. Understanding Contemporary Social Change.* London: Zed Books, 2005.

Olivier de Sardan, Jean-Pierre. "Embeddedness and Informal Norms: Institutionalism and Anthropology." *Critique of Anthropology* 33(2013): 280–99.

Pouliot, Vincent. "The Logic of Practicality: A Theory of Practice of Security Communities." *International Organization*62, (2008): 257–88.

Putnam, Robert D. "Diplomacy and Domestic Politics: The Logic of Two-Level Games."*International Organization* 42 (1988): 427–60.

Reckwitz, Andreas. "Grundelemente einer Theorie sozialer Praktiken." *Zeitschrift für Soziologie* 32 (2003): 282–301.

Rhodes,A. W. Roderick. *Everyday Life in British Government.* Oxford: Oxford UP. 2011.

Rhodes, A.W. Roderick, Paul t'Hart, and Mirko Noordegraaf (eds.). *Observing Government Elites Up Close and Personal.* Houndmills: Palgrave, 2007.

Rottenburg, Richard. *Far-Fetched Facts. A Parable of Development Aid.* Cambridge Mass.: MIT Press, 2009.

Sande Lie, J. Harald. "Challenging Anthropology: Anthropological Reflections on the Ethnographic Turn in International Relations." *Millennium* 41(2013): 201–20.

Sande Lie, J. Harald. *Developmentality. An Ethnography of the World-Bank-Uganda Partnership.* New York: Berghahn, 2015.

Schatz, Ed (ed.). *Political Ethnography. What Immersion Contributes to the Study of Power.*,Chicago, Ill: Chicago UP, 2009.

Schlichte, Klaus, and Alex Veit. "Three Arenas: The Conflictive Logic of External State-Building." In *State-Building or State-Formation?*, edited by Berit Bliesemann, 167-83. New York: Palgrave, 2012.

Schmidt, Brian C. "On the History and Historiography of International Relations." In *Handbook of International Relations,* edited by Walter Carlsnaes et al. 3–23. London: Sage, 2011.

Stepputat, Finn and Jessica Larsen. "Global Political Ethnography: A Methodological Approach to Studying Global Policy Regimes." *DIIS Working Paper* 1/2015, Copenhagen: DIIS. 2015.

Swedberg, Richard 2014: *The Art of Social Theory*, Princeton NJ: Princeton UP.

Te Herdt, Tom, and Jean-Pierre Olivier de Sardan (eds.). *Real Governance and Practical Norms in Sub-Saharan Africa: The Game of the Rules.* New York: Routledge, 2015.

Thelen, Tatjana, Larissa Vetters, and Keebet von Benda-Beckmann (eds.). *Stategraphy. Toward an Relational Anthropology of the State.* New York: Berghahn, 2018.

von Trotha, Trutz. *Koloniale Herrschaft. Zur soziologischen Theorie der Staatsentstehung am Beispiel des "Schutzgebietes Togo."* Tübingen: Mohr, 1994.

Veit, Alex. " International Intervention and the Congolese Army. A Paradox of Intermediary Rule." In *The Political Sociology of Intervention*, edited by Berit Bliesemann de Guevara, 40–56. Statebuilding and State-Formation. London: Routledge, 2012.

Vrasti, Wanda. "The Strange Case of Ethnography and International Relations." *Millenium*, 37,(2008): 279–301.

Wæver, Ole. "The Sociology of a Not So International Discipline: American and European Developments in International Relations." *International Organization* 52, (1998): 687–727.

Weber, Max. *Economy and Society. An Outline of Interpretive Sociology.* New York: Bedminster,1978.

Weber, Max. *Gesammelte Aufsätze zur Wissenschaftslehre*, Tübingen: Mohr, 1988 [1922].

Wedeen, Lisa. "Reflections on Ethnographic Work in Political Science." *Annual Review of Political Science* 13(2010): 255–272.

Part I

NEW VANTAGE POINTS

Chapter 2

Conducting "Field Research" When There Is No "Field"

Some Notes on the Praxiographic Challenge

Christian Bueger

As a political science researcher I have been hanging out quite a while in places such as the city of New York, the Kenyan cities of Nairobi and Mombasa, Djibouti or Victoria, the capital of the Seychelles. Indeed, I even received (public) funding for doing so. Visiting such places is a lot of fun and one learns various things, starting from how to survive Nairobi's traffic jams, what the hottest bars in New York City are, to where one can enjoy an Indian Ocean sunset the best. To gain public funding for these great trips and to justify that they contribute to knowledge, I have relied on the justification that I am doing "field research." This is a conventional, more and more accepted justification in political science. It is also a convenient one for why a political scientist drags himself around elsewhere than the office desk, library, or seminar room he otherwise has to be. In this chapter, I shall challenge the worth of such a justification. I do so in putting forward two strong, and indeed, provocative claims. First, the majority of political scientists, claiming to do field research, do not do field research. Second, the term and justification of working in (or on) a field is a cover-up for all sorts of techniques. By using the field research terminology we prevent an open and reflexive debate on the appropriateness of interpretative methodologies and concepts. Indeed, I want to claim that political scientists frequently (whether intentionally or not) distract and hide the intricate methodological issues that arise by arguing that they do field research.

Now to be clear, my claim is not that political scientists should not be allowed to have a pleasurable time in doing research (exactly the opposite!). Neither is it an argument that the political scientist better sits behind university desks. Gaining practical experience with one's objects of research is vital for solid interpretative research. Nor is it to argue that learning about traffic jams, bars, and sunsets cannot be important for research. Indeed, such experience can be an important device to transcend the boundary between the researching subject and his object. Instead, my claim is that political scientists can only under very rare circumstances justify leaving their desk by the claim that they are doing field research. This is for one reason, namely, that, in the majority of cases, there is no "field." Most of the stuff that today's political scientists are interested in is not bounded by a "field." This is the claim I shall discuss in the following. The problem that there is no identifiable "field" is not merely a semantic one. If it is not a field, then let's call it something else! Instead, by abandoning the concept of field, several genuine methodological problems of interpretive political analysis come to the fore and it is these that require close consideration. To ponder about these problems, I draw on the experience gathered in a multiyear project that studies the global governance of counter-piracy. I do not, however, describe this project and its methodology in detail which has been done elsewhere (Bueger 2015, 2017).

I start with a discussion of what is problematic about the concept of field and the epistemic practice of fieldwork linked to it. I proceed in arguing that once we abandon the concept of field, a range of problems seems less important, while others come to the fore. The problem of access becomes less important. We need to pay particular attention to the practical problems of multiplicity, temporality and proximity. I start out in discussing the problem of movement between different sites, and the question of time. Next, I discuss how one can get closer to practice and if and why proximity to practitioners can be problematic. I then ponder about whether ethnomethodology provides potentially useful guidelines. My core intention is to contribute to conceptual awareness in the dialogue of anthropology and political science, and the need to focus on concrete and practical problems of research practice.

THE CONCEPT OF FIELD AND ETHNOGRAPHY

The meaning of the utterance "I am doing field research" relies on the following claims: First, the claim that a field, which can be researched, exists. The existence of a field can be justified by either asserting or presuming that it does (an objectivist claim), or by making a convincing case of how such a field has been identified through empirical research (an empiricist claim). Second, the utterance is based on the claim that "field research" is a legitimate, worthwhile, and intelligible epistemic practice of producing (scientific) knowledge.

The concepts of "fieldwork" or "field research" are frequently and increasingly used by political scientists (Kapisezewski et al. 2015, 34–81).

They denominate methods and technique that are widely employed across epistemological traditions, and are often seen as crucial in the encounter of anthropology and political science (Gupta and Ferguson 1997, 2, 3). The broad definition of fieldwork as "leaving one's home institution to acquire data, information or insights that significantly inform one's research" (Kapisezewski et al. 2015, 9) is certainly uncontested among political scientists. If a growing body of political science literature sets out to discuss what fieldwork comprises of and to provide guidelines,[1] what is meant by a "field," and what the implications of this concept are in ontological, epistemological, and methodological terms, is, however, hardly scrutinized. For instance, Kapisezewski et al. (2015)'s 400-page systematic overview of fieldwork in political science does not even discuss the concept of field once.[2]

The authority of the concept and its related epistemic practice is usually derived by pointing to the discipline of anthropology.[3] Indeed, anthropology has not only introduced, popularized, and demonstrated the value of "field research" as a social scientific methodology, but the concept of a field was a constitutive concept for (social) anthropology. As Gupta and Ferguson (1997, 1) argue, "Whether a piece of research will be accepted as [. . .] 'anthropological' is the extent to which it depends on experience 'in the field.'" For them, fieldwork is "the single constituent element of the anthropological tradition used to mark and police the boundaries of the discipline" (Gupta and Ferguson 1997, 3). As observed by Stocking (1992) and Kuklick (1997), anthropology's interest in fieldwork is to be located in the later nineteenth- and early twentieth-century works of naturalists. It was to engage in natural history by focusing on the detailed study of a limited area. With the revolution in anthropology established by Bronislaw Malinowski, fieldwork became associated with the study of small-scale societies in their natural state with extended participant observation as the main method.[4] As popularized by Malinowskian anthropology, the archetype of the field was the foreign and strange, detached and well-bounded colonial village in which the lone white male field-worker would live for a year among the native villagers (Stocking 1992, 59). In other words, field referred to a bounded territorial space of social meaning and customs, or "culture." The goal of the anthropologist was then to record the culture of that field. Hence the term "ethnography" as denominator of that challenge, a combination of ethno (culture) and graphy (to record, or write about).

Contemporary anthropologists increasingly took issues with the agrarian metaphor of the field and started to reject it as a useful ontological or analytical category (Amit 2000; Gupta and Ferguson 1997; Faubion and Marcus 2009). There are several reasons for such reconsiderations. The first is the changing character of spatiality and temporality in an age of globalization. The field is a concept which assumes the existence of well-bounded "territory of meaning" stable throughout time. What Tsing (2000) called the "contemporary global situation" sheds doubt on the possibility of fixed boundaries and temporal stability. Today, the colonial village has ceased to exist. Even the most remote village of the planet is afflicted with global developments. Whether we find a Coca-Cola bottle in that village, an NGO who educates the population or provides medical care, environmentalists attempting to preserve the local habitat, communication technology (a television, radio, mobile phone, or even internet access), or indeed an anthropologist from a Western university, our local community will be in some way connected to what happens around the globe. Not only global connections challenge the idea of the field. It is also the importance of movements and mobility. As Appadurai (1991, 191, 196) poses the problem, "As groups migrate, regroup in new locations, reconstruct their histories, and reconfigure their ethnic 'projects,' the ethno in ethnography takes on a sippery, nonlocalised quality. [. . .] The task of ethnography now becomes the unravelling of a conundrum: what is the nature of locality, as lived experience, in a globalized, deterritorialised world?"

To deal with this problem contemporary anthropologists have suggested different topologies that do not rely on ideas of fixed boundaries and appreciate relations, multiplicity, and contingency instead. I shall come back to these proposals in the subsequent sections. For now, it suffices to say that a justification of fieldwork through references to anthropology seems not particularly strong. Even if we treat the field as an essentialist category, as something out there in reality and externally given, in the face of globalization such a claim is weak. The majority of researchers, who claim to be doing field research, most likely will agree with contemporary anthropologists, that a field is not just out there, and will reject an essentialist understanding and appreciate the "field" as an analytical construct instead. If we take this route, we still face an intricate challenge: How do we determine what belongs to the field and what not? How can we set such boundaries? The cynical answer is that fields "appear simply as a natural array of choices facing graduate students preparing for professional careers. The question becomes one of choosing an appropriate site, that is, choosing a place where intellectual interests, personal predilections, and career outcomes can most happily intersect" (Gupta and Fergusson 1997, 11). Borders are then set in an arbitrary pragmatic sense. (I have time to do x interviews, and money to spend x months in this and this place, therefore this is my field.) Another widespread solution is to point to some other established traditional container of meaning, such as the nation-state ("fieldwork in Uganda") or an organization ("fieldwork in the United Nations"), and equate the field with it. The trouble with such a solution is that it leads to a regress, since such containers are equally problematic and their boundaries contested.[5]

There are of course more sophisticated answers to the question of a field's boundary. Field theorists, such as Pierre Bourdieu, have outlined promising conceptual understandings of "field."[6] In such approaches the field is a theoretical concept and implies a distinct methodology. For Bourdieu a field is a social structure held together by practices and by a distinct body of knowledge and rules. Bourdieu's solution was to make the identification of fields a major objective of research. He proposed to do so by studying representations and shared practices as well as the struggles to determine the boundaries of a field. The goal was to gather a map by which one can see the field. Yet, the Bourdieusan way might not be a pleasurable choice for those who want to do field research. As can be seen throughout the writings of Bourdieu, as well as those following his guidelines, mapping is hard work, and often requires no less than a team of researchers collaborating over years.

In summary, the first claim of doing field research (assuming a field) is weak, and the second (making a convincing case that a field can be observed) de facto requires hard work and seems not what the majority of political scientists, claiming to do fieldwork, are actually doing. Indeed, I suggest that the majority of "field-workers" are interested in interpretative methods, they want to understand meaning and how it is made and enacted in practice. Yet, the concept of the field is hardly the appropriate road to do so.

BEYOND AGRARIAN METAPHORS: TOWARD ALTERNATIVE CONCEPTS

What then are alternatives to the concept of "field"? In my research I have been studying the global governance of counter-piracy. I was interested in how various actors respond to the problem of Somali piracy and how they align and coordinate their behavior. This is the work that brought me to Nairobi, New York, Mombasa, or Victoria. It is a fascinating case, and we will come back to that. When I started this research, I initially followed the convention to describe my methods as fieldwork. My intention was to leave the desk and visit the practitioners at the places where counter-piracy is governed. In the study I draw on a relational ontology and a practice theoretical framework.[7] The core idea here is not to focus on the question of who governs, but to understand how governance takes place in practice.

Initially, I described the whole of counter-piracy governance as a field of practice.[8] Thinking about the field metaphor and dwelling deeper and deeper into the empirical material, meeting people and writing about piracy, led me to alternative concepts. Counter-piracy as I was understanding it, simply lacked the coherence, as well as the established boundaries that would justify the use of the field term. Moreover, counter-piracy is an unruly, unsettled structure and in consequence I became interested in emergence and in the ways homogeneity and coherence are achieved among the many elements that make counter-piracy and govern it. Scholars from anthropology, science and technology studies, and organization studies, struggling with similar issues, had advanced useful alternatives. In the meantime, I tend to refer to a range of structural concepts which, I think, provide viable alternatives to the concept of a field. I speak of counter-piracy governance as an "assemblage," "actor network," and sometimes "practical configuration" or "texture of practices." What these concepts have in common is the idea of ontological parsimony. They do not assume to know how a structure looks like, whether it is hierarchical, and what kind of boundaries it has. Instead, they turn such questions into an empirical challenge. The quest becomes one of studying through which practices order and coherence is achieved. In consequence, I think it is also important to abandon the notion of ethnography, since it is not ethno I am interested in, it is praxis. Hence, I think the term "praxiography" is much more useful to describe my endeavor.[9]

MULTISITEDNESS

The first issue that became obvious to me and spurred the need for rethinking the idea of a field was the dispersed character of counter-piracy governance. It does not take place at one site, but at many. Activities at sea by navies and shippers, the work of diplomats in capitals and international organizations, or the work of policemen and legal professionals in prisons and courtrooms in Europe quite obviously mattered. Asking where counter-piracy governance is practiced and its territory is made, hence led me to a quite a number of distinct sites, that is, social spaces where meaning is made and practiced. And behind one site another one seemed to appear. They were connected to each other, but no boundary would contain them. Studying sites required hence to travel to more than one place. In contrast to the traditional anthropologists dream of staying in one village and drawing nice, neat maps, we "have to drag ourselves around everywhere," as Latour (1996: 46) puts it. This is because "behind the actors, others appear; behind one set of intentions there are others; between the (variable) goals and the (variable) desires, intermediate goals and implications proliferate, and they all demand to be taken into account" (Latour 1996, 100). Anthropologists have recognized the problem of the dispersity of meaning for some time. This led for calls to multisited research.[10] As Marcus (1995, 102) programmatically outlined it, such research sees its object of study as "ultimately mobile and multiply situated." It thus explores "along unexpected and even dissonant fractures of social location" (Marcus 1995, 102). For Marcus, "Multi-sited research is designed around chains,

paths, threads, conjunctions, or juxtapositions of locations in which the ethnographer establishes some form of literal, physical presence, with an explicit
posited logic of association or connection among sites that in fact defines the
argument of the ethnography" (Marcus 1995, 105).

Traveling to various sites will mean for many studies primarily traveling
virtually, visiting the websites of the organizations under study regularly,
and connecting with the staff working in and at these sites by e-mail.[11] Yet, it
will also entail to conduct short visits to sites which are fairly easy to reach
(depending on resource constraints) with the primary purpose of speaking to
actors of, in, and at the sites in face-to-face situations. Beyond the immediate
sites chosen to be studied in detail, understanding their practices will also
mean acknowledging other sites and taking their practices into consideration.
The texture in which practices, such as those of counter-piracy governance,
are embedded is rich. However, not all sites and actors can be treated with the
same intensity. Resource constraints simply prevent it.

The phenomena we study in political science are a complex mutually connected multiplicity of various actors, objects, and practices. Coping with this
complexity without deducing it away (e.g., by just assuming a field) is an
intricate challenge. The complex microprocessing of structures of meaning
which are fluid, tenuous, and open is hence demanding. There is no obvious
solution or ideal strategy to cope with this situation. Yet, a range of proposals has been put forward for coping. In my counter-piracy research I have
experimented primarily with one strategy, the strategy of zooming in on sites
with high ordering capacity. My intent was to spend considerable time with
a site with high ordering capacity, a space in which many of the connections
were made and held together.

In the case of counter-piracy governance, four of such spaces were
vital: two established international organizations, that is, the International
Maritime Organization and the United Nations Security Council, and two
sites explicitly created for counter-piracy governance, that is, the so-called
Contact Group on Piracy off the Coast of Somalia (CGPCS) and the Shared
Awareness and Deconfliction mechanism, known as SHADE. At all of these
sites actors come together and develop shared narratives, discuss how to
proceed and how to align their activities. The site that connects the majority
of actors is the CGPCS, an informal governance mechanism in which different types of representatives come together. It was this site that became my
main object of study. Yet, also the CGPCS was not a regular field site. The
CGPCS in essence is a practice. Actors meet physically several times a year
in different locations and in different formats (strategy meetings, preparatory meetings, working groups, and plenaries). In between these times they
coordinate via e-mail or phone conversations. There are no public records of
these meetings, the only immediately accessible textual artifacts are so-called

communiqués finalized at plenary meetings. The individuals participating in the CGPCS change continuously. Some of them stay for years; others participate and represent their organization only once.

TIME

A core problem became time. Where ever I went what I was interested in seemed to have already happened. The meeting was already over, the negotiations closed, the document already published. Or the actors I was interested in were already elsewhere, cognitively or geographically. As Latour and Woolgar (1979, 172) argue, "A major difficulty for the observer is that he usually arrives on the scene too late: he can only record the retrospective anecdotes of how this or that [actor] had an idea." Researchers are involved in a complex microprocessing of the facts. That is, a process of "sifting through the jumble of clues that may enable a reconstruction of the original sequence of events" (Austrin and Farnsworth 2005, 155). Latour (1996, 36) and Law (2004, Chapter 7) underline the importance of uncovering original documents and other artifacts and to assume "that people are right, even if you have to stretch the point a bit" (Latour 1996, 36).

Partially, the problem of arriving too late can be overcome as Latour and Woolgar (1979, 172) suggest "by in situ observation both of the construction of a new statement and of the subsequent emergence of anecdotes about its formation." It was between 2014 and 2017 that I had the opportunity to start observing the actors within the CGPCS in action, how they were deliberating, and how they were drafting their core document, the CGPCS communiqué. Getting immersed in the action further undermined the value of the field metaphor, but also brought new considerations to the fore, that is, the question of the relations between the researcher and the researched, how epistemic hierarchies are constructed, the negotiation of proximity, and the prospects of doing action research in political science. I address these issues next.

ACCESS, ENTRY, AND EXIT

The concept of the field establishes a boundary, usually through its counter-concept, that is, "home." While in the field everything is strange, at home it is familiar. What needs to be known is in the field, and the researcher's interpretation and sensemaking process takes place at home. The idea is to enter the field, record all the strangeness, and once one is at home the interpretation of all the treasures collected in the field starts, with the goal of turning them into knowledge. The field/home dichotomy leads to two discourses, both of which I continue to find problematic. The first is the discourse on field access and on how to enter and exit fields and the second is the epistemic hierarchies established between the researcher and the researched.

One of the intellectual artifacts of the concept of the field is the debate around access, how to enter and how to exit. In political science this has been identified as a major issue, since many subjects that do politics are not easy approachable, they might be simply very busy, or there might be walls of secrecy.[12] Indeed, the problem of access is frequently leveled against ethnography or other forms of immersion as a method. In my own work, I have never thought this to be a problem. Much of the problem, I think, is linked to the metaphor of the field, which assumes a bounded entity, which one has to permeate. Given the multiplicity of sites in which counter-piracy is governed there was always someone to talk to, to exchange e-mails with, or an event to visit. Rather than accessing a field I gradually but persistently moved closer and closer to the practices and became more and more familiar with the practitioners. I was the guy who came back. Yet, I was also lucky. In 2014, the then chairmen of the CGPCS invited me to conduct a lessons learned project for the group.[13] This is what allowed me to study the practices of the group in depth. In attending the meetings of the group and gradually learning the practices, I started to understand that the idea that there is a center or a sort of inner circle one has to penetrate is a myth. There was nothing like an inner circle, yet, there were participants who had been to meetings for longer than others. These people had a better sense of what the group was doing and where it was heading. Yet, each of these participants had also only a partial perspective limited by the organizational interests they were presenting and their personal resources. What changed when I was invited to do a project for the group was primarily my legitimacy in the conversation with the counter-piracy practitioners. If before, I was primarily someone conducting research (the university professor), with the value for counter-piracy ambiguous or unclear, through the commissioned project this fundamentally changed. I was now certified to produce something of value for the actors, and through this recognition I (increasingly) became one of them (their lessons learner).

How bizarre the field/home distinction is became fully clear to me, when the "field" visited me at "home." I had invited counter-piracy practitioners before to give talks at my university; but soon after the lessons learned project was commissioned, the chairmen of the CGPCS, an ambassador from the United States, expressed interest in visiting me at home. In my hometown we hosted her for two days, over the course of which we not only discussed the CGPCS but also went to one of my most favorite pubs and even attended a music concert together. If the quality of the folk music we were exposed to was questionable, the home visit allowed for a co-productive atmosphere in which we could interpret the CGPCS and counter-piracy at large conjointly. Ever since, I have turned inviting my "objects of study" to my home into a useful epistemic practice.

Also, the epistemic boundaries implied by the home/field distinction did not quite hold. To start with many of my interlocutors were not that strange at all. They were well educated, many had studied political science or had a degree in international relations or international law, and some of them had a PhD. In many of the conversations I had, often at some nice hotel bar or in a restaurant, I thought, "This could be me." The main difference between my interlocutor and me apparently was to choose an alternate career path at some stage in life. Moreover, the activities that many of the participants in the CGPCS were engaged in were essentially the same as mine. They were observing and recording what happened in the meetings. They asked others about their impressions and interpretations. They were trying to make sense of the developments in order to report back to the organizations that sent them. From a methodological point of view then, there was not that much difference. Each of us had a partial understanding of what was going on and everyone tried to represent what was happening at the meeting in a different context through developing a narrative. The only difference was, however, that my narratives were meant to be for two audiences, political science as well as the practitioners of the group—I was doing a lessons learned project after all. This brings me to the next point, which I think requires consideration, that is, the status of the narratives we develop in our research.

UNCERTAINTY AND MODESTY

Following leads, multiple actors, and the different stories they tell lead to a construction of a narrative by the investigator. Yet, this is a narrative which foregrounds some aspects and silences others; it gives presence to certain parts of a reality and absence to others (Law 2004; Czarniawska 2008). Whether the investigators narrative is "true," depicting the event "as it was," however, is uncertain. As Latour details over various texts (e.g., Latour 1996), the problem of uncertainty is embedded in the problem that investigations cannot draw on a "foundation" or final justification. As he suggests,

> There is no metalanguage, no master discourse, where you wouldn't know which is the strongest, sociological theory or the documents or the interviews or the literature or the fiction, where all these genres or regimes would be at the same level, each one interpreting the others without anybody being able to judge to say which is judging what. (Latour 1996, 298)

We never know enough to judge actors. For Latour it is the actors who teach the sociologists their sociology (Latour 1996, 168). Classical social science research claims to know more than the actors it researches (Latour 1996, 199). This research presumes to comment on what others say because it has metalanguage whereas the actors only have language. For classical social science research, actors become only informants and research exists above the fray at the same time as it also offers lessons, denounces, and rectifies. As Latour puts it in his strongest attack, "For classical sociology the world is an asylum of fools and traitors, of pretenders and guilty consciences, and half-educated types. In this asylum the sociologist is the director, the only one who has the right to go outside" (Latour 1996, 200).

By contrast, in Latour's account (and others following the core assumptions of practice theory) there are no fixed reference frames and consequently no metalanguage. This language does not know, or presume to know, what the world is made of; instead, it seeks out informants who may (Latour 1996, 200). Latour consequently speaks of an "infralanguage" to designate that the researcher's vocabulary should be understood as a (voluntarily poor) device for organizing research and making things visible without foreclosing possibilities a priori. This also entails being open and modest about the issue that the narratives told by researchers are not certain or can make any claim to be narratives (about what happens at the site) superior to those of the practitioners and participants. Rather is it to add a narrative to the debate, and indeed to add an object (an article, a book) to the existing structures of meaning. Adding a narrative; this is precisely what I did through my descriptions of the CGPCS and counter-piracy governance at large. Adding a narrative, seems modest at first glance, yet it raises new questions.

THE ETHNOMETHODOLOGICAL GAZE: EXPERIMENTING AND ACTION RESEARCH

As Aradau and Huysmans (2013) have reminded us, methods are performative, and they produce certain realities. They are not innocent tools but have effect. As, I suggested earlier, fieldwork, for instance, produces fields.[14] Empirical work in this sense is an intervention in what one is studying. This is, I think, a particularly troublesome observation for much of the traditional methods discussion. The field is what one studies, but one does not intervene in it. The goal is to be objective and impartial after all, and one is to mirror what happens in the field, not create it. With my research I am, however, intervening directly and explicitly, if only by adding narratives. This, I think, requires us to peer for new guidance and new directions. And indeed, there is a long history of discussion in research methodology that argues quite the opposite to the conventional story: a line of thinking developing from Francis Bacon to Kurt Lewin and John Dewey, Harold Garfinkel and contemporary action research suggests that in order to understand we have to intervene and experiment with our objects of study.

Increasingly, I have come to explore whether the form of research I am engaged in can be understood as a type of experimentation and action research. Action research has a long intellectual tradition, but the majority of political scientists are not familiar with it. While ethnography has received quite some consideration in political science in recent years, action research, is, if at all, mainly recognized as a rather radical epistemic practice useful for the study of grassroot organizations, or social movements, and associated with emancipatory or radical projects aiming at assisting the marginalized.[15] Can one do action research with diplomats, naval officers, and lawyers?

I think the answer is yes, and partially, though implicitly, this is what I have been doing in the past years. The lessons learned project I was undertaking for the CGPCS was a sort of hybrid: It was an attempt to only generate knowledge valuable for scholars and for the practitioners that I was studying. Initially, I aimed at conceptualizing this work through the metaphors of "collaboration" and "co-production." I was collaborating with the practitioners, and together we would coproduce knowledge about how the CGPCS works. Although I am still struggling to get my head around it, I think this does not fully grasp it. Over the years, I have given quite some presentations to the CGPCS, and at some of the meetings, I was even asked to act as a personal adviser of the chairmen in the negotiations. I became a participant, and the tools I had developed to understand the group, started to be used by the diplomats as well. For instance, when I started to describe the CGPCS as a laboratory and its practice as experimental this was instantly picked up by the CGPCS chairmen, and members started to describe the group in such terms.[16] In other words, I started to intervene in the work of the group and conducting such experiments gave me a better understanding of how the group works.

The relation between ethnographic political science and action research in political science, I think, deserves some further discussion, in particular, since it radically alters the role of the researcher not as standing outside, but as working within the practices one researches. Moreover, as Eikeland and Nicolini (2011) argue, it can help us to elucidate a new type of theory. A theory which can be used as a resource in action and for action to give practitioners the capacity to liberate themselves from the constraints of a practice they are engaged in, and as such contribute to transformative change.

Importantly, I think it also might give us a plausible answer to the problem of validity.

PROXIMITY AND VALIDITY

Given the considerable time I spent with my practitioners, some colleagues have started to accuse me of losing critical distance and hence validity by becoming too close to the practices I am studying. As we have discussed elsewhere (Bueger and Mireanu 2014), what is required is a well-negotiated proximity to the practices. My main argument is that the core problem of much of political science is not proximity, but too much distance from the practices through which order and meaning is achieved. Yet, when are you too close? As briefly indicated, my role in the CGPCS started to change; I was now giving presentations and literally negotiating and drafting parts of the communiqué of the group. I was not a participant observer anymore; I was actually doing their work. In doing what they do, the benefits for my scientific analysis were not obvious anymore. I stopped recording anything; I was just doing. My initial reaction was "This must be it; this is now the moment where I am too close." Did I give up my academic identity and just acted as if I was a legitimate actor within the CGPCS? The professor turned diplomat? With some critical distance, and more time at my university desk, however, I think differently. What was happening at the meetings was just another episode of me employing the tools I had developed in the joint experiments with the CGPCS practitioners. The philosophy of action research, I think, allows me to argue that such activities are still valid in that they give us an understanding of how the practices of governance work. Conducting such work is to engage in immanent critique by starting out from within an existing practice. It allows, as Eikeland (2007, 60) phrases it, "making explicit tacit knowledge, and inner tensions and contradictions in [. . .] communities of practice or discourse formations provoking and promoting the development, the explication, and the actualization of inherent potentials in the practices."

HAVING A BEER IN MOMBASA

As should have become clear by now, my argument is that once we abandon the term "fieldwork" we can start rethinking our conceptual and methodological practices anew. Concepts such as the field have theoretical and methodological implications, and we should be reflective if we employ them. I tried to sketch out some initial ideas of how we might redirect our research practices through concepts such as assemblage, multisited research, experimentation, and action research. Rather than going to the field to harvest data, what we need to do is to practice. Rather than turning our interlocutors into researched object, we have to appreciate that they are fellow practitioners.

Interpretative research is a complex form of sensemaking. It is an attempt to negotiate and assemble an account of what "really" happened in the incident that explains who did what to whom and why. I sketched a range of problems: time—the investigator usually arrives too late; complexity—new actors, motives, and sites continuously appear; uncertainty—the investigator develops narratives which make certain things present and not others; intervention—the research has an effect on the practices studied; and proximity—the distance and forms of engagement need to be carefully negotiated. These are some of the practical problems that require attention. A discussion of the concrete technologies of understanding we employ is needed. Talking about "field research," justifying our work by the claim to "field research," shadows the important discussion on these issues. Talking about field research is hiding the problems we are facing, rather than bringing them to the fore.

To conclude, I hope I have made a convincing case for abandoning the terms "field," "field research," and "fieldwork" from our analytical vocabulary (unless they are used in the sense of the reconstruction and identification of a field in the Bourdieusian sense). We might want to stop fooling ourselves, our funding agencies, and our colleagues with the field talk, and start a conversation on what we are really concerned about: How to interpret from the experiments we are part of, the observations we make and the talk we listen to. If you find me, however, by some strange coincidence sitting in a beach bar in Mombasa, sipping a cold beer, and enjoying the East African sunset, and ask me, what I am doing, most likely, I will answer, "I am doing field research." Then, I hope you recognize the irony of such a justification and join me in for a drink to talk about multisitedness, proximity, the problems of time, action research, and how to make sense of the experiences in the present environment.

NOTES

1. Including Kapisezewski et al. 2015; Eckl 2008; Vrasti 2008; Sande Lie 2013; Weeden 2010; Kuus 2013; De Volo and Schatz 2004; Stepputat and Larsen 2015; Bueger and Mireanu 2014; and the contributions in Schatz 2009.

2. This is a widespread phenomenon. Some scholars seem to be aware about the problems associated with the concept but do not address it. For instance, Eckl 2008 puts "the field" in quotation marks, but does not further problematize the term.

3. For a telling discussion and critique of how anthropology has been misunderstood in international relations see Vrasti 2008.

4. See Stockin 1992; Kuklick 1997 for the historical reconstruction; for references and discussions in political science, see Sande Lie 2013 and Eckl 2008, 187.

5. See, for instance, for the problematic concept of the state Kratochwil 1986 and Ferguson and Gupta 2002.

6. For a discussion of field theory, see Martin 2003, a useful brief reconstruction of Bourdieu's concept of the field is provided in Nicolini 2013, 53–70.

7. As outlined in Bueger 2014.

8. See Bueger 2013.

9. See Bueger 2014 for a discussion of this concept.

10. Cp. Hendry 2003; Marcus 1995; Nadai and Maeder 2005.

11. For a discussion of such forms of ethnographic research see the contributions in Amit 2000.

12. See, for instance, the discussion in Kuus 2013.

13. A story that I tell in more detail in Bueger 2015.

14. See in particular the contributions in Faubion and Marcus 2009.

15. In this sense, action research shares a similar fate with recent discussions on a "public" or "engaged anthropology," which primarily understands engagement as a form of emancipation, critique of activism aligned with marginalized groups and communities (as reviewed in Low and Engle Merry 2010). While I recognize the parallels between both projects, I reject the claim that there is a justification by which researchers' should align with a particular group of practitioners for moral or epistemic reasons.

16. As discussed in Bueger 2015.

BIBLIOGRAPHY

Amit, Vered. (ed.). *Constructing the Field: Ethnographic Fieldwork in the Contemporary World.* London: Routledge, 2000.

Appadurai, Arjun. "Global Ethnoscapes: Notes and Queries for a Transnational Anthropology." In *Recapturing Anthropology: Working in the Present,* edited by Richard G. Fox, 191–210. Santa Fe: School of American Research Press, 1991.

Aradau, Claudia, and Jef Huysmans. "Critical Methods in International Relations: The Politics of Techniques, Devices and Acts." *European Journal of International Relations,* 20(2013), 596–619.

Austrin, Terry, and John Farnsworth. "Hybrid Genres: Fieldwork, Detection and the Method of Bruno Latour." *Qualitative Research* 5(2005), 147–65.

Bueger, Christian. "Responses to Contemporary Piracy: Disentangling the Organizational Field." In *Modern Piracy: Legal Challenges and Responses,* edited by Douglas Guilfoyle, 91–114. Cheltenham: Edward Elgar, 2013.

Bueger, Christian. "Pathways to Practice. Praxiography and International Politics." *European Political Science Review* 6:(2014): 383–406.

Bueger, Christian. "Experimenting in Global Governance: Learning Lessons with the Contact Group on Piracy." In *Knowing Governance. The Epistemic Construction of Political Order,* edited by Richard Freeman, and Jan-Peter Voß, 87–104. Basingstoke: Palgrave MacMillan, 2015.

Bueger, Christian. "Experts in an Adventure with Pirates: A Story of Somali Piracy Expertise." In *Assembling Exclusive Expertise: Conflict Resolution Knowledge in Practice,* edited by Anna Leander, and Ole Wæver, 40-56. London: Routledge, 2017.

Bueger, Christian, and Manuel Mireanu. "Proximity." In *ritical Security Methods: New Frameworks for Analysis,* edited by Claudia Aradau, Jef Huysmans, Andrew McNeal, and Nadine Voelkner, 118-41. London: Routledge, 2014.

Czarniawska, Barbara. "Organizing: How to Study It and How to Write About It." *Qualitative Research in Organizations and Management: An International Journal* 3(2008): 4–20.

De Volo, B. Lorraine, and Edward Schatz. "From the Inside Out: Ethnographic Methods in Political Research." *PS: Political Science & Politics* 37 (2004): 267–72.

Eckl, Julian. "Responsible Scholarship After Leaving the Veranda: Normative Issues Faced by Field Researchers-and Armchair Scientists." *International Political Sociology,* 2 (2008): 185–203.

Eikeland, Olav. "Why Should Mainstream Social Researchers be Interested in Action Research? " *International Journal of Action Research* 3(2007): 38–64.

Eikeland, Olav, and Davide Nicolini. "Turning Practically: Broadening the Horizon." *Journal of Organizational Change Management* 24(2011): 164–74.

Faubion, James and George E. Marcus (eds.). *Fieldwork is Not What It Used to Be. Learning Anthropology's Method in a Time of Transition.* Ithaca: Cornell University Press, 2009.

Ferguson, James Gupta Akhil. "Spatializing States: Toward an Ethnography of Neoliberal Governmentality." *American Ethnologist* 29(2002): 981–1002.

Gupta, Akhil, and James Ferguson. "Discipline and Practice: 'The Field' as Site, Method, and Location in Anthropology. In *Anthropological Locations. Boundaries and Grounds of a Field Science,* edited by Akhil Gupta and James Ferguson, 1-46. Berkley: University of California Press, 1997.

Hendry, Joy. "An Ethnographer in the Global Arena: Globography Perhaps? *Global Networks,* 3(2003): 497–512.

Kapiszewski, Diana, Lauren. M. MacLean, and Benjamin L. Read. *Field Research in Political Science: Practices and Principles.* Cambridge: Cambridge University Press, 2015.

Kratochwil, Friedrich. "Of Systems, Boundaries, and Territoriality: An Inquiry into the Formation of the State System." *World Politics* 39 (1986): 27–52.

Kuklick, Henrika. "After Ishmael: The Fieldwork Tradition and Its Future." In *Anthropological Locations. Boundaries and Grounds of a Field Science.* edited by Akhil Gupta and James Fergusson, 47-65. Berkley and Los Angeles: University of California Press, 1997.

Kuus, Merje. "Foreign Policy and Ethnography: A Sceptical Intervention." *Geopolitics*, 18(2013): 115–31.

Latour, Bruno, *Aramis, or the Love of Technology.* Cambridge, MA: Harvard University Press, 1996.

Latour, Bruno, and Steve Woolgar. *Laboratory Life. The Social Construction of Scientific Facts.* Beverly Hills: Sage, 1979.

Law, John. *After Method: Mess in Social Science Research.* London: Routledge, 2004.

Low, Setha, and Sally Merry. "Engaged Anthropology: Diversity and Dilemmas." *Current Anthropology*, 51(2010): 203–26.

Marcus, E. George. "Ethnography In/Of the World System: The Emergence of Multi-Sited Ethnography." *Annual Review of Anthropology* 24 (1995): 95–117.

Martin, L. John. "What Is Field Theory?" *American Journal of Sociology* 109(2003): 1–49.

Nadai, Eva, and Christoph Maeder. "Fuzzy Fields. Multi-Sited Ethnography in Sociological Research." *Sociological Research*, 6(2005): art. 28.

Nicolini, Davide. *Practice Theory, Work & Organization.* Oxford: Oxford University Press, 2013.

Sande, H. L Jon. "Challenging Anthropology: Anthropological Reflections on the Ethnographic Turn in International Relations." *Millennium—Journal of International Studies* 41(2013): 201–20.

Schatz, Edward. (ed.). *Political Ethnography. What Immersion Contributes to the Study of Power.* Chicago: University of Chicago Press, 2009.

Stepputat, Finn, and Jessica Larsen. "Global Political Ethnography: A Methodological Approach to Studying Global Policy Regimes." *DIIS Working Paper* 1 (2015): 1–30.

Stocking, W. George. *The Ethnographer's Magic and Other Essays in the History of Anthropology.* Madison: University of Wisconsin Press, 1992.

Tsing, Anna. "The Global Situation." *Cultural Anthropology* 15(2000): 327–60.

Vrasti, Wanda. "The Strange Case of Ethnography and International Relations." *Millennium—Journal of International Studies* 37(2008): 279–301.

Wedeen, Lisa. "Reflections on Ethnographic Work in Political Science." *Annual Review of Political Science* 13 (2010): 255–72.

Chapter 3

The Possibilities and Limits of Ethnography

Two Examples from Syria and Jordan

Sophia Hoffmann

> In a culture of political surveillance, participant observation is at best an absurdity and at the least a form of complicity with those outsiders who surveil. (Feldman 1991, 12)

This chapter describes and compares two research projects I have worked on in the past ten years. The aim of this comparison is to show that although the topics of both projects are quite similar, ethnography was a remarkably good choice of method in the first project, but an impossible choice in the second project. In the process of arguing this comparison, I want to analyze some of the debates surrounding the use of ethnography to research questions of international relations. Some of the current debate offers rich food for thought; however, some of it might have already been overtaken by the adaptation of ethnographers and research participants to what used to be called "globalization."

Overall I argue that ethnography should always be considered as a methodological choice within a qualitative International Relations (IR), which mobilized impressive ethnographic research, also research framework. But I also seek to highlight that there are situations in which ethnography may not help to understand, may not be the best use of time, or may inevitably lead to the production of knowledge overly tainted by power. Ethnography must be regarded as one of several useful and merited research methods, but we should seek to rid it of the "halo" it appears to have acquired in the past decade within IR at least, and the assumption that it will inevitably produce more nuanced, reliable, and ethical knowledge. Importantly, ethnography, even in a fragmented way, can be used as one of several approaches within a multi-method research frame, to unravel complex questions of the international and global.

The two projects that this chapter compares both address the interaction of international and domestic politics surrounding forced migration in the Middle East. The first, my dissertation project, considered the situation of Iraqi migrants in Syria in the years 2003 to 2010 (Hoffmann 2016). In particular, the project analyzed the differences between the way foreign aid organizations managed Iraqis in Syria and the way the Syrian state did, to argue that foreign organizations approached Syria from a completely different understanding of state-society relations than those actually found there. For a number of reasons laid out below, ethnography, combined with a relatively small number of interviews, here proved an extremely useful method, perhaps the only possible method, to carry out this project.

The second project concerns my postdoctoral research. This project honed in on one aspect revealed by my previous work: the social changes brought to the Middle East through the interactions between international aid providers and domestic state and society. Specifically, the project focused on the security measures that aid agencies use to secure their own projects, and how these measures shape the provision of aid, and become layered with other security considerations, such as those for the aid recipients, or those of state authorities. Time and resource constraints clearly played a role in the more modest role planned for ethnographic research in this project from the beginning. Yet in the course of carrying out interviews and a first field visit to Jordan, I came to realize that independent from time constraints, ethnography would not be a good or useful research method for this project, due to the material nature of the field and the knowledge I was seeking to create.

This chapter is split into three parts. The first part engages the debate surrounding the use of ethnography as method for IR, picking up some aspects I regard as most interesting and highlighting some of the debates lacunae. The chapter's second part compares the two abovementioned cases to explain the different roles ethnography was able to play in their construction. The third part concludes the chapter with a forward-looking discussion on the role for ethnographic research in IR.

UNPICKING THE "ETHNOGRAPHY-IN-IR-DEBATE"

Clearly, the rise of ethnography as an admired and sought after research method in IR is linked to a wider backlash against the scientific method paradigm that began in IR since the 1970s. IR scholars working within the scientific method paradigm believe that it is possible for their work to reflect an objectively existing, reality, and to develop models about how, for example, states are likely to behave in a given situation. Exemplary for this approach is game theory, which is a particular approach to understanding the international system of states (Kydd 2015). According to game theory, states are rational actors, whose behavior is determined by a narrow set of interests, which remain constant. On the basis of this assumption, game theorists develop models ("games"), which make it possible to predict how states will behave in certain situations. Such modeling depends, generally speaking, either on statistical analyses of large datasets or on highly abstract mathematical formulas. While game theory and related rationalist approaches to IR[1] develop insights into certain macrostructures that shape international politics, they remain totally unsuited to creating more nuanced knowledge about why, for example, certain interests remain constant at the international level, or how international and domestic politics interact. Such frustrations about the limits of the scientific method paradigm eventually led IR scholars to look for research methods, which would provide them insights into the inner workings of some of the large-scale phenomena that IR is historically interested in. So began the growing application of ethnography within the discipline.

It is important to remember that this lately observed *rise* of ethnography as a method in sociology, politics, and IR was preceded by its *fall*. After all, many of the major and minor giants of social theory and indeed IR—Marx, Gramsci, Weber, Foucault, E. H. Carr, Arendt—arguably base their arguments at least partially on *observations* they made in society, either out of deliberate interest, due to extra-academic employment, or out of personal experience (see also Bierschenk 2014a, 6). IR, indeed, has deep roots in sociology and anthropology. While the approaches of these "elders" did not place ethnography at the heart of their work, they point to an onto-epistemological position that today's proponents and applicants of ethnography-in-IR generally share: that to grasp the *meaning* of social processes, and to understand the *social and political relations* they create, it is necessary to observe their material effects in person. In fact, I believe that such use of ethnography as part of a research bricolage, in which material is (re)assembled to address new and emerging phenomena and questions, is an absolutely justifiable, and sometimes indeed necessary, method that current IR, anthropology, and sociology students can recover from their famous elders. I will return to the idea of a research bricolage toward the end of this first section.

Ethnography is frequently described as primarily a mindset. This proposition refers partially to the onto-epistemological perspective described above. But it also refers to a researcher's personal disposition toward his or her research question: ethnographic research requires the openness of mind to draw connections that a maths formula, based on rational-choice theory, would not see. It requires also, in a way that scientific method does not, a certain trust in one's own intuitions: not just during the analysis phase, but already while conducting research. Finally, ethnography frequently demands humility from the side of the researcher, as access to information depends on negotiating one's way through unfamiliar social environments. Beyond this particular mindset, defining ethnography or ethnographic material is a lengthy exercise, which is best served by reading some of the wonderful textbooks that exist on the topic (e.g., Feldman et al. 2003; Emerson et al. 1995). Ethnography may be conducted among people or archives (Feldman 2008; Stoler 2008; Trouillot 1997; Verdery 2013), and it may result in written texts or in visual material, as in the growing field of visual anthropology. Conducting ethnography belongs to the more general category of fieldwork; however, it is not identical with it, as fieldwork also covers the mere collection of artifacts (as in, for example, archaeology, biology, or linguistics), conducting polls or fielding questionnaires.

The ethnography-in-IR debate addresses the wide-ranging promises and pitfalls of translating ethnographic research from the circumscribed local into the potentially boundless global, and from its disciplinary home anthropology into new fields. A number of challenges have been identified here, of which I will walk through a few, giving examples of how ethnographers have addressed them. For example, Gille and O'Rairi (2002) point out the difficulty of defining *where* and *when* to research a global community that may be constituted as much across physical neighborhoods, as across transnational diasporas, global social networking sites, or international labor markets. Who should be considered a member of such a community, who should be observed, and how, at what kind of sites, and via what kind of communications? Should "becoming part of" a place or a community remain a core essence of ethnographic research in such a situation, and can it (Gille and Riain 2002, 285)? Clearly, the fracturing of community across numerous conceptual and physical sites is a fundamental difficulty confronting the ethnographer of the international or global, which scholars have begun addressing in multiple ways (Marcus 1995).

A fascinating "working through" of this problem can be found in urban sociologist Sudhir Venkatesh's ethnography *Floating City*, in which Venkatesh explores the social relations of New York's underground economy and its international relations (Venkatesh 2013). At the onset of his research, Venkatesh is influenced by his previous ethnographic experience in Chicago, where communities and neighborhoods were geographically fixed and social relations carried out within their boundaries. New York, the global city, he quickly discovers, is different. Here, communities are made up of delocalized networks, which span not just the city, but the world. Sitting in his initial research site, a small porn shop on 9th Avenue, he realizes that while he is observing one end of community networks, he cannot grasp the whole picture without "floating" across the city. He embraces this challenge uneasily, as it upsets much of what he has learned not just about ethnography, but about the functioning of urban society elsewhere. Eventually he finds that by "floating" he is emulating precisely the behavior of his informants and that it is exactly such constant movement through the city that allows him to become a member of New York's global community.

Didier Fassin, in his monumental work *Humanitarian Reason*, which explores the growing influence of humanitarian logic on global politics, on the other hand takes seriously the challenge to conduct ethnographies on the same question in multiple physical locations around the world, including France, Palestine, and Colombia (Fassin 2011). Clearly, this challenge can only be met through expending significant resources, and *Humanitarian Reason* combines the results of a scholar's decade-long curiosity about one broad political trend, being effectively a convincing patchwork of a series of thorough, stand-alone projects. The book is, of course, extremely impressive. However, to me it also shows up the limits of writing a truly multisited ethnography into the confines of a single book, while still maintaining nuance, and connecting singular observations to large theoretical analysis. While this is already intensely challenging within the rich ethnographic context of a single project, it seems to become overwhelmingly so when trying to cover several in significant depth. This, I believe, shows up the challenge of explaining necessarily local observations with reference to global knowledge-power structures primarily via ethnography.

Beyond questions of method, the IR-in-ethnography debate has also covered the thornier ground of what ethnography actually *is*. Here, according to some scholars, researching the global or transnational presents a real danger which, if not addressed carefully, may not just rob ethnography of its principles and essence, but turn it into something pernicious and misleading.[2] For example, in a widely noted article in the IR journal *Millennium*, Vrasti warns of the dangers of turning ethnography-in-IR into a mere "data collecting" machine, which turns on its head ethnography's dissolution of subject-object, method-methodology, and empirical research-theory development divides (Vrasti 2008). Vrasti, who is an IR scholar, decries her colleagues' ignorance of the vital debates about ethnography carried out between anthropologists since the 1970s (see, for example, Paul Rabinows many writings on this topic, for example, Rabinow 1977). These debates critically examined, inter alia, ethnography's colonial heritage, in which the purportedly holistic representation of foreign people via the writings of white, male observers was naively and imperialistically consumed. Since the 1980s, US anthropology has acknowledged that ethnographic research involves a textual translation of fieldwork and can thus never result in an absolute truth, or erase the researcher's personal perspective (Vrasti 2008). This acknowledgment, clearly, is a revolutionary attack on the principles of scientific objectivity, which continue to reign supreme in many IR quarters. On the one hand, it contains ethnography's biggest potential to produce truly original IR research, but on the other hand, it is also what is most at risk of being lost in interdisciplinary translation. This is because peppering academic texts with firsthand observations tends to produce an effect of authenticity (what Vrasti calls "ethnografeel"), which, if not situated with care, will return to naive representationalism, yielding little insight or critique. This danger is indeed only heightened by the assumption, widespread across all disciplines, that ethnography is simply "what one does in the field" and requires little training and theoretical preparation. This, I would strongly emphasize, is false, and I echo the call for more and better qualitative methods training in IR and political science (Menzel 2014).

Arguably, Vrasti's assumption that IR scholars are more likely to wield ethnography crudely is correct, given their reduced exposure to anthropological debate and training. Regarding my area of research, the international relations of the Middle East, I have indeed come across ethnographic IR works that have failed to convince. Here, an overly narrow perspective, or an excessive focus on preset research questions, has appeared questionable. A circumscribed, "instrumentalist" approach to ethnography is not problematic per se, and I have relied on it myself when seeking answers to specific questions, as laid out later. However, in an unfamiliar political or cultural context such an approach is at greater risk to produce wrongheaded results than the slow, long-term research advocated by anthropologists and sociologists. If circumscribed research then combines with tight theoretical frameworks used as explanatory "models" to interpret ethnographic results, this research design may indeed counter much of ethnography's progressive innovations mentioned earlier.

Further, there exists the problem of misinterpreting results of thorough ethnographic work, because of the adoption of an ill-fitting theoretical frame. For example, a dissertation on the Syrian charity sector, which mobilized impressive ethnographic research, also applied a Foucauldian framework, which led to a thorough misinterpretation of the power effect of certain changes to the way the Syrian state managed charities. Also, an article on Shiʻa people in Syria adopted Giorgio Agamben's bare life, together with rich ethnographic work, again leading to a thorough misinterpretation of the way Shiʻa were integrated in Syrian society (Szanto 2012). In both cases, the ethnographic material was not just convincing, but indeed amazing. But analyzing it through an ill-fitting choice of theory, which was elevated to a single, explanatory model, instead of allowing the ethnographic material to lead and to speak, narrowed the author's interpretative frame, desensitized their scholarly instinct, and ultimately led to a stale result. Of course, it takes courage to let the ethnography lead you, rather than leaning on a theory with existing, disciplinary approval. But this courage, and the venturing into the unknown is, I believe, where the relevance and potential of ethnography lies!

In fact, many of the concerns regarding ethnography-in-IR, about the fragmentation of time, place, and community via globalization, have already become obsolete, because researchers—and research participants—today do not confront globalization as a new phenomenon, but have increasingly grown up with it. To them, community has *always* been fragmented, social relations have *always* been carried out as much across cyber as physical space, and place has *never* been particularly attached to geographical location. Thus, to them, many of the essentially comparative problems of Gille and O'Rairi (and others) do not arise, because they are simply developing ethnography as a research tool to fit the reality they encounter. Personally, I am strongly attached to some of ethnography's classic principles as core guiding principles to develop my research methodology. But also, I believe that one reason these principles retain relevance is their adaptability and researchers will and must adapt ethnography to a changing reality (Bierschenk 2014 3). Whether successful, or not, can ultimately only be judged by the written and spoken texts produced by their research: the proof of the pudding remains in the reading.

Before turning to the field studies at the heart of this article, I want to return to the idea of research method as bricolage (or bricolage as a research method), which has also been called "assemblage" (Ong 2006). Bricolage here is a term borrowed from Levi-Strauss's *The Savage Mind*, in which Levi-Strauss opposes "savage thinking," which continually gathers structures and builds reality from the material at hand, to "scientific thinking," which approaches reality via preformulated, goal-orientated questions (Levi-Strauss 1984). Certainly in Middle East studies, the most convincing and celebrated scholarship, assembles a mix of observations, interviews of various kinds, archival research, topographical analysis, legal analysis, architecture studies, and more (Khalili 2013; Wedeen 2008; Weizman 2007, 2012). This mix is woven organically into an analysis and narrative, which is not justified by any explicit methodological choice, but convinces due to the sheer amount and variety of material martialled, and the originality of the arguments generated. What sets these works of excellency apart is precisely their creative, imaginative, surprising, analytical ability to see how a wide range of objects, sites, and people are shaped by the question they seek to elucidate. Adopting a "savage" mindset when carrying out ethnography and allowing the resulting bricolage of material to fall into place, without ignoring its contradictions, but still seeing its common theme, is the work of confident, ethnographic scholarship, which takes its responsibility and skill seriously (Gupta and Ferguson 1997; Vrasti 2010).

COMPARING TWO RESEARCH EXPERIENCES

The research for my dissertation was carried out in Syria's capital Damascus in 2009 and 2010, for around ten months. The topic of the dissertation was the situation of Iraqi migrants in Damascus, with the specific question yet to be developed. I had regularly visited Syria since 2005, including one long-term stay of six months. While there, I had regularly filed stories as a journalist, and completed some research on Iraqi refugees for a policy report of The Brookings Institution, so I could build on relatively strong experience of Syria's research environment (al-Khalidi et al. 2007).

The dissertation research was planned as a curtailed ethnography from the outset, a conscious methodological and practical choice. In terms of method, my previous research experience had taught me that "hanging out" and observing could be a better way to pick up on social developments in Syria than direct questioning. Further, my academic environment at the School of Oriental and African Studies in London, where most academics have a strong regional focus, and where an even stronger tradition of fieldwork exists, contributed to my choice.[3] Finally, there was a practical choice, which related to the fact that the Syrian government did not, or only in very rare cases, award research visas and had a history of expelling researchers it discovered. This meant that my research had to be conducted in manner that would not attract much public attention, and had to be framed in a way that would not raise the ire of intelligence agencies, should they become aware of it. Wide-ranging interviews, focus groups, surveys, and any official contact with government officials were out of the picture. Given that the fearful atmosphere in pre-revolution Syria made people extremely nervous to speak to, let alone be interviewed by, researchers, I also knew that I would have to collect a lot of information through informal conversations and observing.

This situation raised several ethical issues related to ethnographic research, which I discussed with my PhD supervisor. How could I go about being *open* enough as to not deceive the people I was collecting information from, but *discreet* enough as to not attract the attention of authorities? My supervisor gave me the following advice (and I paraphrase): To conduct research ethically, you have to be scrupulously transparent toward those who are less powerful than you. Toward those with more power than you, you do *not* need to be scrupulously transparent. With this guidance, I developed the policy of publicly stating that my research focused on humanitarian aid provided by the Syrian government to Iraqi migrants. Directly toward research participants, I provided much more nuance, adding that I was looking at the general treatment that Iraqis were receiving from different centers of power, or answering whichever questions they had (which generally were surprisingly few, an experience shared by many ethnographers). Indeed, I believe this particular advice about differentiated ethical treatment of research participants can have a wide applicability with regards to the much-discussed question of how to use ethnography to "study up" (this question forms part of the ethnography-in-IR debate, due to the realization that much global policy research involves elites; see, for example, Bierschenk [2014: 15]). I will briefly return to this in the conclusion.

In Damascus, I had prearranged a rented room in a family-owned house in the Christian quarter of the old city, which was a popular choice for foreign students studying Arabic. After arriving and seeking out some existing contacts, I quickly encountered substantial hurdles. First, I discovered that my assumption that research would be made easier by the recent arrival of a dozen international Non-Governmental Organisations (NGOs) working with Iraqi refugees was wrong (Hoffmann 2011; Kraft 2008). Doors slammed in my face right and left as I tried to contact foreign aid workers, and my hope that I would be able to develop a research site at one of these international organizations was soon dashed. In retrospect this false start was lucky, as working through an NGO would have made it much harder to be perceived as an independent researcher. A frightening experience at the Jordan-Syria border, during which a tiny Israeli airline sticker was discovered on my passport (which both the Syrian embassy in London and I had failed to detect earlier), and my readmission to Syria hung on a thread, left me paranoid and unable to conduct any work for two weeks. After a moment of despair, during which the specter of having to move my research elsewhere appeared close, things began to move, if generally, at snail's pace. I moved to a derelict flat in a suburb dominated by recently arrived Iraqis, which opened space for daily observations on Iraqi life in Syria. I made friends with some Iraqis and began to do some voluntary teaching to Iraqi students at a small, informal NGO, which led to yet again more observations. I found a sports group at which expats and Syrians "hung out" together, which lifted my spirits and provided energizing physical exercise. A handful of formal interviews with United Nations High Commissioner for Refugees (UNHCR) managers—who proved less fearful of Syrian authorities than NGO workers—came through. But I still hesitated to ask any of my new, informal connections for interviews, as I worried that the request would shatter our frail social bond and make our relationship appear instrumental. I encountered the full force of ethnography's ethical tensions, which I had until then only read about, and in the intensely charged atmosphere of prerevolution Damascus and the Iraqi reality of recent displacement it occasionally became nearly too much to bear (Feldman et al. 2003; Huisman 2008). How could I confront people, who believed that I was spending time with them as a friend, and who quickly seemed to forget my announcements about being a researcher, with an interview request, which in Syria always carried at least a small security risk? Would it not make them

feel used and abused? What would I do if an interview had negative consequences for them? So, I pushed ahead with observations and "hanging out,"
remaining on research alert in all possible places: squeezed into a collective
taxi, discussing identity with my students, chatting at the juice bar. Any
encounter could end up being meaningful. Eventually, my biggest push on
interviews came in the last month of research, and most were conducted with
people I either specifically met only for the interview or knew only superfi-
cially. Only with one of my close research participants did I actually conduct
a formal interview, collecting the rest of my "data" in field notes (Emerson
et al. 1995).

My postdoc project also focused on forced migration in the Middle East,
which sadly has continued to escalate, now with the Syrian war added to the
Iraqi catastrophe.[4] The project has had a specific focus from the onset: the
content and influence of aid organizations' security management practices.
Humanitarian security today comprises a significant subsector, which is
exclusively focused on developing measures that ensure the safety and security of staff and projects (Bollettino 2008; Burkle 2005; Christian Aid 2010).
My project addressed the question of how these measures shape aid delivery
and interact with the politics and societies of the Middle East. The project's
research methodology was a mix of interviews, conducted via Skype with aid
security managers all over the world, reviews of security-related documentation (i.e., policy guidelines, manuals, etc.), and fieldwork in Jordan, where the
effect of security measures on aid projects and two new refugee camps was
investigated. Eventually, I conducted around thirty interviews and conducted
two weeks of field research in Jordan.

While devising and beginning this project, I was acutely aware and felt
insecure about the fact that, due to time constraints, I would only be able
to conduct very limited ethnographic field research. How would I be able
to adequately look at the effect that security management had on the daily
lives of aid recipients? How would I be able to become familiar with Jordan
as a research environment, that is, become part of the place if even in the
most superficial manner? And how would I be able to extrapolate *anything*
from my findings in Jordan to the wider region? Feeling pressured, I began
to dig into the online world of the aid sector in the Middle East, which was
growing together with the physical aid effort on the ground. Luckily I found
that, UNHCR operates an online portal, which contains masses of data on
the Syrian refugee crisis and where many involved aid organizations upload
a vast range of material. Everything, ranging from detailed camp infrastructure maps at various stages of design, to meeting minutes, to research
reports and statistics, can be found on this portal, especially once I learned
to navigate and search it effectively. Quickly, I became fascinated by the
well-documented planning and design process for the new refugee camp

Azraq, opened in 2014, as it attempted to incorporate several security-related improvements, and was an evident attempt to layer humanitarian concerns with a desire for order and control over a potentially unruly camp population (Care International 2015; International Medical Corps and UNHCR 2014; UNHABITAT et al. 2014). Azraq, it appeared, clearly offered a very obvious and fascinating example for the research puzzle I was trying to elucidate.

The first stint of field research in Jordan took place in March 2015. Due to the limited amount of time, I had prepared quite thoroughly, identifying and contacting relevant interview partners in advance, and collecting advice from other researchers. Aside from interviewing more aid managers, my only firm plan was to arrange visits to two refugee camps, Azraq and Zaatari. There, I hoped to be able to "hang out" at key camp locations, to observe the interaction between security and humanitarian concerns.

Unlike in Damascus, field research in Jordan immediately started off well. The difference in atmosphere, so much less fearful and oppressive than in Syria, thrilled me; simply the ability to openly meet research participants in cafés and talk about (most aspects of) Jordanian politics was an amazing and invigorating experience. I felt the world was my oyster. Similarly, the process of obtaining a permit to visit the refugee camps, which I had hugely worried over, proved a breeze, and was aided by the lucky break that the head of Azraq Camp had immediately responded to my e-mail, and had handed me over to her security advisers. They explained to me how to obtain the permit, who to call and visit, which documents to provide and so forth, and after a few days I had obtained the first permit, for a one-day visit to Azraq Camp. A one-day visit! Which, I discovered, was already lucky, as Azraq was considered to be much more off-limits than Zaatari. At the permit office, I witnessed an NGO worker's difficult negotiation to obtain a *three-day* visit to Zaatari camp, and decided, as this was my first contact with Jordanian authorities, to play it safe and not ask for more than one day. But how was I going to do any significant research in one day? Transport to Azraq, located 120 kilometers outside of Amman, 20 kilometers from the nearest town, proved another challenge. The UN bus was a possibility, public transport complicated, due to my need to arrive early in the morning to make the most of the day visit. In another lucky break, an aid manager I interviewed offered me an early morning lift.

In the meantime, I spent much time walking around West Amman, an exceedingly wealthy area, and picking the brains of researcher friends and other contacts. Jordan was still reeling from the recent killing of a Jordanian airline pilot by Da'esh and I noticed new, nationalistic propaganda posters around town, with slogans such as "Raise your head, you are Jordanian" (Peter Beaumont 2014; Sullivan and Tobin 2014). Such attempts to foment nationalism were significant for my research, as they related to a growing security focus on the Syrian refugee population, and perhaps a greater elite interest to marking this population as different from the Jordanian "nation" (Montoya 2015). Also, I regularly noticed the presence of abandoned or empty houses and flats in West Amman, which struck me as surprising, due to the constant chorus about how Jordan was flooded with refugees. Damascus in 2010 had truly and evidently been a city bursting at the seams, as wealthy and poor Iraqis alike rented or bought whatever property there was available. If Jordan was so overflowing, why were there not wealthy Syrians buying or renting these empty properties in West Amman? Adopting again a modus of constant ethnographic observation and awareness helped me to perceive my surroundings always through the prism of my research focus.

Thus, my Azraq visit began with me clambering into a Toyota jeep at 7:00 a.m. on Sunday morning, a ride through Amman's low-rise suburbs, and two hours on an increasingly remote desert highway. This growing remoteness—empty, blue skies hanging over empty, yellow gravel—became more and more oppressive as we drove on, due to the knowledge that somewhere, out there, 30,000 people were living against their will. The aid manager driving the jeep explained the topography to me, pointing out the air base at 50 kilometers from the camp, which was now being used by international forces to conduct air strikes in Syria and Iraq. Directly opposite the camp was a huge radar stationed used by the Americans. A clerk at AVIS, where he had rented the jeep, had told him that the Americans rented 200 vehicles for use in the enormous station, but he never saw them. What did I think were they doing in there? he asked conspiratorially. Eventually we reached the perimeters of Azraq, driving around it to reach the entrance. Behind barbed wire, rows and rows of little white huts (the innovatively designed "T-shelters" I had read so much about) stretched across the low desert hills. After a brand new road sign indicating "Azraq Camp," we reached the heavily fortified entrance, guarded by an armored vehicle of the military police and several barriers. My permit was closely examined and after a phone call and brief questioning, we were waved through.

Although I had frequently examined maps of Azraq, the significance of its vastness only struck me then. The camp is divided into distinct areas, such as the base camp, where aid organizations' caravans are located; the supermarket; the school; clinics; residential areas; which are all bounded, some by barbed wire, and are at several kilometers distance from each other. Moving between the base camp and the other camp areas would require hours, unless one has a car, as only aid workers and security personnel do. After arriving, I conducted several interviews at base camp, and then managed to hitch a ride into the camp with another aid manager, who took me to the community hall, where a kind of ceremony was taking place to thank a group of donors, who had provided improved solar lamps to the camp. I spent perhaps one hour hanging around the community hall, chatting with a group of camp residents and observing their interactions with camp security and aid staff. Most of the rest of the visit, including the ride back in the UN bus, was spent on recovering from this experience.

Without a doubt, Azraq was the most repressive place I had ever visited and its inhabitants were the most policed, surveilled, and controlled people I had ever encountered. Sandwiched between a fighter jet base and an enormous radar station—visible from nearly everywhere in the camp—surrounded by ditches and barbed wire, housed in prefab units that were spaced out in a way to ensure rapid access for police and military vehicles, and located a two-hour walk through open space from the camp "rulers," Azraq inhabitants were squeezed of as much room for agency as possible. All the while they were being fed, clothed, and their children educated according to humanitarian standards. The layering of humanitarian and security logics was not only evident in Azraq, but the entire camp was an expression of a logic in which humanitarian and security interest merged (nearly) seamlessly (Hoffmann 2015b, 2017).[5]

How do these two research cases speak to the experience of using ethnography as a method to address questions of global or transnational power-knowledge production? In the following paragraphs I will draw out the argument that while ethnography was an excellent method in the first case, it was not a good choice in the second case.

In Syria, ethnography's "fly-on-the-wall" approach allowed me to conduct thorough research in an environment, in which open questions would have placed myself and my research participants at risk. But it was not just ethnography's surreptitious qualities that were beneficial. Equally, observing and hanging out gave insights into the opportunities and limitations that Iraqis encountered in their daily lives as a result of the interventions of the Syrian state and aid organizations, which they did not, as interviews showed, always consciously reflect (Hoffmann 2011, 2015a). Understanding the degree of integration and laissez-faire through which Syrian authorities governed Iraqis was, I am convinced, *only possible* by walking around Damascene neighborhoods, in which vibrant Iraqi communities had rapidly developed. To truly feel and "get" the social impact of, for example, the public electoral campaigning and voting, which Iraqis were allowed to conduct in "their" neighborhoods, and which Syrians of course were denied, was only possible after having become, at least somewhat, a "part of" the Damascene space. Here, ethnography's classic moments of arrival, culture shock, and assimilation all played valuable roles for my ability to perceive and interpret the social developments taking place around me. Importantly, the fact that I was able to openly establish relationships with Iraqi migrants, visit them at their homes, have them visit mine, meet in restaurants and bars was itself an important research result established through ethnography. It demonstrated that in prerevolutionary Damascus, governance had little to do with nationality and citizenship, and much more with individual, financial, cultural, and social resources. Finally, it was the experience of the diversity and richness of Iraqi life in Syria, and the evident contrast it provided to the narrow image and concept of this life held by aid organizations, that eventually enabled me to develop the precise focus of my analysis. Ethnography-led theory development worked in Syria: first, because there were so few other, good sources on Iraqi livelihoods in Syria, and second, because associating with Iraqis was made easy by the type of governance they lived under.

In Jordan today, the obstacles to ethnography lie precisely in the inverse situation of migration governance found there: as Syrian migrants are moving from a position of tolerated migrant to security risk, "hanging out" with Syrians on a broadly reciprocal basis, which, I would argue is a requirement for good ethnographic work, is becoming more difficult. While colleagues looking at the general living conditions of Syrians in Jordan were able to conduct ethnographic work in urban centers, I argue that Azraq, as the most extreme expression of Jordan's new approach to Syrian migrants, is an impossible challenge for ethnographic research. After a single visit, I realized that my plan to conduct ethnography in the camp was doomed. Apart from the obstacles to access and an inability to move around independently, the prime reason for not conducting ethnography in Azraq, I would argue, was its *nonambiguous character*. Ethnography is frequently celebrated for its ability to capture and reproduce the ambiguity of governance, of reality and of scholarship. Here, it is precisely ethnography's erasure of distance between observer and observed, material and theory, knowledge and reality that is embraced as a type of "method," which avoids the fakery and posture of "scientific" social science (Wedeen 1999). But what if a situation is *unambiguously awful*? In a situation of obvious and utter domination, is ethnography an appropriate method to collect information by getting friendly with, and observing the oppressed? In a situation, in which research participants are thoroughly monitored, their daily-life behavior captured and calculated in databases, and surveillance is overwhelming, can *more* observation be carried out without adding to the domination? In Azraq, to me the answer was very obviously "no." Open as well as surreptitious, detailed observation were central methods of control in Azraq, especially toward inhabitants, but also toward anyone moving across the camp's territory (Hoffmann 2017). While this alone would have complicated research far beyond the situation of fear in Syria, the absolute singularity of an independent researcher's position in the camp made the notion of "hanging out" naturally absurd. To me, it appeared that these restraints, added to time- and money-restrictions of my research project, meant ethnographic research would present a serious risk of doing much more harm, and was not justified by the additional insights that were likely to be gained.

CONCLUDING ANALYSIS

Before moving to the final concluding paragraphs, I would like to draw attention to several important challenges confronting ethnographers of the "global," which do not yet seem to have received significant attention, or which emerge from the nature of the "ethnography-in-IR" debate itself. First, and crucially, there appears to be a real danger in this debate *to forget to talk about people*. Astonishingly, one can find in this debate texts about ethnographic methodology, which talk about analyzing, for example, "the life of policies" or "global policy fields" *without referring to people*. Given the centrality of human experience, behavior, voice, perception, indeed physical presence to ethnographic research, this strikes me as absurd. For even if ethnography is no longer about "capturing the native's view" (Sande Lie 2013, 204), is it not one of the most central ethnographic realizations that policies, fields, concepts, and dispositifs are nothing much beyond what humans make of it? And that thus, such structures are always fluid, always an outcome of power relations and struggles? In fact, silencing the "human factor" of ethnographic method precisely means erecting a power structure, allowing ethnographers to ignore not just questions of justice and equality, but also the effect of their own presence and work on such issues. Following a "people-free" approach to ethnography will turn IR scholars into monitory and evaluation specialists at best, and market researchers at worst, and must be guarded against.

The second challenge, which is related to the first, lies in worrying too much about concepts before conducting ethnography. Much of the ethnography-in-IR debate discusses questions such as the boundaries between the local and the global, the hierarchy of scales and levels, even the relation between units of analysis and interpretation! The risk in going down such rabbit holes lies in approaching the research via a set of premade boxes, which research participants themselves do not use to interpret their world, and would possibly even have a hard time grasping when confronted with them. Starting ethnographic research with a head full of scientist worries risks misinterpreting the views and behaviors of research participants, for whom, perhaps, the contradictions and fluidity of global-local relations and material-digital reality merge without much problem. Ethnography teaches the scholar precisely to see the world through an unscholarly lens. The question to puzzle out is, how is this lens built in the first place and what effect does it have on society and social reality? Ethnographers must be led by the worries and confusions that research participants express, which will be complex enough to understand, rather than their own anxieties about a world that may not fit established, disciplinary tools anymore.

Third, across the debate, the issue of "studying up" looms large. The aim to turn a scholarly gaze on those who have most successfully avoided it is highly welcome. Studying up clearly requires a different set of skills and perhaps also a different set of ethics than studying the impoverished and oppressed, and an investigation and exposure of these skills and ethics would be a helpful addition to encourage more scholars to attempt this challenge. In particular, an investigation into methods to counter the ability of the powerful to counter attempts to study their lives appears as a necessary step forward that has not yet been tackled. Surprisingly, the possibility of studying the powerful and the powerless within the same project does not seem to arise as a possibility in the debate, even though in practice it has been done (Khalili 2013; Venkatesh 2013; Wedeen 2008). My own research in Syria focused both on those subject to international intervention and those carrying out this intervention, and it was precisely the interaction between the two spheres that was most productive for analysis.

Fourth, it appears that IR's treatment of ethnography contains a risk to ignore or minimize the emotions or affects that ethnography invariable invokes. It would take a robot to conduct ethnographic research without encountering pleasant, unexpected, awkward, or frightening moments. In anthropology and sociology, the emotional and affective content of ethnography is relatively easily acknowledged and addressed by making explicit a researcher's positionality and including personal anecdotes into the narrative. In IR it seems there is more resistance to such acknowledgment, stemming probably from recognized limitations in the discipline that privilege a neutral, objective style of writing and analysis. Here, again, IR scholars seem to want the ethnographic cake, but only pick out what they see as the raisins: empirical authenticity and a claim to have left the scholarly armchair. And although I have expressed above the belief that ethnography is more adaptable than some of its idealists might believe, erasing ethnography's affective and emotional elements from methodological debate pretends that ethnography can be conducted in the same mental state as adding up statistics in front of a screen. This amounts to a fake assumption of an Archimedean viewpoint and, once again, means turning ethnography on its head.

Fifth, the question of what ethnography-in-IR scholars actually wish to address via ethnography remains under-answered. For some, the focus should be on "travelling blueprints" (Bierschenk 2014, 11), for others on "global policy regimes" (Stepputat and Larsen 2015), for yet others on the state or "development" (Bierschenk 2014a; Oliver de Sardan 2005; Sande Lie 2013). But does all this discussion not evade the heart of the matter, which is that

IR research is interested in power? And that global ethnography is about researching how the few manage to dominate the many, and command the lion's share of global resources? In whatever form, power appears to be central to the "ethnography-in-IR" debate, as a subject matter, but also as something that ethnography is particularly suitable to explore. Instead of making this explicit, IR debates on ethnography skirt around this issue, framing it instead as "normative questions," which can or cannot be considered by research. Acknowledging the centrality of power relations and imbalance to ethnography-in-IR's research focus would do much to push the debate in the right direction.

To conclude, and to return to the comparison at the heart of this article, ethnography, today, is ready to become a regular method of choice for the qualitative IR researcher. Whether to choose it or not should depend on the empirical material available, the questions sought to answer, and the temporal and financial limitations of a project. There may be numerous reasons why ethnography may not end up being the most appropriate method, including, as the example in this article showed, the impossibility of conducting ethnographic research ethically or when the risk of adding to an oppression outweighs the value of the possible knowledge gained. A thirst for knowledge, or the ambition to be at the cutting edge of research, which most scholars will at least understand, has led (and probably continues to lead) ethnographers toward ethnical violations, sometimes of shocking extent. Teaching, seeking out, and debating ethnography's classic and evolved principles, while not considering them as set in stone, will point the way ahead for this important method-methodology in IR research.

NOTES

1. Other examples of such theories include interdependence theory or regime theory.

2. Briefly, the core principles of ethnography may be summarized as (1) living with informants under equal conditions, (2) interacting in the local language, (3) participating in all activities, (4) grasping the "imponderabilia of actual life," (5) embedding phenomena in their multitude of contexts, and (6) perceiving phenomena as singular (Sande Lie 2013).

3. Notably, despite this focus on empirical research at SOAS, my cohort of PhD students was only the second one to receive a course on quantitative and qualitative methods training—confirming the widely held (and false) assumption that method is what one learns in the field. Today, this methods course is firmly established at SOAS.

4. This postdoc project was generously supported by a Marie-Curie COFUND grant and the University of Bremen, Germany.

5. I write "nearly" seamlessly, because both aid workers and security managers occasionally expressed unease with the effect that Azraq had on the living situation of refugees.

REFERENCES

al-Khalidi, Ashraf, Sophia Hoffmann, and Victor Tanner. *Iraqi Refugees in the Syrian Arab Republic: A Field-Based Snapshot.* Washington DC: The Brookings Institution, 2007.

Bierschenk, T. (2014a). *Entwicklungsethnologie und Ethnologie der Entwicklung: Deutschland, Europa, USA* (No. 150; Arbeitspapiere Des Instituts Für Ethnologie Und Afrikastudien Der Johannes Gutenberg-Universität Mainz). Ifeas.

Bierschenk, Thomas. "From the Anthropology of Development to the Anthropology of Global Social Engineering." *Zeitschrift Für Ethnologie* 139(2014b): 73–98.

Bollettino, Vincenzo. "Understanding the Security Management Practices of Humanitarian Organisations." *Disasters* 32 (2008): 263–79. doi:10.1111/j. 0361-3666.2008.01038.x.

Burkle, Frederick M. "Anatomy of an Ambush: Security Risks Facing International Humanitarian Assistance." *Disasters* 29(2005): 26–37.

Care International. (2015). *Factsheet Azraq Refugee Camp.* Care International. http://www.care.org/sites/default/files/documents/CARE_Factsheet_Syria_azraq_camp_April_2015.pdf

Christian Aid. (2010). *Saving Lives Together: A Review of Security Collaboration between the UN and Humanitarian Actors on the Ground.*

Emerson, Robert M., Rachel I. Fretz, and Linda L. Shaw. *Writing Ethnographic Fieldnotes.* Chicago: Chicago University Press, 1995.

Fassin, Didier. *Humanitarian Reason: A Moral History of the Present Times.* Los Angeles: University of California Press, 2011.

Feldman, Allen. *Formations of Violence.* Chicago: University Of Chicago Press, 1991.

Feldman, Ilana. *Governing Gaza: Bureaucracy, Authority, and the Work of Rule, 1917–1967.* Durham: Duke University Press, 2008.

Feldman, Martha S., Jeannine Bell, and Michele T. Berger. *Gaining Access: A Practical and Theoretical Guide for Qualitative Researchers.* Walnut Creek: Altamira Press, 2003.

Gille, Zsuzsa, and Seán Ó. Riain. "Global Ethnography." *Annual Review of Sociology* 28 (2002): 271–95.

Gupta, Akhil, and James Ferguson. *Culture, Power, Place. Explorations in Critical Anthropology.* Durham: Duke University Press, 1997.

Hoffmann, Sophia. "The Humanitarian Regime of Sovereignty: INGOs and Iraqi Migration to Syria." *Refuge* 28: 59–70.

Hoffmann, Sophia. "Humanitarian Sovereignty: The Management of Refugees as Nation-state Politics." In *The Politics of Humanitarianism, edited by* Antonio De Lauri, 147–74. London: I.B. Tauris, 2015a.

Hoffmann, Sophia. "Wen schützen Flüchtlingslager? Care and Control im jordanischen Lager Azraq." *Peripherie* 35 (2015b): 281–302.

Hoffmann, Sophia. *Iraqi Migrants in Syria: The Crisis Before the Storm.* Syracuse: Syracuse University Press, 2016.

Hoffmann, Sophia. "Humanitarian Security in Jordan's Azraq Camp." *Security Dialogue* 48 (2017): 97–112. doi:10.1177/0967010616683311.

Huisman, Kimberly. "'Does this Mean You're not Going to Come Visit Me Anymore?': An Inquiry into an Ethics of Reciprocity and Positionality in Feminist Ethnographic Research." *Sociological Inquiry* 78: (2008) 372–96.doi:10.1111/j .1475-682X.2008.00244.x.

International Medical Corps, & UNHCR. (2014). *Detailed Health Report for Azraq Camp.*

Khalili, Laleh. *Time in the Shadows: Confinement in Counterinsurgencies.* Stanford: Stanford University Press, 2013.

Kraft, Katherine. *Two Changing Spheres: NGOs and Iraqis in Syria.* Brea: Middle East Fellowship, 2008.

Kydd, Andrew H. *International Relations Theory: The Game-Theoretic Approach.* Cambridge: Cambridge University Press, 2015.

Levi-Strauss, Claude. *Das Wilde Denken.* Frankfurt: Suhrkamp, 1984.

Marcus, George E. "Ethnography in/of the World System: The Emergence of Multi-Sited Ethnography." *Annual Review of Anthropology* 24 (1995): 95–117.

Menzel, Anne. "Zwischen Herrschaftswissen und Irrelevanz? Feldforschung und das Ringen mit der Policy Relevanz." *Zeitschrift Für Friedens- Und Konfliktforschung* 3 (2014): 264–83.

Montoya, Katy . "Syrian Refugees Collectivizing in Jordan Becomes a Security Issue." Accessed October 28, 2020. http://www.jadaliyya.com/pages/index/20911/ syrian-refugees-collectivizing-in-jordan-becomes-a.

Olivier de Sardan, Jean-Pierre. "Development Projects and Social Logic." In *Anthropology and Development: Understanding Contemporary Social Change,* edited by Jean-Pierre Olivier de Sardan, 137-49. London: Zed Books, 2005.

Ong, Aihwa. *Neoliberalism as Exception: Mutations in Citizenship and Sovereignty.* Durham: Duke University Press, 2006.

Beaumont, Peter. "Jordan Opens New Syrian refugee Camp." Accessed October 15, 2020. http://www.theguardian.com/world/2014/apr/30/jordan-new-syrian-refugee -camp-al-azraq.

Rabinow, Paul. *Reflections on Fieldwork in Morocco.* Berkeley and Los Angeles: University of California Press, 1977.

Sande Lie, Jon H. "Challenging Anthropology: Anthropological Reflections on the Ethnographic Turn in International Relations." *Millennium—Journal of International Studies* 41 (2013): 201–20.

Stepputat, F., & Larsen, J. (2015). *Global Political Ethnography: A Methodological Approach to Studying Global Policy Regimes* (DIIS Working Paper). Danish Institute for International Studies.

Stoler, Ann L. *Along the Archival Grain.* Princeton: Princeton University Press, 2008.

Sullivan, Dennis, and Sarah Tobin. "Security and Resilience Among Syrian Refugees in Jordan." *Merip Online*, October 14, 2014, http://www.merip.org/mero/mero101414.

Szanto, Thomas. *Bewusstsein, Intentionalität und mentale Repräsentation*. Berlin and Boston: Walter de Gruyter, 2012.

Trouillot, Michel-Rolph. *Silencing the Past: Power and the Production of History*. Boston: Beacon Press, 1997.

UNHABITAT, IFRC, & UNHCR. (2014). Shelter Case Study Jordan—Syria Crisis: Azraq Camp. In *Shelter Projects 2013-14*. UNHABITAT, IFRC, UNHCR. http://www.sheltercasestudies.org/shelterprojects2013-2014/SP13-14_A10-Jordan-2013.pdf

Venkatesh, Sudhir. *Floating City*. New York: Penguin, 2013.

Verdery, Katherine. *Secrets and Truths: Ethnography in the Archive of Romania's Secret Police*. Budapest: Central European University Press, 2013.

Vrasti, Wanda. "The Strange Case of Ethnography and International Relations." *Millennium—Journal of International Studies* 37 (2008): 279–301. doi:10.1177/0305829808097641.

Vrasti, Wanda. "Dr Strangelove, or How I Learned to Stop Worrying about Methodology and Love Writing." *Millennium—Journal of International Studies* 39 (2010): 79–88. doi:10.1177/0305829810371017.

Wedeen, Lisa. *Ambiguities of Domination: Politics, Rhetoric, and Symbols in Contemporary Syria*. Chicago: University of Chicago Press, 1999.

Wedeen, Lisa. *Peripheral Visions: Publics, Power, and Performance in Yemen*. Chicago: University Of Chicago Press, 2008.

Weizman, Eyal. *Hollow Land: Israel's Architecture of Occupation*. London: Verso, 2007.

Weizman, Eyal. *The Least of All Possible Evils: Humanitarian Violence from Arendt to Gaza*. London: Verso, 2012.

Chapter 4

Zooming in Dissolves the Taken-for-Granted and Allows to Reconstruct Its Production

Toward a Political Anthropology of Global Health Governance as Lived Order

Julian Eckl

While often overlooked, the conversation between political anthropology and political science—including its subfield of international relations—started more than half a century ago.[1] Bringing this common past to mind not only shows shared research interests but also helps to appreciate what is particular about current debates. Before turning to my work on global health governance, I will briefly set the stage by revisiting the past and thereby link this chapter to the broader concerns of the edited volume.

Some precursors notwithstanding, 1940 can be seen as the year in which political anthropology emerged in earnest when M. Fortes and E. E. Evans-Pritchard published their edited volume *African Political Systems* (Fortes and Evans-Pritchard 1950). The volume was very British in the sense that it was rooted in British social anthropology in general and in British structural-functionalism in particular. But it was British not only in an academic but also in a practical sense since it addressed some of the riddles that had emerged when the British struggled to establish colonial rule in parts of Africa. The book proved very influential within political anthropology even though important criticisms emerged (Leach 1954) and in spite of the fact that anthropology as such would eventually engage critically with its colonial past (Asad 1973).

What is even more important for the present purpose is that the book also caught the interest of political scientists (Easton 1959) and proved

particularly influential on international relations. The most visible link
between political anthropology and international relations is also a British—
or English—one in the sense that the so-called English School in particular
drew on it.[2] This applies both to structural-functionalist reasoning and to the
basic theme of distinguishing between hierarchical and anarchical *societies*,
that is, societies with and without centralized authority (Fortes and Evans-
Pritchard 1950, 5–6). These two aspects are especially obvious in Hedley
Bull's *The Anarchical Society* (Bull 1977). While Bull agrees with those
authors who argue that the international—or anarchical—society is not simply a "primitive" society on a global scale (Masters 1964), he still draws on
African Political Systems and some of the ideas that emerged in its aftermath
to make the general point that also under the conditions of anarchy order is
possible (Bull 1977, 59–65). Moreover, Bull's way of theorizing draws on
structural-functionalist ideas and terminology to such a degree that he saw
himself obliged to explicitly point out that he was nevertheless not a structural-functionalist (Bull 1977, 74–6). This disclaimer and Bull's concern with
just change notwithstanding, one reviewer in particular felt at times reminded
of "an old-fashioned treatise in anthropology or sociology" and was not quite
convinced by Bull's distancing from structural-functionalism (Mandelbaum
1977, 575).[3]

At least from a British perspective, one could consequently assert that
the conversation between political anthropology and political science/inter-
national relations has been there "from the start" even though this was not
always acknowledged or has been forgotten in the meantime. The central
question is therefore what is specific about the current exchange, and I will
argue that it is the methodological considerations and their consequences
that are key. This claim can be illustrated with Bull's aforementioned *The
Anarchical Society* since it is marked by clear anthropological traits but not
the product of ethnographic field research. Rather, it is obvious throughout
the book that Bull relied much on historical analysis and diachronic comparison. This reliance on history notwithstanding, Bull made even clear at
the beginning of the book that his main focus was not on questions of methodology but on theory building: quoting Samuel Alexander, Bull argued that
"thinking is also research" and seemed to suggest that abstract reasoning or
"thinking it through" was his main research method (Bull 1977, x). As evidenced by Bull's illuminating insights and by the influence of the book, this
approach has its strengths, but it also suggests that the increasing relevance
of (political) ethnography as a research methodology is a novelty indeed. In
other words, while authors like Bull made use of anthropological findings,
ideas, and terminology, a lot of the contemporary interest in political anthropology is a consequence of the methodological fascination with firsthand
encounters with "the political."[4]

RENEWING THE CONVERSATION

These developments illustrate that political anthropology offers multiple sources of inspiration and that international relations as an eclectic subdiscipline of political science might draw divergent conclusions from it. As a consequence, I will not try to answer the very broad question of what political anthropology may or may not have to contribute to international relations, but I will rather draw on methodological changes in my own research on global health governance in order to develop the following argument: while social constructivism and other approaches of the "Third Debate" (Lapid 1989) have been emphasizing for decades that the world around us is the product of human interactions, reification is such a pervasive and persuasive process that it is very difficult for researchers not to mimic the people they study and not to use terms such as "the state," "the military," "the European Union," "the World Health Organization (WHO)," and so forth as if they referred to self-evidently existing entities. One way to work against this tendency is to rely on political ethnography since, by zooming in on the objects of study, ethnographic field research has a tendency to dissolve what was assumed to be circumscribed and fixed. Moreover, building on the newly discovered details and on the estrangement effect that comes along with it, the researcher can start to investigate the question of how the impression of stasis had originally been produced.

Paying attention to and reflecting on the (micro) practices that (re)produce social entities, researchers will probably realize that a lot of the discussions in international relations appear as strangely distant and abstract while there is a very rich anthropological—and sociological—discussion on human interactions that will also help political ethnographers to make sense of their observations. In other words, while I start with the assertion that it is the methodological considerations in particular that make political anthropology interesting for political scientists, I will also argue that this will eventually lead to an interest in anthropological and sociological concepts, models, and styles of theorizing, but these will not start at the level of society as structural-functionalism did and hence it will be approaches of a different kind.

To some extent, the implications of a bottom-up approach to politics had already been mentioned by A. R. Radcliffe-Brown in his preface to *African Political Systems*, but the challenge was not quite taken up by mainstream international relations—even though one could argue that approaches like bureaucratic politics (e.g., Halperin 1972) avoided the lure of taking words such as "the state" for entities and to treat "the state" as a black box. In a much-quoted paragraph, Radcliffe-Brown essentially argued that "the state" as such did not really exist but was "a fiction of the philosophers" (Radcliffe-Brown 1950, xiii). While the philosophers were certainly among those who contributed to a reification of the state, one could add that "we all" engage in it and that an ethnographic take on politics can help us to appreciate how we succeed at it. In short, those political scientists/international relations scholars who want to move beyond the taken-for-granted and to develop a sense for the (re)production of social entities will find that political ethnography and the conceptual discussions that it will inevitably give rise to constitute a particularly productive and inspiring avenue toward this goal.

The remainder of this contribution will be organized in the following way. First, I will explain one of the key considerations for which I moved beyond document analysis and made my research on global health governance more ethnographic; this section will also explicate what my interpretation of ethnography is. Second, I will elaborate on the question of what additional issues and empirical puzzles emerged after the ensuing ethnographic turn, that is, once I had started to try to get to the *"nearest possible vantage point"* (Schatz 2009a, 307 emphasis in original) and began to visit key sites of global health governance. For the present purpose, I will focus the discussion on sites that are related to the WHO, and I will highlight in particular in what sense visiting these sights differed from reading about them in the official records. Third, I will show how the additional issues and puzzles in particular made me revisit approaches that look at social order from a bottom-up perspective, that is, that investigate "lived order" (Pollner and Emerson 2001); in this context, I will also investigate the question of what kind of empirical material the official records actually are, how they are produced, and what role they play for the actors themselves. Fourth, I will address the question of what implications this has for the study of WHO (or other international organizations) and for the conversation between political anthropology and political science/international relations.

PRIMARY SOURCES AND PERSONAL IMMERSION: TWO AVENUES TOWARD RICH EMPIRICAL DETAIL

Historical research promises to help to avoid reification and to remind oneself of the contingent and human-made character of the world around us. While diachronic comparison for the purpose of estrangement or critical reflection is advocated and practiced by various scholars, I have been particularly inspired by power analysis (Foucault 1984; Lukes 2005, 1974), science and technology studies (Bijker 1995), and international political economy (Cox 1986). Actually, as mentioned before, also scholars like Bull relied on historical analysis; however, the authors just quoted emphasized the critical potential of diachronic comparison while Bull and others displayed a tendency to use it primarily to develop ideal types or to construct abstract (structural-functionalist) models of society. In conducting diachronic comparison along the lines suggested by the more critical strand of authors, I found it paramount not to rely on secondary sources alone. Rather, I have always strived to get hold of primary sources as well and in a political science context these were often the official records of public actors as well as media reports and similar sources that commented on political processes. This approach proved helpful both for the analysis of long-term political struggles that lasted over decades and centuries (Eckl 2004, 2010) and for the analysis of individual decision-making processes that lasted for several years (Eckl 2006). A particularly rich source was the analysis of the records and minutes of national and international decision-making fora since they provided a detailed account of the divergent voices that were raised at the time and of the language and frames that were used. The richness of these documents became particularly apparent when I contrasted them with the final documents that were the outcome of the decision-making process or—even more so—when comparing them with the condensed accounts in secondary sources.

The strengths of diachronic comparison based on the analysis of documents notwithstanding, I still developed an increasing concern with this kind of research, in particular since I became more and more dissatisfied with the problem that particularly marginalized voices would not even make it into the official minutes and records. This was a problematic issue since students of power have long argued that the most subtle forms of power are at work if conflicts stay covert or remain latent (Lukes 1974, 2005). Insights from my own research on global health governance reinforced this point; for example, I came across retrospective accounts of WHO's far-reaching—but eventually unsuccessful—decision of 1955 to start a "global" malaria eradication campaign that made the following point: "It was in private talks rather than during the debates, as those present at the time may recall, that the most serious criticisms were expressed, despite the overwhelming result of the vote" (Gramiccia and Beales 1988, 1345, see also 1348–1349 as well as Nájera 1999, 41–42 and Trigg and Kondrachine 1998, 11–12). Similarly, when the Gates Foundation hosted the Malaria Forum in 2007, and when Bill and Melinda Gates declared that it was time to start a new effort to eradicate malaria, criticism was expressed "offstage" rather than in the discussions that followed (Brown 2008; McNeil 2008; Paulson 2007).[5]

In light of these considerations and as a consequence of my increasing focus on contemporary political issues,[6] I concluded that I should supplement my documents-based research with participant observation (and interviews) at the sites at which such decisions are taken in order to bring the aforementioned private criticisms to the fore. In retrospect, I would also add the following point to these considerations: the increasing acceptance of (political) ethnography in general and of participant observation in particular had created an environment that made ethnography a much easier choice than previously. Thinking about it now, I would even argue that I experienced the change firsthand myself but was not fully aware of it then. When I worked ethnographically as a student in the years 2001 and 2002 and when I later suggested an ethnographic case study for my doctoral dissertation in 2006, my ideas were met with a mixture of disinterest and outright rejection. By contrast, when I shared my ideas about doing an ethnographic project on global health governance in 2010, I even felt encouraged to give it a try—although a lot of my colleagues remained skeptical if it was going to be feasible and worth the effort.

My eventual (re)turning to ethnography did not mean that I had to turn away from historical, documents-based analysis at all. Rather, I view my previous approach as—in principle—compatible with an ethnographic one.[7] In other words, when I speak of ethnography, I imply primarily that the project should go beyond an analysis of documents in a particular way; this may or may not include the analysis of additional, non-textual artifacts but will usually comprise an engagement with people and often the people who produced the key artifacts, or are otherwise related to them, are the ones to start with. The preferable way to get in contact with people would be participant observation but sometimes (ethnographic) interviews with only a small element of participant observation constitute the *"nearest possible vantage point"* (Schatz 2009a, 307 emphasis in original; for an example, see Schia 2013). Some authors have suggested the term "immersion" in order to label that element of ethnography that encourages the researcher to get in contact with the field (Schatz 2009a); I would add that one way to describe ethnography would be to say that it rests on three pillars (artifact analysis, interviews, and participant observation) and aims, in particular, at creating situations in which the researcher's own senses can be used as data collection instruments rather than relying merely on data that others have collected.[8]

What makes a project ethnographic then is not that it is limited to participant observation but rather its striving for immersion and its openness for heterogeneous data or material, which the researcher collects and produces in the course of the research process. While the specific way in which the heterogeneous material could subsequently be interpreted and integrated used to be rather mysterious, "grounded theory," in its interpretative strand in particular (Charmaz and Mitchell 2001), has in recent years proven to be a highly compatible methodology and many textbooks on ethnography draw on it explicitly (e.g., Emerson, Fretz, and Shaw 2011; Gobo 2008). Finally, "ethnography" can also refer to a particular style of writing and ethnographic research will often be written up in texts that deviate from the standard template of academic publications (Yanow 2009a).

To summarize, while it was not the only argument in favor of my "personal ethnographic turn," the most important one for the present purpose was an interest in those voices that did not appear in the official records of the relevant governance bodies. By drawing on participant observation in particular, I hoped to be able to document some of the grievances that would be expressed in private conversations—be it in the hallways of official buildings or around the tables of nearby restaurants. As it turned out eventually, however, ethnography not only opens an additional avenue for data collection but also has a profound impact on the conceptual-theoretical dimension of research.

THE PROJECT AND PUZZLING
INSIGHTS FROM THE FIELD

The project that emerged eventually from these and other considerations had the task of investigating global health governance from an "insider's perspective," that is, to address the question of how practitioners come to terms with the fragmented nature of the global health governance architecture.[9] The project was planned as a multisited ethnography and the selection of sites was going to be carried out incrementally, following a logic of holistic reconstruction[10] on the one hand and a logic of comparison on the other hand.[11] While the aforementioned issue of the marginalized voices was still a concern of the project, it had been broadened to the general manner in which global health governance is experienced. The idea behind the project's setup was that the various practical problems that I as a researcher would encounter would also offer insights into the challenges that the practitioners face. For example, not only I but also they would face the challenge of avoiding scheduling conflicts and the task of being at the right place at the right time if they wanted to engage in governance processes and to make their voices heard.

In order to illustrate how my turn toward ethnography led me to rethink much more than anticipated, I will, in the following, focus on what I assumed to be one specific "site," namely the WHO. In a way I felt quite familiar with WHO even before attending any WHO-related meeting since I had engaged with piles of official WHO documents in my diachronic study of the global struggle against malaria (Eckl 2010). WHO resolutions and other official documents from the World Health Assembly (WHA, or Assembly) as WHO's supreme decision-making body had been particularly relevant. I had, of course, also read documents from Executive Board (EB, or Board) meetings but the main focus had still been on the Assembly that takes the authoritative decisions. Moreover, the Board was in a way present at the Assembly, too, since its key documents would feed into the Assembly's decision-making process. In sum, while I knew that the Assembly was not WHO's only decision-making body, I still considered my field trip to the Assembly as my field trip to WHO as such.

This initial assumption was challenged by various empirical observations that amount to the insight that from an insider's perspective, WHO is not a single site but consists of a multitude of (sub)sites which illustrates the broader claim that ethnographic research has a tendency to dissolve the taken-for-granted. There are three aspects to this claim and I will briefly introduce them before elaborating on each of them. First, from the perspective of the individual participant, not even the Assembly is a single site but a frame that holds various processes together, each of which takes place in more specific subsites. For example, delegates conduct their work both in plenary as well as in committee meetings that can run in parallel to one another and might even be accompanied by additional meetings such as meetings of drafting groups. Second, it also turned out that I had not taken the differences between the Assembly and other sites that constitute WHO seriously enough and that even if one focuses on the decision-making (or governance) aspect of WHO, it is more than just one site. In particular, the Assembly is preceded and followed by both closely and loosely connected meetings and activities of which the Board meetings are just one example—albeit an important one. Third, and drawing on the previous two points, probably the most striking observation was that WHO is strangely absent from these governance meetings even though they constitute its supreme governance bodies. In other words, while I had assumed that by attending these meetings I would get to the heart of the organization, this center proved to be void in the sense that it rather diverted me into various other directions which suggested that there is probably no center as such.

THE ASSEMBLY AS MULTIPLE SITES

The first aspect supporting the claim that from an insider's perspective WHO is not a single site is the observation that not even the Assembly is a single site: there could be a plenary meeting in the assembly hall, a committee meeting in one of the large conference rooms, and one or several drafting group meetings in the smaller meeting rooms—not to mention the need to speak to someone in private which also makes it difficult for delegates to actually get into the official meeting rooms. Moreover, there are coordination meetings for regional and other groups, and some delegations even hold coordination meetings exclusively for their own delegates. Finally, over lunch and in the evening in particular, there are also technical briefings and side events. All of these competing meetings would still take place in the same complex of buildings, namely the *Palais des Nations* and most of them would also be announced in the *World Health Assembly Journal*.[12] There is, however, another set of meetings, which is advertised through leaflets, word-of-mouth advertising, direct invitations, and so forth, and takes place outside of the official premises—thereby linking yet other sites to the Assembly. Typical examples would be the meeting rooms of permanent missions, hotels, international organizations, and museums. These rooms allow actors other than states to take on a central role and allow generally for additional forms of interaction and conduct.

The key point about the various meetings at different sites is that both the ones within and the ones outside of the *Palais* contribute to the proliferation of parallel meetings. The ensuing time/place conflicts are felt by the field researcher as well and I started more and more to agree with my interlocutors who warned me that I would have to set priorities and to accept the fact that you cannot be everywhere at the same time. These similarities between the experiences of the participants and my own experiences were extremely helpful for understanding their day-to-day problems.

When it comes to understanding the day-to-day problems of the participants, it is particularly noteworthy that the parallel processes at the Assembly make the overburdening of the smaller delegations strikingly tangible. Moreover, their weakness in the form of understaffing helps the larger delegations also at a very practical level since any seat that is left empty by the smaller delegations can be used by the larger ones in order to fit more than the usual two delegates into committee rooms. In other words, while each delegation is officially assigned two seats in a committee room, delegates tend to sit wherever there are empty seats (and preferably close to their fellow delegates) even if this implies that "overflow delegates" will be sitting behind the name plate of another country. As a consequence, the actual difference between country delegations in terms of capacity and staffing is quite obvious to the trained observer who knows about the actual affiliations of the people in the room while the architectural setup and the seating arrangement in terms of the name plates emphasize the sovereign equality of countries.

A second consequence of the fragmented and parallel nature of the Assembly proceedings is that a substantial part of the delegates does not stay in the individual rooms for the whole working day. While this is in part also attributable to the division of labor within delegations, both in conversations with me and in discussions with each other, delegates have time and again pointed out that they could not stay the whole day—and in particular not without interruption—because of competing responsibilities. The somewhat strange consequence of this is that there are constantly people entering and leaving the rooms while the delegates appear to be playing musical or, rather, thematic chairs. This practice has at times odd consequences for the discussions as such since it is not uncommon that someone contributes to a debate of which he or she did not hear the beginning or that someone makes an intervention but has left by the time at which someone else replies to it.

What these points amount to is that "being there," that is, visiting a site, does not mean that one can cover it "entirely" at all. Both researchers and practitioners face this problem and these lived experiences stand in stark contrast to the impression that the official records had given me. They had suggested in particular that an Assembly was a manageable sequential process that could just as easily be followed "live" as one could simply read the verbatim and summary records from the first page to the last. Similarly, through the list of participants that they contained, the records had conveyed a completely static picture of who participated and mirrored in no way the actual flow of people. In other words, the Assembly as a single site that is attended by a set number of participants exists only in as well as through synoptic written accounts.

THE ASSEMBLY AS ONE OF SEVERAL
POLICY-MAKING SITES WITHIN WHO

While the previous subsection emphasized the fact that the Assembly as WHO's supreme decision-making body is not a single site, this section looks at the relationship between the Assembly and other sites of WHO governance in order to elaborate further on the claim that WHO dissolved into multiple sites once I zoomed in on it. As indicated above, I had obviously been aware of the fact that also the EB (or Board) plays a role in WHO policy making but compared to the Assembly its role appeared much more marginal. For example, in the course of my documents-based research on the global struggle against malaria, both primary and secondary sources would usually refer to resolutions of the Assembly when discussing global policies against malaria. Similarly, the annual meeting of the Assembly in May is the highlight of the global health calendar and thousands of people attend the various events inside and outside of the *Palais*; by contrast, meetings of the Board and other decision-making sites get much less public attention.

In spite of the apparent relevance of the Assembly, several of my interlocutors in Geneva—implicitly or explicitly—suggested to me that the main bulk of the work had been done before the opening of the Assembly and that I had missed a large part of the story by not having been there. From their perspective, I could not really understand the processes if I only attended the Assembly. While these comments came in different forms and had varying implications, the main consequence for my research design was that I decided to not only revisit the Assembly in subsequent years but to systematically visit these other sites as well. This strategy worked in principle but one striking insight of this endeavor was that it turned out to be almost a "regressus ad infinitum" since each meeting seemed to have been preceded by another—potentially more relevant—meeting; usually these preparatory meetings were meetings of a subset of the participants. For example, when I attended a meeting of the Board, I learned that the meeting had been preceded and prepared by a meeting of the Board's Program, Budget, and Administration Committee (PBAC) and when I attended a meeting of WHO's Regional Committee (RC) for Europe, I learned about the much smaller but crucial Standing Committee of the Regional Committee (SCRC). In other words, while my visit to the Assembly made it obvious that other sites of policy making were also important, none of them would by itself qualify as "the real" center of decision-making.

To be sure, I could have learned about the mere *existence* of these other sites also by studying documents, but regarding *relevance* I found it still remarkable that the picture that emerged from an engagement with the participants was almost the mirror image of my previous impression where the Assembly was key and all other sites served merely a supplementary role. It also changed my perception of WHO activities and decisions since it became clear that policy making takes place virtually the year round but comes in various formats that vary by key features such as their inclusiveness. (For example, all 194 member states have a seat and an equal vote at the Assembly while the Board has thirty-four members and PBAC only fourteen.)[13] Moreover, in order to understand the lived reality of policy making it was also important to try to attend these meetings myself since it drew my attention to some of the challenges that these—at least in sum—frequent meetings create.[14]

While I had to overcome additional challenges such as getting access as a researcher, a large part of my own experiences overlapped with those of other participants. Most importantly, everyone faces the challenge of being at the right place at the right time, which is similar to the task of being in the right room at the right time during the Assembly. Even the representatives of states do not always meet this challenge and some interlocutors missed individual meetings (i.e., decision-making sites) beyond the Assembly because they underestimated their relevance or because other reasons prevented them from doing so; typical obstacles for attending were scheduling conflicts, restrictions on the annual amount of business trips/lack of travel funding, or the problem that their country was not an elected member of a particular forum; division of labor and a poor flow of information could also be an issue, that is, the meeting was attended by someone else who represented the same country but did not meet the expectations. Moreover, it turned out that I was not the only one who was struggling to understand the role of the various sites of decision-making. Similarly, not only I had underestimated the degree to which the individual meetings are highly prestructured: several interlocutors told me that either they personally or people they knew were not able to contribute to the discussion of an existing agenda item or to bring up an entirely new agenda item since they had not understood the way in which the agenda was set or because they did not know when and where certain topics were discussed in depth.

Overall, WHO policy making turned out to be much more of a moving target than the routine reference to the Assembly as the supreme decision-making site suggests. Typical examples of other relevant sites are the Board, PBAC, and the RCs, all of which can be considered as being part of a core annual policy cycle; but there are even more sites including special-purpose intersession meetings, advisory committees, and other much less formal gatherings. As just indicated, this means that the people involved in the policy-making process might vary and it poses various challenges for the participants that have consequences for questions of transparency and inclusiveness. Actually, one could say that both the multitude of parallel processes at the individual sites (at the Assembly in particular) and the multitude of meetings throughout the year have the consequence that member states that have limited resources and/or that are not elected members of the additional bodies will find it particularly difficult to actively engage. At the same time, it has to be pointed out that the various additional bodies that are marked by a small number of participants are often consequential since one of their main tasks is to reach consensus before the subsequently following larger meeting is opened. It is in this context that the Board has started to become a "mini-WHA" that has absorbed some of the work of the Assembly while some decisions of the Board are merely nodded through by the Assembly.[15]

To summarize, there is no quintessential center at which all WHO policy-making processes take place but they have to pass through important bottlenecks at which they become visible and are formalized. The Assembly is the most important of these bottlenecks and it is particularly important from an outside perspective since its outcomes are communicated to an external audience. However, it is quite likely that by the time a process reaches this bottleneck, all important decisions have been taken, while the memory of the actual complexity of the course of events starts to fade away and a streamlined version of the process is preserved in the official records.[16]

THE ABSENCE OF WHO AT WHO MEETINGS

In this subsection, I elaborate further on the claim that WHO kind of dissolved in the course of my field research. I do this by discussing the strange absence of WHO during WHO governance meetings. This does, of course, not mean that WHO was completely absent but it was less present than expected or present in a way that was different from the one that I had anticipated. Moreover, there was not one WHO that was present but it manifested itself in different forms and roles. Some of them were subject to self-efficacy and others were more easily recognizable. I start with one of these roles before I expand on the absence of WHO at WHO governance meetings. While I focus on the Assembly, most of these arguments hold also for other governance meetings.

The first role in which I encountered WHO in the context of an Assembly meeting was the role of a gatekeeper. In preparing for my initial trip to the Assembly, I had to figure out what the possibilities and conditions for attending governance meetings were. While I tried first to register as an academic observer and later as a journalist, my e-mails and phone calls to the people listed on the WHO website as contact persons remained long unanswered. Only eventually and in a piecemeal fashion was I able to obtain the relevant information and at the end of a time-consuming process it turned out that the best option would be to obtain a public badge by queuing up early in the morning at WHO headquarters. This option worked also in practice but it was cumbersome since it had to be done for every single day and since there was only a limited number of public badges available, which made it compulsive to arrive among the first. But also from the perspective of delegates who attend the Assembly, WHO has a certain gatekeeping role since WHO sets the terms of the registration procedure and issues the badges that allow delegates to enter the *Palais*.[17]

This gatekeeping role can be seen as one aspect of WHO's larger role as the host of governance meetings, a role in which I repeatedly encountered WHO during my visits to the Assembly. Actually, if one takes the perspective of the delegates and if one looks at the Assembly from a very practical angle, one could argue that WHO is primarily a conference host that has the responsibility to allow for a smooth policy-making process among member states. There are various aspects to this hosting role and in addition to gatekeeping, there is another key aspect that has to be taken care of even before the Assembly starts: the timely provision of the documents on which the discussions will be based; this aspect proved particularly important and the late availability of these documents (in particular in languages other than English) was actually a recurring point of contention.

In addition to the multitude of documents that were made available on the website before the opening of the Assembly, WHO also produced documents during the Assembly; these included the *World Health Assembly Journal*, conference papers, revised versions of draft resolutions, and other accompanying material. At a more infrastructural level there is an endless amount of things that have to be prepared before and taken care of during meetings—from planning and indicating the seating arrangement to approving, scheduling, and conducting side events. Even though each of these steps might seem like a small contribution to the overall goal of WHO governance they are still among the very concrete manifestations of WHO that delegates encounter during their time in Geneva. Interestingly enough, a lot of the WHO staff who are present at the meetings and contribute to this hosting role are actually temporary employees or interns.

The relevance of these observations becomes particularly clear once one realizes the somewhat strange disconnect between the role of WHO as the host of governance meetings and the general idea that the Assembly would be WHO's supreme decision-making body (rather than primarily a multilateral forum). Actually, most of the people at the Assembly and at other WHO governance meetings consider themselves as delegates of collective actors other than WHO and while WHO is spoken *about* a lot, it comes across much more as a "defining other" rather than a "collective we." This "speaking about WHO" addresses WHO in at least two different roles of which the role as a host is only one. The other one is the role of WHO as something that is entirely external to the meeting but has to be controlled by it, that is accountable to it, and that should do something for member states. This role of WHO manifests itself in different ways but the most important ones are as follows: first, written reports by the secretariat that are submitted to the Assembly; second, operative paragraphs of resolutions in which the Assembly requests the director general to do certain things; third, representatives of WHO who participate in the meetings and, during specific sequences, take on an active role. The latter are much less numerous than the delegates, have no right to vote, and act in a very specific capacity. In other words, they are there but "not part of the crowd."

For example, the director general reports to the Assembly not only through a written annual report but also through an address in the plenary that is followed by a general discussion. In committee meetings, assistant directors general (ADGs)—at times also the director general—and other relevant WHO representatives would often respond to the comments made by member states once the discussion of a specific agenda item has come to an end. What this comes down to is that WHO is certainly not completely absent but the proceedings of the Assembly (or of other governance meetings) are primarily conversations among the delegates of member states[18] while WHO holds simultaneously the role of a self-effacing host that does the background work and the role of a listener that is addressed both directly and indirectly.[19] To be sure, the director general in particular can also make decisive interventions—for example, when the delegates of member states cannot reach an agreement—and, depending on personality as well as the agenda item, WHO representatives can become the center of attention; but the overall impression remains still that WHO's supreme decision-making body is something external to WHO. Moreover, by meeting multiple people who enact WHO in multiple ways, one realizes that there probably is no WHO "as such."

What the three preceding subsections of this section amount to is that I hardly recognized the Assembly even though I had thought I knew it well from the documents that I had previously analyzed. By the same token, the "live version" of WHO came across quite differently from the WHO that presents itself in, say, the *Handbook of Resolutions and Decisions of the World Health Assembly and the Executive Board* or in the other official records. Most importantly, this discrepancy did not only apply to those parts of the proceedings that are undocumented—for example, the side events—but even to those parts that are documented in summary and verbatim records. In other words, while I had initially planned to focus on collecting empirical material in addition to the official records, the official records themselves appeared increasingly as estranged and noteworthy in the course of the research process. This key point will be taken up in the subsequent section that will start off by discussing the role of the official records, the production of which is actually an important part of WHO's role as a host of governance meetings.

HOW THE IMPRESSION OF STASIS HAD ORIGINALLY BEEN PRODUCED OR HOW ORDER IS LIVED ACROSS SITES

The previous section has already shown that the role of WHO as a host requires continuous work both before and after the meetings themselves. A central area of work that continues also after the closure of the meetings is the production of the official records. In the case of the Assembly, the records are traditionally published in three volumes: Volume I would contain resolutions, decisions, and annexes; Volume II would contain verbatim records of plenary meetings and a list of participants; and Volume III would contain summary records of committees and reports of committees.[20] These seemingly sober and precise accounts of past events appear in a completely new light if looked at from an ethnographic perspective that compares them with the impression that one gets through participant observation.

First of all, in consideration of the absence of WHO during governance meetings in the sense that was discussed before, it is quite striking that WHO plays a leading role in the production of the records and that the cover sheet of each of the three volumes displays the wording "World Health Organization" and a WHO emblem, both of which mark them as documents of WHO. This appropriation of the proceedings by WHO is certainly not the only mechanism through which processes that appeared as external to

WHO from a participant perspective become part of WHO but certainly a particularly illustrative one. It shows how quotidian self-representations of the practitioners can create a spotless wide-angle version of the phenomena that—from a zoomed-in ethnographic perspective—appear as only loosely connected activities.

Complementing my own experience as a reader of these documents and as a participant at the meetings with conversations I had with people who are involved in the production of the official records, I would, however, go even one step further. The official records are not only an important means that turns all of the things that the representatives of member states did into activities of WHO; rather, like any account, they also produce a particular version thereof. For example, as mentioned above, while the Assembly is marked by parallel events and a constant flow of people, each list of participants conveys a static picture of who participated at the Assembly and gives the impression of the Assembly as a single site that is attended by a set number of participants. Consider also what different image would be created if the cover sheet displayed the flags of all 194 WHO members instead of a single WHO emblem. Another illustrative example for the effects of the official records is the summary records of committee meetings—but this requires a brief elaboration.

Summary records are produced in a work-intensive process that involves précis-writers, reviewers, and editors; moreover, the text is first cleared within WHO and then—in the form of so-called provisional records—by member states. At the end of this process, the finalized summary records emerge as the authoritative account of the proceedings. This account is, however, a highly condensed version of the actual proceedings. Not only is it limited to what happened in the room and focused on what was said; even the spoken words are only partially preserved since the records are meant to be concise and since the instructions for précis-writers require that what was said by the participants has to be reduced by around 70 percent. This implies inevitably that the summary records contain a highly streamlined version of the proceedings. In particular, since the précis-writers are requested to concentrate on those elements of an intervention that were to the point and to account for those events that contributed to the eventual outcome of the deliberations, the discussions will come across as much more focused and rational than they actually were. The implicitly retrospective nature of the summary records that are written at a time when the outcome is known stands in stark contrast to the experience of the participants, however, for whom the process will have appeared as much more contingent and unpredictable. Moreover, subtleties in the statements as well as potentially unarticulated tensions that could be felt in the room will also remain unaccounted for. In other words, from the perspective of the people who produce the official records, they have to record the essence of the proceedings and an interesting side effect of this is the essentialization and reification of WHO.

For the present purpose, the key insight from these considerations is that while WHO manifests in multiple as well as unexpected ways at sites of governance, it manifests in a highly streamlined and in this sense seemingly self-explanatory fashion in the official records. Since these official records are simultaneously the authoritative account, a central message beyond the content of the decisions is that the meetings were obviously conducted in accordance with the rules and that the decisions are consequently legitimate. It is in this sense that the official records contain not only policy documents but also polity documents: they contain a very important manifestation of the WHO-in-action—and it is this manifestation that is preserved, remembered, and communicated across sites. It is such recorded "polity outcomes" in particular that make it seem plausible to speak of "the WHO" as a self-evidently existing entity even though the official records are merely identical with themselves.[21]

At least to some extent, delegates at governance meetings seem to tacitly and implicitly acknowledge that these policy-polity outcomes are dearly needed. What I have in mind here is delegates' omnipresent drive to conclude discussions and to reach at least some form of an agreement even in contentious areas. This lowest common denominator (or common cause) is one important reason for the aforementioned tendency to search for agreement even before meetings start or in parallel to the official proceedings. The relevance that is attributed to it becomes also obvious in the language of the participants who want to avoid "blockades," "standstills," and related dangers that could stop a process before it reaches its designated end point; and for all practical purposes, this designated end point is usually a resolution (or some other formal decision) of the appropriate governance body. As a consequence, it is not uncommon that the passing of resolutions is welcomed with applause. Finally, if one looks at the passing of such resolutions from the perspective that governance meetings produce not only policy outcomes but also polity outcomes, a new light is shed on the often made claim that WHO would pass too many resolutions: resolutions are not only the starting point for implementation procedures but visible affirmations of the continuous existence and successful operation of WHO. In other words, it is not surprising that there is a proliferation of resolutions since this is crucially important reproductive work.

These considerations show that an ethnographic perspective has not only the important side effect of dissolving the taken-for-granted but that it also allows researchers to reconstruct its production. While we have just seen that the official records play a key role in the case of WHO, the reconstruction of the production of social reality as such was not at the center of attention when the early works in political anthropology were considered by scholars of international relations like Hedley Bull. As suggested by Radcliffe-Brown's comments in *African Political Systems*, this would have been a possibility but the reasoning went more along the lines of structural-functionalism. Since the renewed discussion between political anthropology and international relations is, however, based on methodological considerations in general and on the potential role of ethnography in particular, "reconstruction of production" as a previously overlooked line of investigation is likely to become increasingly important and it will inevitably also lead to an introduction of theoretical-conceptual discussions that can account for processes at the microlevel.

A suitable tradition to draw on in these theoretical-conceptual discussions is ethnomethodology (Garfinkel 1967; Pollner and Emerson 2001) and I will briefly illustrate to what extent ethnomethodology can help to make sense both of the zoomed-in and of the wide-angle version of WHO. Ethnomethodology differs from structural-functionalism in that it does not presuppose social reality and social order but considers them as an active accomplishment of direct and indirect human interactions (Abels 2013, 88). Thus, social order is not conceptualized as a monolithic phenomenon that is "out there" and determines the actions of people but considered to be lived in distinct ways by specific people at individual sites and at particular moments (Pollner and Emerson 2001, 119). From the perspective of this bottom-up approach, it is consequently expectable that WHO manifests itself in specific and divergent ways and it is therefore not surprising that I got the impression that WHO dissolved once I zoomed in on it.

The more puzzling question is consequently, how the wide-angle notion of a monolithic WHO became the self-evident, taken-for-granted understanding of WHO in first place. While the question was answered above with the role of the official records, ethnomethodology can put the answer into a broader context. From an ethnomethodological perspective, people negotiate reality constantly and systematically but are usually not aware of this process. This unconsciousness explains why things are taken for granted even though other interpretations would have been possible. Moreover, people are even very quick at interpreting although their interpretations are based on sparse and ambiguous information or, if you like, on very thin empirical evidence. An important source of this situated empirical evidence comes from the activities and utterances of other people who are present, who are equally making sense of a setting, and who are in this sense involved in the negotiation of reality. What makes the quick and unconscious interpretations of the evidence possible is that people start from the assumption that there is an unproblematic and patterned reality which leaves them "merely" with the question of what this reality looks like.

In addressing this question, people draw on tacit background knowledge that allows them to see the phenomena around them as indications of a larger whole; but while this means that the character of the larger whole was to some extent already contained in the background knowledge, to them, the process appears like the uncovering of something that preexisted. Similarly, the process is generally marked by reflexivity where interpretations serve as the basis for further interpretations which means that mutually supportive "evidence" is created along the way. Since ethnomethodologists anticipate that individual phenomena will be seen as evidence for a larger whole and that multiple phenomena will be subsumed under one umbrella, it becomes straight forward that the official records are seen as evidence for WHO and as a persuasive account of how WHO works. By the same token, it becomes also plausible that the people at various sites see their work as part of WHO even though there is no place at which WHO "as such" can be found. In other words, unless the negotiation of reality is seriously challenged by some of the participants, people find the idea that something like a monolithic WHO (or any other collective actor) should exist little puzzling, and while even a few documents with a WHO emblem on them would be seen as sufficient evidence of its existence, the more common consequence is that a multitude of phenomena are related to a larger whole and in this sense seen as visible traces of a self-evidently existing WHO.[22]

This leads to the conclusion that from the perspective of practitioners, "reality" is commonly unproblematic and that the question of how it was produced will appear as rather odd. While this perception is likely to change in times of crisis, ethnographers and ethnomethodologists would generally emphasize that the apparently unproblematic nature of social reality is an accomplishment of lived order (Turner 1974, 11). It requires constant work and is made possible since people link events in concrete settings prospectively, simultaneously, and retrospectively to larger wholes. In light of these considerations, the practical work of producing and consuming official records has to be seen as a central mechanism that makes it possible to live order across sites.

IMPLICATIONS AND CONCLUSIONS

The official records of each governance meeting are the product of the collective work efforts of a multitude of people—from précis-writers via editors to delegates—but the records' front matter suggests otherwise; rather than listing the contributors and their respective roles, the texts simply "self-identify" as WHO documents. Similarly, the story that is contained therein does not seem to be told from any particular perspective. It is a synchronic, timeless, and synoptic account by an invisible and omniscient observer.[23] There is no other account like it and it is also unlike the experience of a participant observer or of any other participant.

Ethnography and ethnomethodology regard such "inconsistencies" as valuable insights and put the plurality of lived order center stage; as a consequence, they develop research puzzles that are rather different from much of the classic scholarship on WHO or on other international organizations. Since very broad phenomena like "reality" and "order" but also more specific ones like "WHO" are seen as an accomplishment, researchers in this tradition are not surprised that constant reproductive work has to be carried out and that it will often not be possible to continuously sustain the spotless wide-angle image that the work-intensive self-representations of the participants create at times. In other words, while much scholarship on international organizations asks, whether the member states as the principles can control a particular international organization as the agent, how a particular line of conflict among member states impacted on the work of an international organization, or how the fragmentation of an international organization developed historically,[24] the microlevel puzzle is more what holds the constituent parts of these disputes together and why there are not even *many more* visible conflicts and fragmentations. By the same token, in the context of my own research one could say that from a participant perspective, global health governance is fragmented at a much more fundamental level than just at the level of competing collective actors.

While the empirical sections of this contribution focused on the governance side of WHO, it became still obvious, that there is more than just one WHO and that not all WHO processes are part of WHO in the same way. First of all, WHO is mainly spoken *about* at governance meetings and WHO holds more than one role at these meetings: WHO as a conference host (or as a forum) differs from WHO as an agency that executes policies and supports implementation. Similarly, it became also clear that from a participant perspective, WHO's governance bodies are not so much bodies of WHO but meetings of member states and that even this part of WHO comprises multiple processes that are dispersed across different sites; during individual meetings like the Assembly, processes run at different subsites and in parallel; in the course of the annual policy cycle, processes move between sites in a sequential fashion. Finally, WHO speaks with multiple faces at governance meetings including the director general and several ADGs; this multi-headedness at the leadership level not only reinforces the point that there is more than one WHO but also reminds us that the recognizable faces of WHO have to be seen as the tip of the iceberg while large parts of WHO as a (widely branched) secretariat remain invisible at governance meetings.[25]

In other words, while classic scholarship on international organizations starts commonly with a conceptual-theoretical argument in order to make the point that the actions of international organizations should not be equated with the interests of their members or that individual international organizations are both a forum and an agency (or an actor), the ethnographic perspective leads to a proliferation of observed fragmentation and organizational manifestations: an individual international organization consists inter alia of *multiple* forums and *multiple* agencies (or administrative units). Similarly, an ethnographic perspective would be interested not just in the question of successful control by member states but also in the consequences of the control efforts on organizational self-representations; the constant pressure that is put on WHO in this regard is exemplified by the recurrent discussions at governance meetings on the availability of and on the format of written accounts— accounts through which WHO (including lower parts of the iceberg) becomes visible and accountable. Among other things, these discussions in turn seem to contribute to the proliferation of documents and to foster the turn toward quantification and the search for measurable results—in the form of output, outcome, and impact.

Another puzzle that emerges from an ethnographic perspective and would warrant further investigation—but goes beyond the scope of this contribution—is the question of how member states and their positions are successfully enacted. While some practical challenges in terms of following the process have already been mentioned, there is also the issue that delegations usually comprise a multitude of people and that these people have different backgrounds—for example, they might work for different ministries and institutions, they might be from different professions, some might be recently appointed interns, others might have decades of experience, they might be from different generations, and they are commonly not just sent from the capital/the home country but also based at the permanent missions in Geneva. To continuously and consistently represent a national position under these circumstances is no small achievement, and, actually, it casts a new light on the very idea of national interests or national preferences; interests and preferences are less something that self-evidently exists but rather something that is dearly needed as a *practical tool* that provides the individual delegates with some guidance (i.e., a rule of thumb) on how to act under various circumstances.

To be sure, the abovementioned approaches to international organizations produce intriguing research and, as the earlier discussion on historical analysis has shown, ethnography is not the only means through which the taken-for-granted can be dissolved and questioned. I am primarily arguing that ethnography is very likely to have this effect and to defamiliarize apparently known phenomena. Moreover, I argue also that an engagement with ethnography is likely to require some conceptual rethinking—as was illustrated with the juxtaposition of structural-functionalism and ethnomethodology, both of which are concerned with order but each of which looks at it from a different angle. In light of this strong link between methodology and conceptual-theoretical issues, the ever-rising interest in ethnography will also leave some conceptual-theoretical traces. At some point, it might even converge with the equally rising interest in practice theory, which is highly compatible with ethnography and can address various concerns that emerge from a microlevel perspective.[26] If this is to be the case, the current exchange between political anthropology and political science/international relations might retrospectively look like one important aspect of a larger process, namely the simultaneous rise of ethnography and practice theory.

NOTES

1. The question of whether international relations is a discipline of its own or a subfield of political science can spark controversial debates and the answers will vary according to different national traditions. Personally, I am inclined to view it as a subfield of political science that draws eclectically on a multitude of other disciplines.

2. For an introduction to the English School that contains a discussion of its name, see Navari and Green 2014.

3. While a classic criticism of structural-functionalism is its propensity to emphasize equilibrium and to be biased in favor of the social status quo, Bull was well aware of the potential clash between order and (differing perspectives on) justice; consequently, he saw, in principle, the need to allow for just change but was also concerned that the call for change should not lead to the unrestrained use of violence.

4. The discussion about the potential role of ethnography for international relations is not a completely new one. While there are some elder texts and studies (e.g., Barnett 1997; Cohn 1987; Gusterson 2001), the debate has intensified since then (e.g., Brigg and Bleiker 2008; Eckl 2008; Jackson 2008; Neumann 2005, Neumann 2007; Schatz 2009a, b; Schia 2013; Yanow 2009b). In spite of this increasing interest, ethnographic research has still not reached the scholarly mainstream in political science/international relations (Schatz 2017) while other disciplines have relied on it for decades.

5. For a more detailed account and comparison of the events in 1955 and 2007, see Eckl 2014.

6. The increasing focus on contemporary political issues was relevant since, in the case of decades-old processes and decisions, extensive archival research would have been an avenue toward digging up some of the less vocal voices.

7. For examples, where I combined participant observation with historical analysis, see Eckl 2017a and Eckl 2017b.

8. This focus on the researcher as a data collection instrument or, to put it differently, this focus on the researcher's own experiences implies that it would actually

be possible to do an ethnographic study even in the absence of other people. For example, if one wanted to do an ethnography on living as a hermit, shadowing a hermit would not be the only alternative. Rather, the researcher could live solitarily in a hermitage and engage primarily with artifacts (such as religious texts, cookware, and the built environment). This engagement could either be of an experimental kind, that is, the researcher could try to simply get along, or it could be of a reenacting kind, that is, the researcher could try to do things according to "hermit practice" as it is documented in written sources or transmitted orally.

9. There are various strands of literature that, in one way or another, work with the notion of "insider's perspective" or "practitioner's perspective." Alternative terms include the following ones: "emic perspective," "native's perspective," "subject's perspective," "(social) actor's perspective," and "member's perspective."

10. Holism or the holistic reconstruction of a local community is a classic ethnographic ideal. Usually, this implied not only that rather small communities were studied but also that the internal structure and logic of each community was at the center of attention while its relations to "the outside world" were neglected. The prejudice that there were self-contained and primordial communities did often not hold empirically but this way of thinking about ethnographic field research and about local communities came under serious pressure only when contemporary globalization drew the scholarly attention to the pervasive interconnectedness of human life around the globe. One answer to this challenge was the notion of multisited ethnography (Marcus 1995). From this perspective, ethnography offers still a valuable research approach but has to follow the actual flow of people, ideas, things, and so forth rather than limiting itself to the study of stationary phenomena. In one sense this was a radical departure from previous assumptions but in another sense the ideal of holistic reconstruction was merely transferred from local communities to global processes. This transferred or transformed version of holistic reconstruction also reverberates in the writings of scholars of international relations and (international) politics who have added "policies" to the list of phenomena to be followed in the course of an ethnographic study (Yanow 2009b).

11. While comparison as such is probably the most basic research method of all, the logic of comparison as it is understood in the present context has been elaborated upon particularly clearly by proponents of "grounded theory" in their discussions on the constant comparative method and on the idea of incremental research designs (or sampling strategies) that allow researchers to select cases in the course of the research project while following a logic of maximal and minimal contrast (Mey and Mruck 2009, 2011). Similarly, authors who have developed Karl Mannheim's "documentary method" further emphasize the need to systematically work with empirical horizons of comparison that allow researchers to see or to recognize things without having to rely on preconceived theories that threaten to force themselves upon the empirical material (Bohnsack 2010).

12. There are a few meetings that are announced in the *Journal* and take place at WHO headquarters rather than at the *Palais*.

13. Both the Board and PBAC are also attended by some nonmembers but these do not enjoy the same rights.

14. As indicated earlier, I revisited not only the Assembly but also visited—either in person or via webcast—the Board, PBAC, regional committees, and advisory committees.

15. For a more extensive discussion of these changes that also puts them into a broader context, see Eckl 2017b.

16. While it would go beyond the scope of this contribution to discuss the matter in detail, it should be mentioned that not all text documents that WHO produces have to pass through the Assembly even though it is the most important of these bottlenecks when it comes to governance by member states. Guidelines, for example, are produced without direct involvement of the governance bodies who might, however, request their development. The rules for guideline development are at times revisited and have proven to be a contentious issue—as evidenced, for example, at the 136th and 137th meeting of the Board in 2015 (see also document EB137/5 [2015]).

17. Access control as such is then conducted by the United Nations security personnel at the *Palais*.

18. They comprise, however, also comments from other organizations, including nongovernmental organizations and other non-state actors.

19. Inside of the meeting rooms the hosting role becomes particularly visible through the support that WHO gives to the president of the Assembly and to the chairs of the individual meetings. For example, both in the case of plenary meetings and in the case of committee meetings, the presidence at the front end of the room would usually include a legal counselor and a secretary—both of whom are WHO staff.

20. While it would go beyond the scope of this contribution to discuss the historical changes of this practice extensively, it should be noted that an important change in recent years was that, as of Assembly 64 (WHA64) in 2011, the print version of Volume II was discontinued. The verbatim records of plenary meetings were replaced with online audio recordings while the list of participants is now published as a part of Volume III.

21. Stephan Hirschauer makes the intriguing point that even audio recordings and transcripts are merely identical with themselves since they represent conversations that, from the perspective of the participants, never took place in this specific form; in particular, no method of preservation can capture the simultaneously present complexity of social reality and the constant interplay of conscious and subconscious interpretations (Hirschauer 2001, 434–436).

22. Even though not all of the concepts are mentioned explicitly, the discussion in this and in the previous paragraph builds on "indexicality," "reflexivity," "accounts," and "documentary method" as key ethnomethodological concepts. For a more extensive and explicit treatment of these concepts, see Abels 2013 as well as Pollner and Emerson 2001.

23. For instructive reflections on texts and social organization that draw on ethnomethodology, see Smith 1984.

24. For important contributions that address these issues, see Chorev 2012, Graham 2014, and Hanrieder 2015. For a classic edited volume on delegation and agency, which also contains a chapter by Cortell and Peterson on WHO, see Hawkins et al. 2006. For a comprehensive collection of research on international organizations,

which contains a chapter on WHO by Hanrieder, see Conceição-Heldt, Koch, and Liese 2015.

25. Although a detailed analysis of the secretariat would go beyond the governance focus of the present contribution, it should be mentioned that the ADGs could actually serve as an excellent starting point for further investigations: if one followed individual ADGs to the clusters and programs they direct, it could be shown in what sense also WHO as an agency (or as a bureaucracy) consists of a multiplicity of parallel sites that are marked by very different lived realities.

26. On the increasing interest in microlevel theory and analysis, see Chakravarty 2013. On practice theory in international relations, see Adler and Pouliot 2011 and Bueger and Gadinger 2014.

BIBLIOGRAPHY

Abels, Heinz. "Ethnomethodologie." In *Handbuch Soziologische Theorien*, edited by Georg Kneer and Markus Schroer, 87–110. Wiesbaden: VS Verlag für Sozialwissenschaften, 2013.

Adler, Emanuel, and Vincent Pouliot. "International Practices." *International Theory* 3 (2011): 1–36.

Asad, Talal, ed. *Anthropology and the Colonial Encounter*. London: Ithaca Press, 1973.

Barnett, Michael N. "The UN Security Council, Indifference, and Genocide in Rwanda." *Cultural Anthropology* 12 (1997): 551–78.

Bijker, Wiebe E. *Of Bicycles, Bakelites, and Bulbs: Toward a Theory of Sociotechnical Change*. London: MIT Press, 1995.

Bohnsack, Ralf. *Rekonstruktive Sozialforschung: Einführung in qualitative Methoden*. Opladen: Budrich, 2010.

Brigg, Morgan, and Roland Bleiker. "Expanding Ethnographic Insights into Global Politics." *International Political Sociology* 2 (2008): 89–90.

Brown, David. "Eradicating Malaria Worldwide Seen as a Distant Goal, at Best." *The Washington Post*, April 26, 2008. https://www.washingtonpost.com/wp-dyn/content/article/2008/04/25/AR2008042503504.html.

Bueger, Christian, and Frank Gadinger. *International Practice Theory: New Perspectives*. Basingstoke: Palgrave Macmillan, 2014.

Bull, Hedley. *The Anarchical Society: A Study of Order in World Politics*. London: Macmillan, 1977.

Chakravarty, Anuradha. "Political Science and the 'Micro-Politics' Research Agenda." *Political Sciences & Public Affairs* 1 (2013): e103.

Charmaz, Kathy, and Richard G. Mitchell. "Grounded Theory in Ethnography." In *Handbook of Ethnography*, edited by Paul Atkinson, Amanda Coffey, Sara Delamont, John Lofland, and Lyn Lofland, 160–74. London: Sage, 2001.

Chorev, Nitsan. *The World Health Organization between North and South*. Ithaca: Cornell University Press, 2012.

Cohn, Carol. "Sex and Death in the Rational World of Defense Intellectuals." *Signs: Journal of Women in Culture and Society* 12 (1987): 687–718.

Conceição-Heldt, Eugénia da, Martin Koch, and Andrea Liese, eds. *Internationale Organisationen: Autonomie, Politisierung, interorganisationale Beziehungen und Wandel, PVS Sonderheft 49.* Baden-Baden: Nomos, 2015.

Cox, Robert W. "Social Forces, States and World Orders: Beyond International Relations Theory." In *Neorealism and Its Critics*, edited by Robert Keohane, 204–54. New York: Columbia University Press, 1986.

Easton, David. "Political Anthropology." *Biennial Review of Anthropology* 1 (1959): 210–62.

Eckl, Julian. *Die politische Ökonomie der Wissensgesellschaft: Geistige Eigentumsrechte und die Frage des Zugangs zu Ideen.* Marburg: Tectum, 2004.

———. "Das Scheitern des Vorschlags für eine EU-Richtlinie zur 'Patentierbarkeit computerimplementierter Erfindungen': Einige Erklärungen und eine Bewertung." Paper presented at the conference "Governing the Knowledge Society," Hamburg, October 12 and 13, 2006. http://www.alexandria.unisg.ch/Publikationen/Julian_Eckl/56096.

———. "Responsible Scholarship After Leaving the Veranda: Normative Issues Faced by Field Researchers—and Armchair Scientists." *International Political Sociology* 2 (2008): 185–203.

———. "Cross-sector Partnerships and World Politics: Institutional Dynamics in the Global Struggle against Malaria." PhD diss., University of St. Gallen, 2010.

———. "The Power of Private Foundations: Rockefeller and Gates in the Struggle against Malaria." *Global Social Policy* 14 (2014): 91–116.

———. "The Social Lives of Global Policies against Malaria: Conceptual Considerations, Past Experiences, and Current Issues." *Medical Anthropology* 36 (2017a.): 422–35.

———. "Successful Governance Reform and Its Consequences: How the Historical Drive for Shorter Meetings and More Time Efficiency Reverberates in Contemporary World Health Assemblies." *Global Health Governance* 11 (2017b): 40–56.

Emerson, Robert M., Rachel I. Fretz, and Linda L. Shaw. *Writing Ethnographic Fieldnotes, Second Edition.* Chicago: University of Chicago Press, 2011.

Fortes, M., and E. E. Evans-Pritchard, eds. *African Political Systems, Fourth Impression.* London: Oxford University Press, 1950.

Foucault, Michel. "Nietzsche, Genealogy, History." In *The Foucault Reader*, edited by Paul Rabinow, 76–100. New York: Pantheon Books, 1984.

Garfinkel, Harold. *Studies in Ethnomethodology.* Englewood Cliffs, NJ: Prentice-Hall, 1967.

Gobo, Giampietro. *Doing Ethnography.* London: Sage, 2008.

Graham, Erin R. "International Organizations as Collective Agents: Fragmentation and the Limits of Principal Control at the World Health Organization." *Journal of International Relations* 20 (2014): 366–90.

Gramiccia, Gabriele, and Peter F. Beales. "The Recent History of Malaria Control and Eradication." In *Malaria: Principles and Practice of Malariology*, edited by Walther H. Wernsdorfer and Ian McGregor, 1335–78. London: Churchill Livingstone, 1988.

Gusterson, Hugh. "The Virtual Nuclear Weapons Laboratory in the New World Order." *American Ethnologist* 28 (2001): 417–37.

Halperin, Morton H. "The Decision to Deploy the ABM: Bureaucratic and Domestic Politics in the Johnson Administration." *World Politics* 25 (1972): 62–95.

Hanrieder, Tine. *International Organization in Time: Fragmentation and Reform.* Oxford: Oxford University Press, 2015.

Hawkins, Darren G., David A. Lake, Daniel L. Nielson, and Michael J. Tierney, eds. *Delegation and Agency in International Organizations.* Cambridge: Cambridge University Press, 2006.

Hirschauer, Stefan. "Ethnografisches Schreiben und die Schweigsamkeit des Sozialen: Zu einer Methodologie der Beschreibung." *Zeitschrift für Soziologie* 30 (2001): 429–51.

Jackson, Patrick Thaddeus. "Can Ethnographic Techniques Tell Us Distinctive Things About World Politics?" *International Political Sociology* 2 (2008): 91–3.

Lapid, Yosef. "The Third Debate: On the Prospects of International Theory in a Post-Positivist Era." *International Studies Quarterly* 33 (1989): 235–54.

Leach, Edmund Ronald. *Political Systems of Highland Burma: A Study of Kachin Social Structure.* London: Bell, 1954.

Lukes, Steven. *Power: A Radical View.* London: Macmillan, 1974.

———. *Power: A Radical View*, 2nd Ed. Basingstoke: Palgrave Macmillan, 2005.

Mandelbaum, Michael. "[untitled review of 'The Anarchical Society: A Study of Order in World Politics' by Hedley Bull]." *Political Science Quarterly* 92 (1977): 574–75.

Marcus, George E. "Ethnography in/of the World System: The Emergence of Multi-Sited Ethnography." *Annual Review of Anthropology* 24 (1995): 95–117.

Masters, Roger D. "World Politics as a Primitive Political System." *World Politics* 16 (1964): 595–619.

McNeil, Donald G. "Eradicate Malaria? Doubters Fuel Debate." *The New York Times,* March 4, 2008. https://www.nytimes.com/2008/03/04/health/04mala.h tml?_r=1&pagewanted=2

Mey, Günter, and Katja Mruck. "Methodologie und Methodik der Grounded Theory." In *Forschungsmethoden der Psychologie: Zwischen naturwissenschaftlichem Experiment und sozialwissenschaftlicher Hermeneutik, Band 3: Psychologie als Natur- und Kulturwissenschaft: Die soziale Konstruktion der Wirklichkeit,* edited by Wilhelm Kempf and Marcus Kiefer, 100–52. Berlin: Regener, 2009.

———. "Grounded-Theory-Methodologie: Entwicklung, Stand, Perspektiven." In *Grounded Theory Reader, 2. aktualisierte und erweiterte Auflage,* edited by Günter Mey and Katja Mruck, 11–48. Wiesbaden: Springer, 2011.

Nájera, Jose A. *Malaria Control: Achievements, Problems & Strategies, WHO/CDS/ RBM/99.10, WHO/MAL/99.1087.* Geneva: World Health Organization. 1999. http: //www.emro.who.int/rbm/publications/mc_najera.pdf.

Navari, Cornelia, and Daniel M. Green, eds. *Guide to the English School in International Studies.* Chichester: John Wiley & Sons, 2014.

Neumann, Iver B. "To Be a Diplomat" *International Studies Perspectives* 6 (2015): 72–93.

———. "'A Speech That the Entire Ministry May Stand for', or: Why Diplomats Never Produce Anything New." *International Political Sociology* 1 (2007): 183–200.

Paulson, Tom. "WHO Chief Joins Gateses' Call to Eradicate Malaria: Some at Seattle Meeting See Risk in High Expectations." *Seattle Post-Intelligencer*, October 17, 2007. http://www.seattlepi.com/health/335869_malaria18.html.

Pollner, Melvin, and Robert M. Emerson. "Ethnomethodology and Ethnography." In *Handbook of Ethnography*, edited by Paul Atkinson, Amanda Coffey, Sara Delamont, John Lofland, and Lyn Lofland, 118–35. London: Sage, 2001.

Radcliffe-Brown, Alfred. R. "Preface." In *African Political Systems, Fourth Impression*, edited by Meyer Fortes, and Edward. E. Evans-Pritchard, xi–xxiii. London: Oxford University Press, 1950.

Schatz, Edward, ed. *Political Ethnography: What Immersion Contributes to the Study of Power*. Chicago: University of Chicago Press, 2009a.

———. "Introduction [to the Symposium 'Ethnographic Methods in Political Science']." *Qualitative & Multi-Method Research* 7 (2009b): 32–3.

———. "Disciplines That Forget: Political Science and Ethnography." *PS: Political Science & Politics* 50 (2017): 135–138.

Schia, Niels Nagelhus. "Being Part of the Parade—'Going Native' in the United Nations Security Council." *PoLAR: Political and Legal Anthropology Review* 36 (2013): 138–56.

Smith, Dorothy E. "Textually Mediated Social Organization." *International Social Science Journal* 36 (1984): 59–75.

Trigg, Peter, I., and A.V. Kondrachine. "Commentary: Malaria Control in the 1990s." *Bulletin of the World Health Organization* 76 (1998): 11–6.

Turner, Roy. "Introduction." In *Ethnomethodology*, edited by Roy Turner, 7–12. Harmondsworth: Penguin, 1974.

Yanow, Dvora. "Dear Author, Dear Reader: The Third Hermeneutic in Writing and Reviewing Ethnography." In *Political Ethnography: What Immersion Contributes to the Study of Power*, edited by Edward Schatz, 275–302. Chicago: University of Chicago Press,2009a.

———. "What's Political about Political Ethnography? Abducting Our Way Toward Reason and Meaning." *Qualitative & Multi-Method Research* 7 (2009b): 33–7.

Part II

LOCAL ARENAS OF INTERNATIONALIZED POLITICS

Chapter 5

Emic Security

An Anthropological Approach to Security

Tessa Diphoorn

For a long time, the term "security" was equated with national security, associated with the military rule of the state, and reserved for "security studies," a subfield within political science and international relations. Yet throughout the past decades, numerous other disciplines, such as anthropology, have increasingly paid attention to the concept of "security" and have provided tremendous insight into the numerous ways in which security is performed, enacted, perceived, and understood, both conceptually and empirically. In many ways, security has acted as a topic of convergence and dialogue between the two disciplines: anthropologists have frequently resorted to political science for intellectual inspiration, and in turn, political scientists increasingly appreciate an "ethnographic turn" (Schwartz-Shea and Majic 2017) when understanding security.

In this chapter, I will explore the "anthropology of security" and outline how anthropology, both conceptually and methodologically, has provided a distinctive way of analyzing security that other disciplines, such as political science, can benefit from. I will do so by drawing from my own fieldwork on private security and policing in South Africa and Kenya. In the first section, I will briefly discuss how security has traditionally been defined outside of anthropology as a discipline and then highlight how the anthropological approach to security has provided a "bottom-up" and emic perspective that focuses on everyday practices, performances, and experiences. I will highlight how this anthropological approach is simultaneously methodological and conceptual. In the second section, I will emphasize my anthropological approach by presenting three different empirical cases from my ethnographic fieldwork conducted in South Africa (2007–2011) and Kenya (2014–2016). These three vignettes demonstrate how the use of particular methods, with participant observation in particular, yielded certain data and in turn, particular conceptual insights into the pluralized nature of security. In the last section, I will provide some concluding remarks about the role that (political) anthropology plays in understanding security that other disciplines, such as political science, can draw from.

SECURITY IN SECURITY STUDIES

Security is a sexy and political topic: it is frequently used in public debates and habitually the focus of global media headlines to cover a wide array of topics. In fact, the term has become such an intricate part of public debate that it is often used as a synonym to refer to anything related to safety, danger, and the general well-being of individuals, and thus includes anything from health care to military action, crime, and migration.

In academia, studying security was largely reserved for the subfield of "security studies," whereby the provision of security was regarded as the prerogative of the state and thus analyzed under the scope of national security and within an international state system. Largely drawing from Hobbes's idea of the state of nature, security was regarded as the inevitable (and desired) outcome result of unified efforts, materialized through the formation of modern states. Security was thus analyzed in rather "narrow" terms and with a focus on military-political conflicts. After the Cold War, the (analytical) scope widened beyond interstate military affairs and security increasingly referred to threats that emerged from numerous other domains, such as the environmental and economic sector. With this encompassing perspective, security is understood as a response to any type of threat to a society. A clear example of this wide approach is the all-inclusive concept of "human security" that broadly defines security as the "freedom from want and freedom from fear" (UNDP 1994). Such sweeping concepts have in turn been criticized for equating security to almost anything and producing "conceptual haziness" (Pedersen and Holbraad 2013, 10).

As part of a critique against both the extreme "wideners" and the traditionalist (narrow) approach, IR scholars Barry Buzan and Ole Wæver developed what is now known as the *securitization theory*, and sometimes referred to as the leading paradigm of the Copenhagen School of security studies.[1] The main aim of these scholars was to simultaneously debunk the state-centric (traditionalist) approach to security that focused on war and the military and to criticize the all-encompassing analysis of security that regards security as "a kind of universal good thing—the desired condition toward which all relations should move" (Buzan et al. 1998, 4). In contrast, their approach to security specifically focuses on the processual enactment of security and its intersubjective nature. By drawing from speech act theory, the authors regard "security" as a social construction and a process whereby a collective conception of security is created that identifies something as a particular threat. In their own words, securitization is "constituted by the intersubjective establishment of an existential threat with a saliency sufficient to have substantial political effects" (25).

The securitization theory has been appealing to anthropologists, particularly due to its emphasis on "security as a particular manner of *politicizing* issues" (Pedersen and Holbraad 2013, 11, emphasis in original), which stresses the crucial role that power structures play in determining who and what is defined as a threat. The securitization theory has been regularly employed by anthropologists to analyze the processes in which security is presented, performed, and interpreted across localities (see Low 2013; Sarkar 2017). However, it has also been met with criticism, particularly from political scientists who advocate an anthropological approach to security. One example is Didier Bigo (2014), who argues that the securitization theory "is still attached to a mode of reasoning that prevails in political science" (191). Furthermore, Browning and McDonald (2013) highlight that it does not encapsulate the diverse way in which security is understood and performed across the globe and that it overlooks the "varied social, historical and political contexts in which security is constructed" (241). This discussion in political science, largely steered by proponents of critical security studies, has moved toward using a practice approach (see Bueger 2014; Hansen 2006) to develop an understanding of "everyday security" (Guillaume and Huysmans 2013) in order to comprehend how mundane security practices, taking place in the everyday, are experienced and performed (Crawford and Hutchinson 2016). This shift has been welcomed by many, and interestingly, these scholars are those that welcome an anthropological approach, such as Bueger and Mireanu (2014, 2), who argue that critical security studies should be "a project of proximity which entails close engagements with the flow and the infrastructures of the everyday and the mundane and with those discriminated by security practices." In understanding contemporary security, political science research is increasingly experiencing an "ethnographic turn" (Schwartz-Shea and Majic 2017).

SECURITY IN ANTHROPOLOGY

In anthropology, the words "security" and "insecurity" can be found in early anthropological texts, but in-depth accounts were rather scattered. The discipline lacked a concrete theoretical operationalization of security and there was often a rather implicit and unspoken idea of what was meant by security (Pedersen and Holbraad 2013, 1).[2] In early anthropological work, particularly in twentieth-century British social anthropology, security was also analyzed within a "narrow" perspective, associated with "rule" and "order," and regarded as something that could only be established through intervention—often coercively—by an overarching authority (Pedersen and Holbraad 2013, 4–6). Although this was not always a modern state (and thus not necessarily within a Hobbesian analysis) and could be exerted by other collective governing entities, such as tribes, security was inherently regarded as something to be implemented top-down, rather than something that was developed from "below." Furthermore, the implementation of security was often regarded as something that inherently accompanied violence and social struggle, and was thus very often framed in terms of *in*security.

Throughout the past two decades, this has changed substantially and the "anthropology of security" has emerged as a focus within the discipline that regards security as "a critical object of study in its own right" (Glück and Low 2017, 283). Limor Samimian-Darash and Meg Stalcup (2016) have, rather helpfully, divided this focus into four main fields of research. The first field is that of "violence and state terror" and refers to the extensive work conducted on violence, war, and social suffering that emerged during the 1990s and 2000 and dominated much of political anthropology (see Farmer 2003; Feldman 1991; Nordstrom and Robben 1995; Scheper-Hughes and Bourgois 2004; Schmidt and Schröder 2001). In a similar vein, rapid urbanization in many parts of the world, particularly Latin America and Africa, gave rise to a heightened focus on urban insecurity, fear, and social exclusion (see Caldeira 2000; Koonings and Kruijt 2007; Low 2004; Perlman 2010). Combined, many of these groundbreaking ethnographies powerfully portray the complexity of violence and its structural and everyday nature. Yet they also predominantly centered around the experiences of individuals and often overlooked the collective nature and experience of (in)security (Pedersen and Holbraad 2013). Furthermore, they primarily focused on the victims of violence and on various forms of *in*security, rather than security.

This can also be said for the second field—"military, militarization, and militarism"—wherein anthropologists moved away from a focus on victims toward one on perpetrators, and an understanding of how organizational cultures condone or maintain the imposition of violence. This includes studies on state armed forces, such as the military (Ben-Ari 1998; Grassiani 2013; van Roekel 2020; Winslow 1997) and the state police (Beek et al. 2017; Fassin 2013; Garriot 2013; Hornberger 2011; Jauregui 2016; Karpiak and Garriot 2019), and the links between civilian and military life (see Gusterson 2007; Lutz 2002).

The third field includes studies dealing with "para-state securitization," namely various forms of security that are produced "outside" the state under and through diverse processes of democratization, neoliberalism, and globalization. These studies analyze the crucial role that non-state security actors play and how citizens look to them for providing security, such as gangs (Jensen 2008; Rodgers 2006; van Stapele 2015), vigilante organizations (Bakker 2015; Buur 2006; Harnischfeger 2003; Pratten and Sen 2007; Smith 2019), community policing initiatives (Kyed 2009; Ruteere and Pommerolle 2003), and increasingly also private security companies (Diphoorn 2016; Grassiani and Volinz 2016; Konopinski 2014; Larkins 2017; Mynster Christensen 2017; Stockmarr 2015). In this field (and similar time period), we also find Daniel Goldstein's (2010) call for a critical anthropology of security, a text that is regarded as pioneering in the "anthropology of security." In this piece, Goldstein encourages anthropologists to further uncover the "multiple ways in which security is configured and deployed—not only by states and authorized speakers but by communities, groups and individuals—in their engagements with other local actors and with arms of the state itself" (2010, 492). Therefore, in addition to calling for further theorization of the concept of "security," Goldstein's approach also entails one of widening, that is, to focus on practices and actors outside and beyond the state.

Goldstein's call has been answered by a growing body of work that comprises in-depth ethnographic fieldwork, but also sophisticated theoretical conceptions, such as several edited volumes (see Diphoorn and Grassiani 2019; Low and Maguire 2019; Maguire et al. 2014, 2018; Pedersen and Holbraad 2013; Hurtado and Ercolani 2013) and special issues in journals such as *Etnofoor* (2015), *Conflict and Society* (2017), *Qualitative Sociology* (2017), and *Anthropological Theory* (2017). Combined, these studies have critically assessed the predominant state-centric approach to security and the need to regard security as plural and globalized. This assessment has emerged alongside and in conclave with other important developments in anthropology, such as the reconceptualization of sovereignty (see Hansen and Stepputat 2006; Humphrey 2007; Oosterbaan and Pansters 2015), citizenship (Holston 2008; Lazar and Nuijten 2013; Ong 1999), and the everyday workings of the state (Das and Poole 2004; Sharma and Gupta 2006; Jaffe 2013). Taking all of this together, the idea that empirical data yielded from an ethnographic approach cannot be used for cross-cultural comparison has been refuted by many, most notably by Holbraad and Pedersen (2013). They specifically show how security can act as a useful medium to make cross-cultural comparisons, and thus how to use detailed, in-depth empirical data from various sites to say something larger about "the world."

Amid this growing work, which Limor Samimian-Darash and Meg Stalcup (2016) argue still remains to focus more on insecurity rather than security, the authors advocate for an assemblage approach to security, which is the fourth field they discuss. In this field, security is regarded "as an assemblage of forms of governance and power" (11) and includes "objects, concepts, and rationalities related to different security forms of action as well as the ethical mode of the anthropologist" (12). This push for an assemblage approach has occurred alongside a larger momentum within anthropology: largely drawing from Deleuze and Guattari (1980), an assemblage framework has been increasingly employed to understand a variety of phenomena (Ong and Collier 2005). Yet despite its popularity, the idea of an "assemblage" has also been critiqued for being far too encompassing to act as a concrete analytical tool (see Diphoorn and Grassiani 2016; Marcus and Saka 2006).

The fact that the assemblage approach has also emerged and been utilized in the field of political science is not a coincidence, but similarly points toward an intellectual exchange across the disciplines. One of the leading studies is that by Rita Abrahamsen and Michael Williams (2011): their notion of the "global security assemblage" has been used to comprehend security across diverse localities and disciplines (see Aradau and Blanke 2015; Berndtsson and Stern 2011; Schouten 2014). Yet I argue that despite the conceptual convergence, the contribution from anthropology differs by being a more localized, bottom-up, and emic approach that gives voice to the perspectives, experiences, and practices of individuals. For example, Abrahamsen and Williams (2009) convincingly portray the presence of a global security assemblage in the diamond mining industry in Sierra Leone and the oil production industry in Nigeria. Yet their work does not shed in-depth insight into how the people in the assemblage, such as the private security guards, the miners, and the affected citizens in the area, experience the multiplicity of the security providers and how this shapes their daily lives. Similarly, Schouten's (2014) analysis of security at Schiphol airport as "controversy" is innovative, yet we are left wondering how the users of the airport experience this "controversy" and how their perceptions fit into the reassembling process, despite the fact that the author states to consider security "anthropologically."

ETHNOGRAPHIC APPROACH TO SECURITY

It is this domain where I believe the merit of an anthropology approach comes into play, namely by providing an *emic* perspective to security. This entails understanding how the individual users and providers of security give meaning to performances of security, how this (re)configures their daily lives, how power dimensions shift and are contested, and what the political and social consequences are. Security is therefore understood as something relational, as something that is continuously in flux and shaped by everyday practices that are performed by a wide range of state and non-state actors that move within, between, and beyond the traditional public-private divide of security. This emic approach is evident in my own work on private security in South

Africa: between 2007 and 2013, I researched armed response companies in Durban, South Africa (Diphoorn 2016). In addition to analyzing the various interconnections between the diverse security providers (what one could perhaps call an assemblage) and understanding how security is performed along the blurry lines of public-private, legal-illegal, and formal-informal and what this means for authority and legitimacy, my main objective was to understand how the security providers themselves, armed response officers in my case, experience their line of work and how their everyday performances of security are subjected by ordinary citizens. My primary framework—twilight policing—does not only encapsulate punitive policing practices that emerge from a simultaneous process of collaboration and competition between different actors, but also includes the emotional and experiential dimension of policing: twilight policing also refers to a constant state of uncertainty and unpredictability. This dimension is rarely found in other texts on private security stemming from disciplines such as political science and criminology.

This emic perspective is primarily made possible through the practice of ethnographic fieldwork, which has, especially for those outside of anthropology, often been the defining marker of the discipline. Within anthropology, there is an ever-lively discussion of what constitutes ethnographic fieldwork and it is increasingly recognized that anthropology should not be equated to ethnographic fieldwork (Ingold 2008). Although I recognize this debate, I want to emphasize here how my ethnographic fieldwork on private security in South Africa and Kenya has been central to how I define myself as an anthropologist, but even more importantly, how it has shaped my understanding of security. For me, one of the defining elements has been my extensive use of a particular method, namely participant observation.

Participant observation is defined as "a method in which a researcher takes part in the daily activities, rituals, interactions, and events of a group of people as one of the means of learning the explicit and tacit aspects of their life routines and their culture" (DeWalt and DeWalt 2002, 1). Participant observation is often regarded as the means in which anthropologists distinguish themselves from other social sciences. Yet numerous scholars, such as Ingold (2008) and Forsey (2010), highlight that participant observation should not be equated with ethnographic fieldwork: it is a method that largely defines ethnographic fieldwork, but it is one method among many, and almost all anthropologists combine this method with others. Furthermore, participant observation, like all other methods, is suitable for particular research goals and questions, and not for all.

Elsewhere (Diphoorn 2017), I outline how I define participant observation as a larger tool kit that primarily consists of the following seven elements: (1) actively participating in daily activities and "hanging out," (2) using and regarding everyday conversations as a form of interviewing, (3) continuously observing one's surrounding, (4) systematically recording the observations made, (5) living in a particular area for a substantial amount of time, (6) establishing rapport, and (7) being reflexive. I argue that these seven elements constitute participant observation as a method and thus highlight that participant observation is more like a toolbox that conjunctively forms a single method. It is therefore about the *combination* of the seven different elements. For example, participating in events without making field notes or observing a meeting without being reflexive is not participant observation. Furthermore, interviews—which often act as a distinct research method—are inherently part of participant observation: we talk with people while we observe and participate, and these informal interviews are crucial to further uncovering people's perceptions, experiences, and behavior.

In the following section, I will present three different cases that occurred during my ethnographic fieldwork in South Africa and Kenya and were made possible through the usage of participant observation, as a larger tool kit. Combined, the three cases not only shed light into some of the empirical data from my research, but they (1) underline how particular methodological choices yield certain types of data, and thus (2) how this resulted in a particular understanding and approach to security, and allowed me to develop my framework of twilight policing.

Case 1: Active Policers

Throughout my research on security, I encountered numerous "active policers," which refers to individuals that are actively engaged in numerous policing activities by inhabiting various roles, such as acting as the chairman of a neighborhood watch and working as a police reservist (see Diphoorn 2016, 183–184). In South Africa, I met a particular active policer named Harry,[3] who I encountered in 2008 during an anti-crime meeting organized by the local municipality in Durban. I had heard of his name several times by others and he was described as an "engaged citizen," one who "cares for the community," and "works well with *other* crime fighters" (emphasis added). During our first encounter, he told me that he was the chairperson of a community policing cluster (which was also the specific role he had during this event) and the founder and chairman of a small neighborhood watch that operated in his residential neighborhood. For my own analytical and organizational purposes, I had placed him under the category of "community policing" within my (administrative) list of informants.

Throughout the next three years of my research in Durban, I met Harry on numerous occasions and this involved both prearranged semi-structured interviews and randomly bumping into him during security-related events. And although our semi-structured interviews were worthwhile and he always seemed to be rather forthcoming, it was during the sporadic encounters that I was able to fully uncover his role as an "active policer." For example, on one Saturday afternoon, I was accompanying several police officers on their shift and when we stood down to meet their colleagues who were on duty in another vehicle, I was surprised to see Harry there, on duty as a police reservist. I did not know that he was a police reservist, because he had not shared this information with me during our previous interviews. And by the end of my fieldwork, it became clear that he was a former police officer, a police reservist who worked regular eight-hour shifts at a particular police station, the owner of a small private security company that provided investigative work, and a "consultant" who assisted other resident-based policing initiatives in setting up a security arrangement. He thus had stakes and networks in various different security domains: the state, the community, and the private. Although I met several similar individuals that I label as "active policers," Harry's case and his participation in policing affairs by far exceeded those of others I met during my fieldwork.

I argue that I was able to uncover these various roles through the use of particular methods and several elements of the tool kit that comprise participation observation. The first dimension concerns time: participant observation is a method that generally needs to be carried out over a longer period of time and requires a substantial amount of "being there" (Becker 1970; in DeWalt and DeWalt 2002, 13). The idea is that more time provides more immersion: research participants get more used to your presence and become more willing to discuss particular issues. Furthermore, it takes time to acquire local knowledge and understand the various "tacit" elements of a research population. And perhaps, more importantly, it takes time to build up rapport, a key term in anthropology that is both a goal and a tool (DeWalt and DeWalt 2002, 40). Although rapport is defined in many ways, I use it to refer to "a particular type of relationship between the researcher and the researched, whereby they share a common goal and feel comfortable with each other to communicate, so that the researcher can collect data from the researched" (Diphoorn 2017, 13). Trust is very often the most important component for establishing rapport, and it requires time to establish this.

With regards to the case of active policers, I argue that being in South Africa for a long period of time allowed me to not only build trust with my informants but literally see individuals in different settings and in diverse (social) networks. Does it matter that Harry has different roles in the policing world? Yes, I believe it does. Not only did it allow me to develop the idea of the "active policer," but it shows the ways in which certain individuals participate in and move along various policing domains. By observing Harry in these different roles and habitats, I was able to analyze his behavior and see how his knowledge, skills, social capital, and essentially also his physical body moved throughout and across various policing domains. If we want to understand the various ways in which security is constituted and how certain objects and skills are circulated within the larger assemblage, concentrating on such individuals is crucial. And more importantly, such a focus can best be done through participant observation, whereby we meticulously observe people over a long period of time.

Case 2: A "Herd of People"

In November 2008, I accompanied Freddy, an Indian armed response officer who works for a large private security company in Durban, South Africa, for a day shift. As Freddy is a supervisor—a higher-ranking officer—we spent most of the day checking up on his colleagues who are stationed throughout the city. As we were driving toward the south end of the city at the end of the shift, we heard over the radio that there was a break-in in one of the neighborhoods where the company Freddy works for has a lot of clients. We received this notification from William, the operations manager of a leading community policing initiative from that neighborhood, who was apparently, in his own words, "managing the situation." Freddy started to drive much faster in order to provide assistance, yet before we arrived at the site of the break-in, we could see from a distance where the entire ordeal was taking place: there were four vehicles that belonged to three different private security companies, two police vehicles from the local police station, a vehicle managed by a community policing initiative, and a specialized dog unit from the regional police unit. We quickly found out that two men were (suspected) responsible for the break-in: one had already been arrested and the other was being chased by, what one of the security officers called, "a herd of people."

Throughout the following two hours, we witnessed how this "herd of people," which was a mosaic of diverse individuals with different colored uniforms and branded vehicles, interacted through coordination, competition, and friction, to eventually arrest the suspect. Without delving into the details of what occurred during those two hours, there are three elements I want to point out here. The first is that this incident—the chase and arrest of the two suspects—was one of the several cases that I witnessed during my fieldwork when several security providers came (and worked) together. In this incident, we see how members from a community policing initiative, various private security companies, and several police officers—from two different units/ departments—were all involved in addressing crime and providing a certain state of security. Again, this highlights the relational nature of security: security is not simply performed by a particular person or body, but it is practiced by numerous individuals who often possess and employ certain skills and/ or objects and whose practices influence each other. It is such incidents that lead me to the conclusion that security is a *joint performance*: it consists of various practices that are shaped by various interactions between different actors (Diphoorn 2016).

The second is that, on top of this being an example of a security arrangement, there were very clear power hierarchies at play during this incident. In this case, it was the community policing initiative that coordinated and managed the event: not only did William himself state this, but it was also supported, both verbally and physically, by others. This counterclaims the rather predominant conception of the state and its armed forces as the steering and authoritative figures of various security arrangements. Furthermore, it also points toward a growing trend in South Africa, namely the prominent role that citizens play in shaping everyday security practices, particularly when efforts are exerted through collective entities, such as community policing forums and neighborhood watches. Furthermore, it highlights the numerous entanglements between private security companies and citizen-based forms of policing (Diphoorn and Kyed 2016).

The third point is a methodological one: I argue that these insights were gained through my methodological approach. More specifically, this is an example of how participant observation, which in my case entailed accompanying security officers on their patrols and observing their practices and interactions, provides access to understanding various networks and power dynamics that define the performance of security. Furthermore, the writing up of field notes is a crucial part of participant observation and this case is a fine example of this. After experiencing this incident, I returned home and spent hours elaborately writing down what I had witnessed during those few hours, particularly the names of the companies and officers. This meticulous process of note-taking, which often takes up a large portion of the *work* of fieldwork, allows one to grasp the small details that not only assist in remembering things along the line but also often define the beauty of ethnographic writing that allow the emic perspective to come to life and be shared with others.

Case 3: Policing Partnerships in Kenya

During my fieldwork in Kenya, I focused on a formalized partnership between the Diplomatic Police Unit (DPU), a particular unit of the Kenyan police that serves the diplomatic community, and several private security companies operating in a particular geographical area. This policing partnership comprises two main elements: (1) joint patrols whereby police officers patrol with the private security companies in their vehicles and (2) the sharing of crime intelligence during monthly meetings (see Diphoorn 2019). My fieldwork initially started with interviewing several individuals involved in this partnership, whereby they all stressed the formalized and organized nature of this partnership and described it as a highly structured system between the companies regarding the joint patrols, with company A conducting patrols on Monday night, company B on Tuesdays, and so forth. However, when I eventually went on some of these joint patrols, it became evident that much of this structure was nonexistent. In fact, I realized that some companies were not conducting patrols at all, that some companies patrol on different nights and thus not on the same day every week, and that most of this was very ad hoc and informal. Therefore, what was presented as a very formalized and structured policing partnership was in fact not the case.

I contend that participant observation allowed me to discover this discrepancy. In fact, throughout my fieldwork, both in Kenya and South Africa, I observed things during my stints of participant observation that differed from what individuals told me during interviews. As I discuss elsewhere (Diphoorn 2017), participant observation provides insight into what people say *and* do and the potential differences between them. The tweaking of interviews or the lack of full disclosure by informants during interviewing is certainly not uncommon and does not necessarily imply that these interviews are not valuable or worthwhile. However, by also being able to witness what people do, we are given the opportunity to firsthand analyze one's behavior and compare this to what is being said. These differences are not simply glitches or disparities. Rather, I argue that they are, for the case and content of my research, fundamental insights into how non-state security operates. Knowing whether police officers and security officers patrol weekly within a structured system or on a very ad hoc basis is significant to know when analyzing how state and non-state security actors interact with each other to shape the pluralized security landscape. It is therefore not about catching people in a lie, but it is about uncovering data that has conceptual implications. Through participant observation, I was able to discover particular practices and processes that determined my conceptual contribution to the scholarly work on (private) security.

CONCLUDING REMARKS

In this paper, I have tried to demonstrate how the "anthropology of security" is a growing field in anthropology that has contributed to our understanding of security, both conceptually and methodologically. By presenting three empirical cases from my own fieldwork in South Africa and Kenya, I have tried to show the type of empirical data that ethnographic fieldwork can yield and thus the type of conceptual insights that emerge from this.

Combined, an anthropological approach to security centers around providing an emic perspective and gaining insight into the ways in which individuals experience, feel, and perceive their surroundings and thus give meaning to their social—and security—realities. This emic perspective relies on the use of certain methods, particularly participant observation, and thereby produces certain conceptual understanding of security. An anthropological approach to security is thus not solely about "closeness," "immersion," and getting away from one's desk by entering "the field." Embracing the "ethnographic turn" is not only a matter of "methodological pluralism" (Bigo 2014; Schwartz-Shea and Majic 2017), but it also includes embracing the way in which theoretical frameworks are developed due to the choice of these methods.

This claim is not entirely new, of course. In the field of private security, for example, scholars outside the discipline of anthropology are increasingly conducting ethnographic fieldwork (see Chisholm 2014; Higate 2011; Rigakos 2002). Furthermore, many political scientists appreciate the ethnographic approach, despite the so-called practical challenges it may have (Schwartz-Shea and Majic 2017). Therefore, although I concur that "security demands anthropological attention" (Maguire et al. 2014, 1), this attention should be shared and conducted in conjunction with scholars from other disciplines. The "anthropology of security" is still in its infancy, after all, and there is much more room for further theoretical development that will surely benefit from a political science perspective.

NOTES

1. For a more detailed discussion of the "wide" versus the "narrow" debate in security studies, see the introductory chapter in Buzan et al. (1998).

2. In fact, Pedersen and Holbraad (2013, 4) argue that security has always been a key area in anthropology, although it was not presented as such, due to the habitual focus on insecurity. They contend that the anthropology of security is not "a new subfield of political anthropology," but that rather, "security lies at the heart of the anthropological disciplines as a whole" (Pedersen and Holbraad 2013, 4).

3. Harry, along with all the other names used in this chapter, is a pseudonym.

REFERENCES

Abrahamsen, Rita, and Michael C. Williams. *Security Beyond the State: Private Security in International Politics*. Cambridge: Cambridge University Press, 2011.
———. "Security Beyond the State: Global Security Assemblages in International Politics." *International Political Sociology* 3 (2009): 1–17.
Aradau, Claudia, and Tobias Blanke. "The (Big) Data-Security Assemblage: Knowledge and Critique." *Big Data and Society* 2 (2015): 1–12.

Bakker, Laurens. "Illegality for the General Good? Vigilantism and Social Responsibility in Contemporary Indonesia." *Critique of Anthropology* 35 (2015): 78–93.

Beek, Jan, Mirco Göpfert, Olly Owen, and Jonny Steinberg. *Police in Africa. The Street Level View.* London: Hurst, 2017.

Ben-Ari, Eyal. *Mastering Soldiers. Conflict, Emotions and the Enemy in an Israeli Military Unit.* New York: Berghahn Books, 1998.

Berndtsson, Joakim, and Maria Stern. "Private Security and the Public-Private Divide: Contested Lines of Distinction and Modes of Governance in the Stockholm-Arlanda Security Assemblage." *International Political Sociology* 5 (2011): 408–25.

Bigo, Didier. "Afterword. Security: Encounters, Misunderstanding and Possible Collaborations." In *The Anthropology of Security. Perspectives from the Frontline of Policing, Counter-terrorism and Border Control,* edited by Mark Maguire, Catarina Frois, and Nils Zurawski, 185–205. London: Pluto Press, 2014.

Browning, Christopher S., and Matt McDonald. "The Future of Critical Security Studies: Ethics and the Politics of Security." *European Journal of International Relations* 19 (2013): 235–55.

Bueger, Christian. "Pathways to Practice: Praxiography and International Politics." *European Political Science Review* 6 (2014): 383–406.

Bueger, Christian, and Manuel Mireanu. "Proximity." In *Critical Security Methods: New Frameworks for Analysis,* edited by Claudia Aradaau, Jef Huysmans, Andrew McNeal, and Nadine Voelkner, 118–41. London: Routledge, 2014.

Buur, Lars. "Reordering Society: Vigilantism and Expressions of Sovereignty in Port Elizabeth's Townships." *Development and Change* 37 (2006): 735–57.

Buzan, Barry, Ole Wæver, and Japp de Wilde. *Security. A New Framework for Analyses.* Boulder: Lynne Rienner Publishers, 1998.

Caldeira, Teresa P.R. *City of Walls: Crime, Segregation, and Citizenship in Sao Paulo.* Berkeley: University of California Press, 2000.

Chisholm, Amanda. "Marketing the Gurkha Security Package: Colonial Histories and Neoliberal Economies of Private Security." *Security Dialogue* 45 (2014): 349–72.

Christensen, Maya M. "Shadow Soldiering: Shifting Constellations and Permeable Boundaries in "Private" Security Contracting." *Conflict and Society* 3 (2017): 24–41.

Crawford, Adam, and Steven Hutchinson. "Mapping the Contours of "Everyday Security": Time, Space and Emotion." *British Journal of Criminology* 56 (2016): 1184–1202.

Das, Veena, and Deborah Poole (eds). *Anthropology in the Margins of the State.* Santa Fe: School of American Research Press, 2004.

Deleuze, Gilles, and Felix Guattari. *A Thousand Plateaus: Capitalism and Schizophrenia.* Minneapolis: University of Minnesota Press, 1980.

DeWalt, Kathleen M., and Billie R. DeWalt. *Participant Observation. A Guide for Fieldworkers.* Walnut Creek, California: AltaMira Press, 2002.

Diphoorn, Tessa. "'Arms for Mobility': Policing Partnerships and Material Exchanges in Nairobi, Kenya." *Policing and Society* 30 (2019): 136–52.

Diphoorn, Tessa. "An Ethnographic Approach to Non-State Security: Participant Observation among Private Security Officers." In *Researching Non-State Actors in International Security: Theory & Practice*, edited by Andrea Schneiker, and Andreas Kruck. London: Routledge, 2017.

———. *Twilight Policing. Private Security and Violence in Urban South Africa.* Berkeley: University of California Press, 2016.

Diphoorn, Tessa, and Erella Grassiani (eds). *Security Blurs: The Politics of Plural Security Provision.* London: Routledge, 2019.

Diphoorn, Tessa, and Erella Grassiani. "Securitizing Capital: A Processual-Relation Approach to Pluralised Security." *Theoretical Criminology* 20 (2016): 430–45.

Diphoorn, Tessa, and Helene M. Kyed. "Entanglements of Private Security and Community Policing in South Africa and Swaziland." *African Affairs* 115 (2016): 710–32.

Farmer, Paul. "An Anthropology of Structural Violence." *Current Anthropology* 45 (2003): 305–25.

Fassin, Didier. *Enforcing Order: An Ethnography of Urban Policing.* Cambridge: Polity Press, 2013.

Feldman, Allen. *Formations of Violence: The Narrative of the Body and Political Terror in Northern Ireland.* Chicago: Chicago University Press, 1991.

Forsey, MArtin G. "Ethnography as Participant Listening." *Ethnography* 11 (2010): 558–72.

Garriot, William (ed). *Policing and Contemporary Governance. The Anthropology of Police in Practice.* New York: Palgrave MacMillan, 2013.

Glück, Zoltán, and Setha Low. "A Sociospatial Framework for the Anthropology of Security." *Anthropological Theory* 17 (2017): 281–96.

Goldstein, Daniel M. "Toward a Critical Anthropology of Security." *Current Anthropology* 51 (2010): 487–517.

Grassiani, Erella. *Soldering under Occupation: Processes of Numbing among Israel Soldiers in the Al-Aqsa Intifada.* New York: Berghahn Books, 2013.

Grassiani, Erella, and Lior Volinz. "Intimidation, Reassurance, and Invisibility: Israeli Security Agents in the Old City of Jerusalem." *Focaal* 75 (2016):14–30.

Guillaume, Xavier, and Jef Huysmans. *Citizenship and Security: The Constitution of Political Being. PRIO New Security Studies.* London: Routledge, 2013.

Gusterson, Hugh 2007. "Anthropology and Militarism." *Annual Review of Anthropology* 36 (2007): 155–75.

Hansen, Lene. *Security as Practice: Discourse Analysis and the Bosnian War.* London: Routledge, 2006.

Hansen, Thomas B., and Finn Stepputat. "Sovereignty Revisited." *Annual Review of Anthropology* 35 (2006): 295–315.

Harnischfeger, Johannes. "The Bakassi Boys: Fighting Crime in Nigeria." *Journal of Modern African Studies* 41 (2003): 23–49.

Higate, Paul. "'Cowboys and Professionals'": The Politics of Identity Work in the Private and Military Security Company." *Millennium—Journal of International Studies* 40 (2011): 321–41.

Holston, James. *Insurgent Citizenship: Disjunctions of Democracy and Modernity in Brazil* Princeton: Princeton University Press, 2008.

Hornberger, Julia. *Policing and Human Rights. The Meaning of Violence and Justice in the Everyday Policing of Johannesburg.* New York: Routledge, 2011.

Humphrey, Caroline. "Sovereignty." In *A Companion to the Anthropology of Politics*, edited by David Nugent, and Joan Vincent, 418–36. Oxford: Blackwell Publishing, 2007.

Hurtado, Fina A., and Giovanni Ercolani (eds). *Anthropology and Security Studies.* Univesidad de Murcia, Nottingham Trent University and College of William and Mary, 2013.

Ingold, Tim. "Anthropology is Not Ethnography." *Proceedings of the British Academy* 154 (2008): 69–92.

Jaffe, Rivke. "The Hybrid State: Crime and Citizenship in Urban Jamaica." *American Ethnologist* 40 (2013): 734–48.

Jauregui, Beatrice. *Provisional Authority: Police, Order, and Security in India.* Chicago: University of Chicago Press, 2016.

Jensen, Steffen. *Gangs, Politics and Dignity in Cape Town.* Oxford: James Currey Ltd., 2008.

Karpiak, Kevin G., and William Garriott (eds). *The Anthropology of Police.* London: Routledge, 2018.

Konopinski, Natalie. "Borderline Temporalities and Security Anticipations: Standing Guard in Tel Aviv." *Etnofoor* 26 (2014): 59–80.

Koonings, Kees, and Dirk Kruijt. *Fractured Cities. Social Exclusion, Urban Violence and Contested Spaces in Latin America.* London: Zed Books, 2007.

Kyed, Helene M. "Community Policing in Post-War Mozambique." *Policing and Society* 19 (2009): 354–71.

Larkins, Erika R. "Guarding the Body: Private Security Work in Rio de Janeiro." *Conflict and Society* 3 (2017): 61–72.

Lazar, Sian. and Monique Nuijten. "Citizenship, the Self, and Political Agency." *Critique of Anthropology* 33 (2013): 3–7.

Low, Setha M. *Behind the Gates: Life, Security, and the Pursuit of Happiness in Fortress America.* London: Routledge, 2004.

———. Securitization Strategies: Gated Communities and Market-rate Co-operatives in New York. In *Policing Cities: Urban Securitization and Regulation in a 21st Century World*, edited by Randy K. Lippert, and Kevin Walby, 222–30. London: Routledge, 2013.

Low, Setha M., and Mark Maguire (eds). *Spaces of Security: Ethnographies of Securityscapes, Surveillance and Control.* New York: New York University Press, 2019.

Lutz, Catherine. *Homefront: A Military City and the American Twentieth Century.* Boston, MA: Beacon Press, 2002.

Maguire, Mark, Ursula Rao, and Nils Zurawski (eds). *Bodies as Evidence: Security, Knowledge and Power.* Durham: Duke University Press, 2018.

Maguire, Mark, Catarina Froisand, and Nils Zurawski (eds). *The Anthropology of Security. Perspectives from the Frontline of Policing, Counter-terrorism and Border Control.* London: Pluto Press, 2014.

Marcus, George E., and Erkan Saka. "Assemblage." *Theory, Culture & Society* 23 (2006): 101–09.

Nordstrom, Carolyn, and Antonius C.G.M. Robben (eds). *Fieldwork Under Fire. Contemporary Studies of Violence and Survival.* Berkeley: University of California Press, 1995.

Ong, Aihwa. *Flexible Citizenship: The Cultural Logics of Transnationality.* Durham: Duke University Press, 1999.

Ong, Aihwa, and Collier Stephen J. (eds). *Global Assemblages: Technology, Politics, and Ethics as Anthropological Problems.* Malden: Blackwell Publishing, 2005.

Oosterbaan, Martijn, and Wil G. Pansters. "Sovereignty and Social Contestation— Between Violence and Alternative Sociocultural Orders." *Conflict and Society* 1 (2015): 125–28.

Pedersen, Morten A., and Martin Holbraad (eds). *Times of Security. Ethnographies of Fear, Protest and the Future.* London: Routledge, 2013.

Perlman, Janice E. *Favela: Four Decades of Living on the Edge in Rio de Janeiro.* Oxford: Oxford University Press, 2010.

Pratten, David, and Atreyee Sen (eds). *Global Vigilantes.* London: Hurst, 2007.

Rigakos, George S. *The New Parapolice. Risk Markets and Commodified Social Control.* Toronto: University of Toronto Press, 2002.

Rodgers, Dennis. "The State as a Gang: Conceptualizing the Governmentality of Violence in Contemporary Nicaragua." *Critique of Anthropology* 26 (2006): 315–30.

Ruteere, Mutuma, and Marie-Emmanuelle Pommerolle. "Democratizing Security or Decentralizing Repression? The Ambiguities of Community Policing in Kenya." *African Affairs* 102 (2003): 587–604.

Samimian-Darash, Limor, and Meg Stalcup. "Anthropology of Security and Security in Anthropology: Cases of Terrorism in the United States." *Anthropological Theory* 17 (2016): 60–87.

Sarkar, Swagato. "The Illicit Economy of Power: Smuggling, Trafficking and the Securitization of the Indo-Bangladesh Border." *Dialectical Anthropology* 41 (2017): 185–99.

Scheper-Hughes, Nancy, and Philippe Bourgois (eds). *Violence in War and Peace. An Anthology.* Oxford: Blackwell Publishing, 2004.

Schmidt, Bettina E., and Ingo Schröder (eds). *Anthropology of Violence and Conflict.* London: Routledge, 2001.

Schouten, Peer. "Security as Controversy: Reassembling Security at Amsterdam Airport." *Security Dialogue* 45 (2014): 23–42.

Schwartz-Shea, Peregrine., and Samantha Majic. "Introduction: Ethnography and Participant Observation: Political Science Research in this 'Late Methodological Moment'." *PS: Political Science and Politics* 50 (2017): 97–102.

Sharma, Aradhana, and Akhil Gupta (eds). *The Anthropology of the State: A Reader.* Oxford: Blackwell Publishing, 2006.

Smith, Nicholas. *Contradictions of Democracy: Vigilantism and Rights in Post-Apartheid South Africa.* Oxford: Oxford University Press, 2019.

Stockmarr, Leila. *"Turning Swords into Silicon Chips: The Israeli Homeland Security Industry and Making of Jewish Nationhood."* PhD Dissertation: Roskilde University, 2015.

United Nations Development Programme (UNDP). *Human Development Report 1994.* New York: Oxford University Press, 1994.

Van Roekel, Eva. *Phenomenal Justice: Violence and Morality in Argentina.* New York: Rutgers University Press, 2020.

Van Stapele, Naomi. *"Respectable 'Illegality': Gangs, Masculinities and Belonging in a Nairobi Ghetto."* Unpublished PhD dissertation: University of Amsterdam, 2015.

Winslow, Donna. *The Canadian Airborne Regiment in Somalia: A Socio-Cultural Inquiry: a study prepared for the Commission of Inquiry into the Deployment of Canadian Forces to Somalia.* Ottawa: The Commission, 1997.

Chapter 6

Dynamic Security and the Scientific Exotic

Vernacularization and Practical Norms in Ugandan Prisons

Tomas Max Martin

This chapter relays the merits of the mid-level concepts that anthropology can bring to the table of the study of the internationalized politics, which this volume seeks to investigate. It is argued that anthropology's relationship with exoticism, which is subject to an ever-present disciplinary self-critique (Kapferer 2013), also entails a fruitful capacity to churn out mid-level concepts that explore "the middle," or the interface, between global forms and local action (Knauft 2006). To operate at this level entails a conceptual framework that is open-ended and encourages inductive discovery. Mid-level concepts do not aspire to produce either high theory or exhaustive ethnographic detail. They support the researcher's efforts to "creatively lever and explore issues that resists or complicates poles of received opposition" (ibid: 425). These concepts are "not-too-hot-not-too-cold," as Vered Amit puts it, and "this mid-range conceptualization is something that anthropologists, wary of abstractions that soar too far from the ground they are trying to explain, have been usually good at" (Amit, Anderson et al. 2015, 3). As such, these mid-level concepts illustrate that anthropology is not simply ideographic. Rather, anthropology's capacity and tradition of developing and applying mid-level concepts enable in-depth ethnographic research that link the messiness of everyday life to larger questions of social change.

Based on case material from an ethnography of prison reform in Uganda,[1] the chapter shows how two such mid-level concepts—"practical norms" (de Herdt and Olivier de Sardan 2015) and "vernularization" (Merry 2006)— help to unpack the concurrent mutation and persistence of the governance of everyday life in Ugandan prisons. Practical norms denote the set of tacit local rules with which bureaucracies are governed. Vernularization describes the processes whereby global norms—most notably human rights—concurrently form and take form from local social lifeworlds. Jointly, these concepts animate an analysis of the changes and continuities of positions of power amid grand stories of reform in Ugandan prisons as well as the equivocal side effects of one particular flotsam of internationalized politics: dynamic security. Dynamic security is a prison management paradigm that encourages investment in constructive staff-prisoner relations in order to make prison life more just and humane and thereby also more stable and safe (UNODC 2015). Dynamic security has become a prominent part of the catalog of human rights reform of prisons in the Global South, including Ugandan prisons. As I will argue below, dynamic security is vernacularized in Ugandan prisons through the pragmatic-cum-aspirational appropriation by staff and strong prisoners in order to both reproduce and update bureaucratic power.

The chapter is structured as follows: First, I will present the notion of the scientific exotic as a basic orientation of anthropological thinking, which bring forth explorative mid-level concepts like "practical norms" and "vernacularization," and I will show how these two concepts have grown out of the anthropological critique of development and human rights. The chapter then offers a comprehensive description of the system of prisoner self-governance in Ugandan prisons—the katikiro system—and leads into an analysis of the actual, on-the-ground appropriation of "dynamic security" in that context. In conclusion, I will then argue that the vernacularized notion of dynamic security allows Ugandan prison actors to situate themselves in a situation of exigency—staff-prisoner ratios of 1:20 in prisons without fences—which in fact legitimizes their ensuing reliance on practical norms of intermediation to meet custodial imperatives. The internationally acclaimed and inherently positive notion of dynamic security offers a progressive language for this practice. By deploying the language of dynamic security to describe persistent practices of prisoner self-governance, Ugandan prisons can be seen to humanize themselves through material crisis. This venularization process is not just a calculated form of opportunism. It is a form of agency and a process of transition. However, it is a pragmatic transition, which is contingent upon local exigencies and people's tactics for professional or personal survival.

THE SCIENTIFIC EXOTIC

Schatz succinctly suggests that ethnography entails a characteristic "immersion" in the field of study, which affords a distinct "sensibility" that cares "to glean the meanings that the people under study attribute to their social and political reality" (Schatz 2009, 5). The immersion and sensibility—classically brought about by long-term, in-depth fieldwork—attunes ethnography to the face-to-face, the informal, and the everyday. Anthropological knowledge is sought and created, not in dissecting the grand "production" of societal schemes, but in picking up the multiple and small-scale human "consumption" of these schemes—and its effects (de Certeau 1984). A distinguishing consequence of this approach is a propensity not to take grand theoretical concepts for granted, let alone as point of departure for anthropological analysis. This propensity has deep roots in anthropology's disciplinary history as the study of "primitive societies." In contrast to sociology and its scrutiny of Western society, the founding mothers and fathers of anthropology did not find that the grand theories of modernity applied so easily to study of kinship and other noncapitalist forms of human organization beyond the West. Instead they pursued a more inductive, qualitative, and phenomenological approach to their science. Latour argues that this division of labor with sociology has had a commendable upside for anthropology, which still lives on: "Anthropologists with pre-moderns and were not requested as much to imitate natural sciences, were more fortunate and allowed their actors to deploy a much richer world" (Latour 2005, 41). However, anthropology's particular dealings with the premoderns, as Latour lackadaisically puts it, is also the discipline's exotic scandal. The ability and authority to discern the different "other"—albeit often in a relativistic effort to challenge racisms—was also an inherently problematic process of exoticizing people and rendering them governable. Consequently, postmodern anthropology has been quite self-critical/reflexive of enduring new and recurrent forms exoticizing that anthropologists might find themselves in the middle of (Clifford and Marcus 1986; MacClancy 2002). Yet, Kapferer inspiringly suggests a rehabilitation or reconfiguration of the exotic as a methodology for discovery and understanding—what he refers to as "the scientific exotic":

> [The scientific exotic] refer to the exotic as the appearance of a previously unknown phenomenon of existence or else a perturbation in the behaviour, creation, or formation of phenomena that deviates from the expectations or predictions based in the current knowledge, opinion, or theory. (. . .) More than difference, the exotic and its recognition have to do with the challenge to understanding and (. . .) can be as much a property of the familiar or what appears to be known as of that which is external or outside. (Kapferer 2013, 818)

What is emphasized here is anthropology's potential to discover and to explore what it actually means to be human in this place at that time by insistently tilling empirical soil in order to uncover relationships that have not been explicitly spelled out in theoretical formulations (Wilson and Chaddha

2009). And it is not only the ethnographic practice of long-term fieldwork that facilitates this discovery. It is also the discipline's ability to churn out relevant concepts. Anthropology may of course contribute to international-ized politics with the classical concepts of the discipline like ritual, magic, sorcery, or kinship. "By calling on metaphors imbued with a sense of the exotic" (Kapferer 2013, 828), anthropology may break up the rationalities of description and explanation that dominate conventional domains of the politi-cal, the economy, or the social—for example, by approaching the study of the state as magical (Taussig 1997), or the study of ethnic violence as exorcism (Kapferer 2012). Yet, what I want to focus on here is rather a seemingly lesser order of anthropological mid-level concepts hinted at above. These concepts do not necessarily have profound explanatory power as grand theory, but they can be put to work in the field for explorative purposes. They work as heu-ristic devices, that is, "as set of conceptual tools, which, rather than telling us anything substantive about the world, suggests ways of approaching it" (Lund 2014). They are focusing on the problem at hand and facilitate an engagement with institutional policies and practical interventions (Knauft 2006). These concepts are agency-friendly and attuned to pick up the volatility, heteroge-neity, and equivocality of everyday life and as such quite helpful in practicing the scientific exotic.[2] To illustrate this point, I will turn to the two concepts of "vernacularization" and "practical norms" that have guided my analysis of the appropriation of human rights reform in Ugandan prisons. But first, I will introduce the anthropology of development and of human rights, from where these concepts stem.

THE ANTHROPOLOGY OF DEVELOPMENT AND PRACTICAL NORMS

To me, a certain strand in the anthropology of development has been quite inspirational in dealing with the encounter between global forms and local action. Most especially, Tania Murray Li's notion of "the will to improve," that is, shifting programs of trusteeship that lay claim to enhance the lives of others (Li 2007). From historical and ethnographic material, Li shows how the will to improve has driven a civilizing mission toward Indonesian forests populations, but her ambition is to launch "the will to improve" as a grand theoretical concept, denoting a civilizing mission that has mutated and persisted as a modality of government from colonial and into postcolonial programs of improvement. To become a program—that is, to lend itself to practice—the will to improve must first of all take a form that allows it to problematize. It must amply and aptly spot deficiencies, that is, people, phenomena, or spaces to improve on. Second, it must render these problems technical—that is, meaningfully lift the problems out of fundamentally political and revolutionary questions of structural relations and into issues of enhancing capacities through reform, in practice depoliticizing social problems and expanding bureaucratic power (Li 2007, 277).

In such programmatic forms, global discourses like human rights have a long and unfolding history of being forcefully exported into particular localities, mounted on an elite donor regime, armored by money and institutions and accelerated by moral claims. Albeit tooled up as an institutional change agent, global discourses are not just either internalized or resisted by people. As argued by Tsing, global discourses need to mobilize people to gain traction locally (Tsing 2005). Global discourses might induce massive change, but they are cut to size and adjusted to the given locality by the people who appropriate the ideas and technologies on offer. As Mosse also argues, development policies are productive and gain traction locally not due to their prescriptive qualities, but due to their capacity to enroll participants and stabilize managers', consultants', field-workers', community leaders', and stakeholders' interpretation of development events (Mosse 2004). Consequently, policy "can only be understood in terms of the institutions and social relationships through which they are articulated" (Mosse 2004, 666).

Together with a group of seasoned West Africa scholars, Olivier de Sardan has developed a comprehensive body of empirically based work that takes up exactly this challenge of understanding policy implementation from below and the forms of governance it produces (Blundo and Olivier de Sardan 2006; Lund 2006, Blundo and Le Meur 2009; Olivier de Sardan 2011; Bierschenk and de Sardan 2014; de Herdt and Olivier de Sardan 2015). The notion of "practical norms" offers a way to explore this actual form of governance. Practical norms are the repertoire of rules and values situated at the midpoint between the collective, abstract social norms and the explicated official norms, which are spelled out and formalized in policies, laws, codes, and standards (Olivier de Sardan 2008, 2009). Divergence from policy prescriptions is, in practice, systematically regulated by such practical norms,[3] that is, "a series of refined, invisible, implicit and subterranean regulation," akin to "tacit, shared road rules" of bureaucratic practice (Olivier de Sardan 2008, 13). Practical norms are locally produced and their importance for actual everyday governance demands an empirical attention that global programs of governance cannot afford inside their own logic. Thus, if we want to understand how different instantiations of "the will to improve"—like human rights reform in Ugandan prisons—take effect in local institutional landscapes, we need to discern how the norms and techniques of these global programs in fact resonate with the practical norms of everyday bureaucratic practice.

THE ANTHROPOLOGY OF HUMAN
RIGHTS AND VERNACULARIZATION

So, one global program with which forms of government or regulation are attempted to be applied "par excellence" is most definitely human rights. There is scholarly consensus that human rights not only constitutes a normative and regulatory framework, but that the concept has also expanded "to a full blown moral-theological-political vision of the good life" (Wilson 2007, 349)—or, as Sam Moyn, flatly states, human rights has become our latest utopia (Moyn 2010).

To my knowledge, the standard take on this proliferation of human rights within political science and international relations studies is to examine to what extent human rights perform (or underperform) according to their own logic. One well-known example of this kind of research is the work of Kathryn Sikkink and her colleagues, who have developed the "boomerang-spiral model," which explains domestic human rights change by the interaction between transnational and national advocacy (Keck and Sikkink 1998; Risse-Kappen et al. 1999). Human rights are of course insightfully reflected upon within such research, but, from a distinct theoretical point of departure that offers a considerable certainty about what human rights are: realists reject human rights as window dressing, liberalists inspect the potentials of human rights as a normative institution, and so on.

On the face of it, this finite approach to human rights is not so surprising. Human rights are fairly well defined. As political scientist Jack Donnelly simply puts it, human rights "are the rights one has because one is human" (Donnelly and Howard 1987, 1), which basically captures the most common and acknowledged definition of human rights. Yet, a significant motivation for the anthropology of human rights has been to question and critically inspect the empirical manifestations and the ambiguous forms that this powerful and expanding discourse takes in everyday practices in the Global South (Goodale 2006; Hornberger 2010). Wilson and Mitchell refer to this line of scholarly enquiry as a study of "the social life of rights"—that is, looking at "rights at the level of social practice: how are rights applied—and what are they applied *for*?" (Wilson and Mitchell 2003: 5, emphasis in original). It is a common understanding across such empirical and practice-oriented studies that the local appropriation of human rights is productive and enabling. This focus on appropriation transcends simple pro- and antagonistic stances on whether and how human rights is a success or a failure (Wilson 2006, 82). And this polyvalence is central to the global proliferation of human rights as it allows them to be appropriated in diverse social processes by diverse social actors (Dembour 1996; Merry 2006).

Ethnographies of human rights have examined this circulation and transplantation, often under the rubrics of "localization" or "translation" of human rights into practice (Merry 2006; Hornberger 2007; Wilson 2007; Jefferson and Jensen 2009). Sally Engle Merry's notion of "vernacularization" is probably one of the most influencing concepts to both capture and direct this body of research. Vernacularization simply denotes "the reconfiguration of global human rights ideas into terms that are relevant and coherent within local life worlds" (Merry 2017, 149). It is, I suggest, an example of a mid-level concept that makes a virtue out of being open-ended and agnostic as it approaches this thing we call human rights. It compels the researcher to consider human rights as an empirical question and builds an argument from the ground up of what human rights then are in a particular place and at a particular time. It is this perspective that has guided my analysis of human rights reform in Ugandan prisons.

THE KATIKIROS OF UGANDAN PRISONS— PRACTICAL NORMS OF INTERMEDIATION

The Uganda Prison Service (UPS) has gone through an applauded, human rights-based reform process and the prison system seems to be changing accordingly. Headlines like "A taste of hell in Uganda prisons" (*The Independent*, April 13, 2010) and "Prison staff accused of hanging inmate" (*Daily Monitor*, March 9, 2010) are not uncommon in Ugandan media, but violations of prisoners' rights are also seen to be decreasing according to independent human rights watchdogs, "to be a centre (...) Africa" \ budgets have increased, management tightened, and material progress has been felt across the institutional landscape. A new law and new policies of imprisonment explicitly draw upon human rights standards and UPS has formally adopted the vision statement: *"To be a centre of excellence in providing human rights based correctional service in Africa."* Staff have been subject to human rights training and managers, staff, and prisoners alike have begun to qualify change in human rights terms with institutional procedures—from budgeting to complaint handling—being formally framed by human rights.

On the basis of in-depth ethnographic research, I have elsewhere argued that human rights reform was being forcefully exported into Ugandan prisons, but the powerful global discourse of human rights was significantly vernacularized in the process through the agency of prison actors, who appropriated human rights talk, law, and technologies and put them to local use (Martin 2014a, b, 2015, 2017). One example of this vernacularization concerns the ambiguous uptake of the notion of dynamic security and its resonance with the practical norms of intermediation, that is, of outsourcing power and privilege to strong prisoners called katikiros.

Distributive and Disciplinary Power

In the overcrowded and communally organized space of a Ugandan prison, prisoners are almost always in groups: as they squat awaiting court, as they sit packed together in their wards, as they are herded two by two in rows to the fields to work, as they stand in line for food, as they gather for parades, etc. But there are a few who stand out as individuals from the masses of confined men and seem better dressed and more relaxed. They move about in the prison with the determination of an official on an errand, or they hang out lazily in a shady spot. They interact seriously or in a friendly manner with staff and they always seem to be around the office of the head of the prison, the gate, the storeroom, the kitchen, and the reception. And they often organize the activity when a truck with firewood is unloaded, when Christian Non-Governmental Organisations (NGOs) hand out bibles, or when confused and scared newly remanded prisoners are marched before the receptionist for admission. These prisoners are known as the "katikiros" of Ugandan prisons.

In the UPS the term katikiro is used for prisoners with some form of staff-sanctioned administrative or disciplinary function—often referred to in English as "leaders" or "bosses."[4] The katikiro system is an institutionalized and essential part of prison management, yet it has no legal basis and there are no official records whatsoever in the Ugandan Prison Service which mention, let alone define and circumscribe this system.[5] The delegation of power to selected prisoners is historically a very common, but also highly criticized way to manage prisons. Throughout the history of imprisonment, reformers have continued to challenge prison administrators' opportunistic interest in using privileged prisoners as a means of control in order to save money and to maintain a brutal and authoritarian regime—often against penal policies and legal obligations (Henriques 1972, 62; McGovern 1995, 80–83). Today, the delegation of disciplinary power to prisoners is also in direct contradiction with human rights standards (UN 1955, Art. 28), and the Ugandan prison act similarly states that "a prison officer shall not employ a prisoner in the punishment of a fellow prisoner" (UPS 2006, Art. 97). Yet, in Ugandan prisons, prisoners to a wide extent govern themselves. *"Prisoners have their own system"* or *"their homemade discipline,"* staff say. *"You cannot run a prison without the katikiros,"* even the top managers of UPS flatly stated. When I asked a newly appointed junior officer about the role of the katikiros, he thought about it for a while and then said, *"Theirs is 80%. Ours are only 20%."*

According to my own rough estimates about 10 percent of all Ugandan prisoners (approximately 3,000 people in 2011) are assigned to different managerial positions as katikiros. When compared to the uniformed staff strength of 6,419 prison officers, it is safe to say that katikiros make up a considerable part of the system of governance in UPS. Katikiros broadly comprise three categories: (1) ward leaders, who manage and administer the wards; (2) "RPs," (supposedly short for Reserve Police) who police; and (3) cleaners, who have manual and organizational tasks in the prison.

Ward leaders distribute tasks, services, privileges, and resources in the ward. This includes, for instance, appointment to attractive and unattractive posts in the ward hierarchy; distribution of food, blankets, and mats; designation of sleeping places; and the collection and administration of joint stocks of basic necessities and utensils. Ward leaders thereby run the ward economy. The extraction of resources from prisoners can be explicitly violent and threatening. Newcomers are routinely initiated into this economy through an introductory bullying called "karaka" in Swahili. A prisoner, who later became a senior katikiro, explained in length his first night in prison. He arrived from court late in the afternoon and was taken to his ward. After lockup the "karaka" started:

> They told me to stand underneath the light bulb: *"You go under the light!"* A certain man stood up—the police, the RP—and he told me: *"Look at me! Put your eyes on me."* Then I looked at him. *"Tell me your names"* and he is very serious and rude, and he is speaking like he is on a parade. (. . .) I thought it was a joke. I was looking at him smiling. He came and slapped me: *"Is this your home? Am I your wife? Why do you smile at me? You have to be serious here. You have to mean business. Do you know the reason why I am telling you to stand there?"* Then I had to ask for forgiveness. I told him: *"I am sorry,"* and I didn't know how to address him because I was calling him: *"Sir, sir, sir, sir."* Again, that was a case. *"Am I your sir? I am a prisoner and you are calling me sir? The 'sirs' are left outside!".* (. . .) Every question he asks I have to answer. *"Why were you brought here?"* This caused me problems again, because I was telling them: *"Somebody has forged an allegation* [against me]." And they told me: *"No, don't say that!!"* and not peacefully! They gave me two strokes. They caned me and I was in tears. *"Everyone who is brought in prison has passed through the magistrate, and there is no way you can tell us: 'they have forged an allegation.' No! You say: 'I have done ABCD.'"* So, I was forced to say that I did ABCD. And their interest was to know about money. If you stole and you are charged of theft, what did you steal? So, [my case] was obtaining money by false pretense, [and they asked:] *"How much?"* I told them two million. So, they started asking me: *"How much have you come with?"* I was telling them: *"I did not steal the money, but you have forced me to say that I stole. But now even if I had stolen, money is not allowed in here."* So, they were telling me: *"Do you think we are fools to make you stand there? Were you not told that you will be*

asked for money inside here?" I told them: *"I have been checked to an extent of even removing my pant. Now, where could I hide that money? You know I am new in prison. I have never been in prison."* So, they told me: *"You have to pay for a place to sleep. You have to pay if you want to go for short-call or long-call* [i.e., use the toilet], *you have to pay . . ."* many things like that: *"You are not the person, who goes for food from the kitchen. There are some people who are supposed to do that, and we pay them. We need soap for the ward, so, if you say you don't have money, then you are looking for trouble. Promise us, when will you pay?"* So, I had to tell them that unless I get visitors—and that is when the man started to speak to me peacefully saying: *"Okay, do you expect visitors?"* I said *"Yes." "When?" "This very week." "Okay,"* he said *"that is okay. Tell us about your family. Are you married?"* I said: *"Yes I am married." "Is it in church or you just found a girl?" "I am married in church,"* I said. So, they are asking this to discover if you are a responsible person outside. Do you have a work? If yes, what kind of work? Are you educated? All those questions, they asked me. Now after that, they said to me: *"Because you don't have money, you will not sleep."* We were about 65 that night in one ward. So, they made me sleep in the middle because I did not have money.

However, the exercise of katikiros' distributive power also has a more indirect and subtle side. An experienced ward leader put it like this:

It is not crude. Oh no. It's much more subtle. A prisoner needs to "behave"— meaning to pay and appreciate. You find yourself being transferred from ward to ward and after some time you think: *"Why can I not settle like the other guys?"* And then you get a loaf of bread from a visitor and bring it to the prisoner leader and ask if he doesn't want some, and then some donuts, some sugar. And then you find yourself settling. It is subdued—otherwise it cannot be sustained. Demanding openly is not good.

This subtle, mutual exchange is especially directed toward visibly affluent prisoners with access to considerable and stable funds. Such prisoners are not necessarily coerced and beaten upon arrival at the ward, but smoothly approached by katikiros, who offer their guidance and protection and find them a nice spot to sleep. This distributive power that katikiros hold is inherently discriminating as it systematically transforms rights to basic needs into unequally distributed privileges (cf. Bandyopadhyay 2010, 207).

Katikiros also have disciplinary powers. At ward level prisoners constitute their own courts, which handle infractions of ward discipline and, as illustrated in the "karaka" session above, the breaking in of new ward members. These courts include posts like judge, prosecutors, and police. Staff do not directly engage with these courts.[6] From the staff's point of view, the courts and ensuing rules, roles, and sanctions are the prisoners' own concern—as long as security is not disrupted. Ward rules are to a great extent drawn directly from the prison rules and standing orders, which hold elaborate lists of prison offences (mainly related to custodial restrictions, but also to issues of theft, fighting, contraband, and labor), and as such part of the repertoire of official norms. However, prisoners also have to abide by a register of prison rules that staff considers the prisoners' own. These rules consolidate katikiro power and facilitate housekeeping and include disrespect toward leaders, talking at ward meetings, not following katikiros' orders, and rules about indecency and lack of hygiene (including very particular rules prohibiting the squashing of lice or the crossing of others' property while wearing sandals). These local ward rules are not official, but they are also not implicit, and they are often written down on boards, posters, or walls. If these rules are broken, katikiros dispense different forms of punishment to fellow prisoners: fatigues, caning, loss of privilege and transfers. Fatigues are punitive manual tasks, most often cleaning and water carrying, and this is the most common form of punishment. Prisoners can also "receive strokes" and "be caned"—that is, ordered to lie on the ground facing down and be hit a designated number of times on the buttocks with a stick or a plastic tube called a "Black Mamba." This type of caning is according to my findings common in most prisons, but in a few prisons katikiros argued that it was only the staff who caned the prisoners. In addition to fatigues and canes, prisoners can be punished by humiliation and communal mocking in the ward, and privileges such as extra blankets or rations or a preferred sleeping place can be withdrawn.

Intermediation

The actual competencies and power of the katikiros make plain that their importance to the governing of Ugandan prisons is indisputable. They control essential resources and are tasked to produce a stable regime as quasi-bureaucrats. Their power is assigned to them by staff in a bureaucratized form, unlike the informal systems of gangs that characterize prison governance in South African and Latin American prisons (Steinberg 2005; Skarbek 2010; Gear 2012; Lindegaard and Gear 2014; Garces and Darke 2017). This delegation of violence to privileged subjects is a distinct legacy of the pragmatic and brutal colonial prison. Colonial authorities systematically lacked linguistic and cultural skills fundamental to the exercise of government and relied heavily on *intermediaries*, that is, indigenous translators and auxiliaries to implement colonial policy and to make alien institutions and structures settle and function with some level of elite consent (Lawrance et al. 2006). Sherman argues the hybrid figure of the colonial convict warder rests in this gap: "Situated on the edge of two worlds," Sherman writes, local native warders (the uniformed as well as the enlisted convicts) "epitomise the ambiguity of the colonial violence for they reveal the extent to which many of the colonial state's coercive mechanisms relied on a small number of the colonised population who, reluctantly, willingly, or cunningly, were instruments of colonial dominance" (Sherman 2009, 662). These gaps between the formal, legal, and idealized imagery of the state and the real practices of bureaucracy have been recast in postcolonial Africa, expanding and consolidating the role of the intermediary. Blundo and Olivier de Sardan find that all the contemporary practices and institutions of public services that they study only function through the commonplace and naturalized facilitation of intermediaries, who support or complete the tasks of regular personnel by adopting certain specific roles:

> [Intermediaries] help to *accelerate procedures* (at the costs of those users who do not have access to their services). They can *protect their clients*, avoiding sanctions or multiplying the latter's chances of winning a legal case or asserting their rights. They also *facilitate the personalisation* of the administrative procedures while reassuring the citizen dealing with an administration perceived as omnipotent. On the other hand, they reproduce the "local professional culture" with its habits, tricks and strategies and schemes. (. . .) While they may not be the systemic vectors of corruption, they can nevertheless *contribute to the euphemisation of illicit practices* and making them commonplace. (Blundo and Olivier de Sardan in Olivier de Sardan 2009, 65, my emphasis)

The intermediaries offer personalized but thereby also inherently unequal access to state services—not least in terms of protection from the chaotic and adverse effects of formal bureaucratic practice. They possess the skills and position to merge formal bureaucratic technologies and structures with local relations and processes into a marketable mix, allowing informalization to both thrive and function. By looking at UPS as such a bureaucratic context, the katikiros can be conceptualized as such "intermediaries" and coproducers of bureaucratic governance.

Unlike the intermediaries that generally hang around African bureaucracies, katikiros notably also wield disciplinary power. In the closed world of the prison, prisoners, who seek intermediation, have little opportunity to choose between brokers. As shown above, ward leaders are positioned to press their facilitation onto the desperate and frightened users of the penal bureaucracy, who more often than not fear for their life and their future. Yet, intermediation is an established bureaucratic form—a practical norm—that offers regulated roles between sellers and buyers of bureaucratic survival. Such intermediation is a role that katikiros can draw on to establish legitimacy and therefore also, to some extent, a role that they can be held accountable for.

This intermediary role was very much part of katikiros' own understanding of their position and task. They often referred to themselves as *"the link"* between prisoners and staff. One katikiro put it like this:

> The best word to use would be to say that we are coordinators. We coordinate the administration and the inmates. What the administration wants us to pass to the inmates, we take it, what the inmates want us to take to the administration, we take it, so we coordinate—we are in between. (. . .) We need to be of sound mind, look at issues critically and think about them. If it's necessary, we forward them.

Katikiros term themselves *"the eyes"* of the administration. They have to police prison life and deliver discipline and security by enforcing and bending written and unwritten prison rules. However, katikiros also argue that they are *"the voice"* of the prisoners. They cannot only *"be on the side of staff,"* as they put it. As intermediaries they need to package and present prisoners' claims in pragmatic ways that both optimize the prospects of addressing actual problems and consolidate the power structures which they are part of. They have to be able to manage the ward and produce information so that staff are relieved of handling petty issues and so that escapes and riot situations are avoided. Although their power is directly based on the ability to exercise physical violence, katikiros also have to lead, to have authority. And it is in order to consolidate this authority that katikiros (and the staff that rely on them) reach out for the global program of human rights and infuse it with practical norms of intermediation through processes of vernacularization.

FROM POWER TO AUTHORITY—THE VERNACULARIZATION OF DYNAMIC SECURITY

It is characteristic of the katikiro system in Uganda that the negotiated ordering between staff and prisoners is set within an explicitly bureaucratic form. The katikiro system is referred to as an "administration," interchangeably with the administration by staff, and I have many times during interviews had to ask which administration a katikiro or a prison officer was in fact talking about: the prison administration or the prisoner administration? As quasi-bureaucrats they form committees, conduct meetings, second decisions, take minutes, and forward reports. They are office holders, whose positions are recorded in ledgers and assigned to them by agents of the state, and this bureaucratic character also enables katikiros to join UPS's institutional embrace of human rights.

All the katikiros and staff that I talked to were quick to stress that the katikiro system was in the process of being reformed. A common phrase to indicate this change for the better was that my informants pointed out to me that *"katikiros no longer carry sticks."* According to my observations, katikiros still carried sticks—but maybe to a lesser degree than earlier. Many of the sticks they carried were often twiglike things used for pointing and herding rather than actual weapons, but they carried sticks and I observed katikiros lashing out at prisoners who were slow to sit or stand more than once. The absence of sticks was nevertheless repeatedly underlined as an indicator of the taming of katikiro violence. These narratives of change were unequivocally stressing the cessation of caning. *"The system of caning is now removed. Now we use the mouth,"* a senior katikiro in a larger up-country prison told me. A katikiro from another prison added,

> People are not children. There is no need to be harsh! You need to be friendly and don't be far—otherwise you will not get information. A good Overall [the most senior katikiro] is someone who doesn't beat, but says "you bring your cases to me." The former Overall would even run after prisoners with a stick and beat them to get them into the wards.

In one of the larger prisons in the Ugandan capital, Kampala, a group of katikiros claimed that it had traditionally been police officers and army men that the administration had appointed as leaders. Now katikiros were rather teachers and medical officers, they said. The majority of ward leaders that I spoke with were in fact former teachers. They referred to themselves as *"leaders"* and highlighted *"reasoning"* as the key management skill that they had to possess. A beating would not make a prisoner understand his wrongdoing but just make him fearful, resentful, and likely to reoffend, they claimed, whereas a reasoned correction accompanied by the clarification of regulations would make the offending prisoner accept the authority of the katikiro and abide by the rules. A senior katikiro compared the prison where he was now with another prison, where he had been severely tortured and threatened some time back. He qualified the difference between those two places with the notions of *"power"* versus *"authority,"* and I asked him to explain the difference:

> Here leaders are given authority. When they appoint leaders, they are looking upon these counselling kinds of qualities. Somebody who has undergone a training, because when you are doing counselling, they teach you how to handle human beings. You don't have to harass everybody. (. . .) What I call authority, is that you use a word. If a prison has set up laws, we have to follow them, and everyone has been educated about them. So, you just tell them: *"Do*

this"—authoritatively! You call them—authoritatively!—because they know the consequences: "*If we fail to do ABCD; ABDC shall be done to us.*" (. . .) Somebody who uses power comes and says: "*Come do this!*" and on top of that he begins to cane you. You are a leader, but you don't respect yourself and the work you are doing. You want to use power to show off that you are the man. You are the one caning, pushing somebody on the ground: "*Lie down! Lie down!*" Sometimes you end up even fighting with fellow prisoners, because you are doing something which you are not supposed to do.

A shift from power to authority is a shift away from unmediated, crude physical violence. It is a shift toward lawfulness and the exercise of mandated authority. It entails the application of new technologies of counseling acquired through formal training. Another experienced katikiro described this change from power to authority more graphically. Two years back, when he had been imprisoned, the prison had been "*very hostile*," as he put it. The Overall had been a former condemned prisoner, sentenced to death, who had been sixteen years in prison—"*a beast that had lost all sense of humanity*," the katikiro argued. The katikiro regime had been violent, he said. "*They even used to put down people forcefully!*" Prisoners were stretched out on the ground by force and held like animals as they were caned. Now, things had changed. Caning had been reduced significantly, and when it was administered nowadays, people lay down voluntarily, he argued.

By identifying themselves with a change from power to authority, from army men to teachers, from caning to counseling, katikiros seek to position themselves against a brutal and unlawful past and as part of a new era of reform and bureaucratic professionalism. I posit that this positioning takes place through the vernacularization of the policy of dynamic security that draws explicitly on the official norms of modern, human rights-based reform. To prison staff, dynamic security offers a discourse that may position their vilified subordinate auxiliary staff—the katikiros—in a more progressive light.

Dynamic Security and a Semblance of Order

In the reporting of national and international watchdog NGOs, it is stressed that incidents of torture and inhuman and degrading punishment and treatment in Ugandan prisons are systematically committed by katikiros (HRW 2011). In human rights terms, katikiros are guilty of criminal assault, while it is the prison authorities that fail their duty to protect the prisoners from abuse from fellow prisoners. From a legal point of view, UPS violates prisoners' rights by omitting to intervene in the prisoners' disciplinary system, but more gravely by unofficially commissioning the katikiros to discipline fellow prisoners. Thus, donor agency representatives and human rights-oriented NGOs are quick to problematize and strongly criticize the katikiro system as unlawful, archaic, and a breeding ground for corruption, brutality, and abuse. *"This is where we cannot enter,"* a donor representative lamented in an interview with me, stressing the challenges of intervening in an informal system armed only with formal tools of law reform and training. One of the few positive appraisals of katikiros from professional critics came from the director of a local prisoner support NGO. Despite the fact that katikiros could be abusive and punitive and that the system was undemocratic, *"katikiros are good,"* he told me. He argued that katikiros were instrumental in mobilizing prisoners and facilitating that prisoners' needs and requests reached staff. They also simplified the work of staff, he claimed, by feeding staff with information, and *"if there was any misbehavior,"* he stressed, *"it was handled."*

A similar cautious and pragmatic praise of the katikiro system was clearly the dominant discourse among prison staff. Senior staff generally acknowledged their awareness of the katikiro system as informal and, as such, in principle illegal, but, as mentioned above, in practice they praised katikiros as indispensable to the maintenance of a safe and stable regime in the context of weak infrastructure and inadequate resources. This positive spin on katikiros as a sensible response to exigency was given form through the localized discourse on "dynamic security."

The concept of dynamic security was originally formulated by UK prison governor Ian Dunbar in 1985 (Dunbar 1985). Dunbar argued that the *physical security* of walls, cuffs, and cameras and the *procedural security* of searches, categorizations, monitoring practices, etc. would be more effective, less needed, and less harmful, if prison regimes also developed and expanded *dynamic security* (ibid.: 23). Dynamic security is defined as the maintenance of meaningful relationships between prisoners and staff through which knowledge of prison life can be developed and shared. It is argued that such relationships and knowledge enable staff and prisoners to jointly prevent and resolve conflicts and to address problems promptly and with a shared sense of fairness. In this original form, dynamic security was presented as a counter-reaction to the tough-on-crime policies that dominated British approaches to imprisonment in the 1980s and 1990s, and which tended to overemphasize physical and procedural security at the expense of human interaction and thus, critics argued, increased penal harm. Dynamic security brought the human factor back in.[7]

Dynamic security has since been included in the human rights-based reform vocabulary to describe a prison regime's commendable focus on ordering prison life through "high quality staff–inmate contacts, relationships and communication" and as a means to make prisons less authoritarian and more fair (Smit and Snacken 2009, 262–263).[8] The emphasis on human interaction "gives prominence to justice and caring, which strengthens the legitimacy of prison regimes, reduces violent conflicts and enhances human rights" (ibid: 263). In Uganda and in other African countries challenged by poverty, dynamic security has later been introduced as the label for a progressive policy with a similar emphasis on relationships and knowledge and a just, humane, and rights-respecting regime.[9] Consequently, dynamic security has become an established management concept in UPS.

In a training session on dynamic security for junior staff, which I sat in on during fieldwork, the senior officer who conducted the training started out by listing three imperatives of prison work on a flip chart: "(1) Security, (2) Order, and (3) Discipline and Punishment." *"If you don't have these—and in that order—you will have teargas in your stations,"* he said, and went on to define the topic of the session:

> Dynamic security is where you can make your input in the face of circumstances of lack of gates and fences. (. . .) [It is] to interact to solve prisoners' problems faster and better. (. . .) Officers-in-Charge who don't want to listen are wrong. If you want peace in your station you must listen (. . .) being dynamic is doing your part. Prisoners are vulnerable. They think that we cannot listen. Get up from you chair and shake his hand and say that you are sorry for his problems. Give him consolation. Say: "Don't worry. We are together. You are part of humanity." (. . .) Every small favor for a prisoner is five times more than favors outside. (. . .) You need to create an atmosphere where the prison is not part of the prisoners' problems.

First of all, it is evident that the security imperative is reconfirmed as the underlying concept or master objective of prison work. The lecturing senior officer did not include "humaneness," "trust," or "fairness" on his initial flip chart, but rather "security," "order," and "discipline and punishment." Yet, dynamic security is in this particular context also about conflict resolution through closer relations with prisoners. In a talk with a UPS top manager he enthusiastically listed the pressing problems of prisoners that UPS tried to address, including increased access to justice, decongestion of prisons, and the abolition of the death penalty. *"All this is part of dynamic security,"* he said. *"We are on the inmates' side and they know it. It's like a cat. You give it love and food and it will even follow you like a dog."* However, as shown in the example from the training session above, such close relations between prisoners and staff were argued for as a response to a *"lack of fences and gates."* This linkage between dynamic security and a situation of deficits and exigency also concerned the problem of *"numbers"* (i.e., overcrowding and understaffing). In a public speech, the Commissioner General of Prisons cautioned his staff about over familiarizing with prisoners and their relatives. *"Because of numbers, we have applied dynamic security to contain inmates at a personal level,"* he said, *"but it seems that it has extended to relatives. That is familiarity. It is an offence!"*

When asked directly about dynamic security, a senior officer in a large urban prison answered that it was not a policy, but more a way to make life as normal as outside: to *"minimize the stark contrast,"* and as such, he concluded, dynamic security was *"a linking together of human rights, humane treatment and rehabilitation."* Junior staff also referred to dynamic security as a way of studying prisoners and consequently *"to handle them by listening to their problems."* Another said, *"With dynamic security you talk things out. And you also get information."*

As much as dynamic security emphasizes humane and cordial relationships—*"dynamic security is that thing of being tactful"* a junior prison officer suggested, when I asked him to define it—UPS managers have taken up dynamic security from an entirely different vantage point than their British colleagues, who originally launched the idea. In UPS, dynamic security is not a program to diminish the dominance and adverse effects of walls, locks, searches, and tight regimes. It is rather a strategy of—temporarily—compensating for the absence of physical and procedural security.

During an interview, a senior officer tried to set out the katikiro system for me. He noted that in this particular prison the ratio of prisoners to staff was one to twenty. *"This [katikiro] system was developed so that there can be some semblance of order. Otherwise there is no way."* He then pointed out that in order for prisoners to get out of their cells you needed katikiros to guard and organize them—*"to see the sun."*

> It is just a mechanism of being human and it is that dynamic security. If you lock-up 24 people in one room, they are definitely going to start hatching plans and making schemes. And there is no real fence in this place, as you see. If a hundred of them decided to jump over the fence, there is nothing much we can do. Really, that is the reality of it all.

The UPS top managers equally linked katikiros to the concept of dynamic security, but they were also quick to voice reservations about the katikiros. A top manager referred to the katikiros as *"the last frontier—this dynamic security. If we break that,"* he said, *"we manage our vision"*—that is, the vision of changing UPS from a punitive to a corrective institution. His superior also voiced reservations about katikiros due to their formal illegality and their potential for bullying. They eventually had to go, he said, *"but we need to have our numbers up a bit."*

CONCLUSION

In the absence of a formal vocabulary to draw upon when talking about katikiros, UPS staff's presentation of their role and function is equivocal. Top managers and senior officers, seemingly concerned about the illegality and general vilification of katikiros, present them somewhat defensively as a temporary measure necessitated by resource deficits. Junior staff and middle-level officers, who seem less preoccupied with external criticism, rather stress the pragmatic utility of katikiros in terms of actually enabling prison governance. These two perspectives tentatively merge with the rise of dynamic security as a label for a reformed approach to prison management in Uganda. The compensation for physical and procedural security which the katikiros provide is not talked of as archaic brutality and unlawfulness, but as an acceleration of attention to prisoners' needs. In reality, the katikiro system is the locus of the practical norms of intermediation and thereby also the locus for exactly the negotiated relations, intimate knowledge, and mutuality that dynamic security aims to increase and give legitimacy to. Top managers are therefore also quick to emphasize the temporary and compensatory character of dynamic security. The ambition is still to get staff numbers up—and the walls, I might add—that is, to quicken physical and procedural security as resources flow in. Yet, the vernacularization of dynamic security offers a discourse that helps prison actors to make current necessities more virtuous and make practical norms of prison life resonate with a human rights approach. The shift from power to authority that the katikiro above talked about can be seen as part of such a process of pragmatically updating prison governance in Uganda. The katikiros position themselves in contrast to the established stereotype of the prisoner leader as a brutal exploitative criminal and present themselves as "counselors" rather than "caners." The katikiro system is in transition as human rights reform gives prominence to a shift from "using the stick to using the mouth." As human rights reform gains traction in Ugandan prisons, they go along with the project and seek to shift their "distributive and disciplinary power" toward a "distributive and disciplinary authority," which is less violent and more lawful.

The application of the explorative mid-level concepts of "vernacularization" and "practical norms" enables an analysis of human rights reform in Ugandan prisons as exotic in the "scientific" variant that Kapferer calls for above. These concepts provide a lens for approaching prison reform without making far-reaching assumptions about its substantive nature (cf Lund 2010, 28). They render human rights and prison governance "exotic" and subject for discovery rather than for a priori normative or theoretical assessment. This form of exploration is a particularly pertinent way to unpack the local effects of a universally "self-explanatory" concept as human rights. The received wisdom of what human rights (and dynamic security in particular) are is thereby questioned. By analyzing local actors' productive ways to consume grand normative regimes to achieve a pragmatic resonance with a subterranean catalog of local rules (that, in fact, make the "bureaucratic bumblebee" fly on a daily basis), we see human rights reform in a new light. Human rights reform is at once feebler and more powerful than it first appears. It is not a righteous normative blueprint that either succeeds greatly or fails miserably. It is rather a supple raw material that lends itself to a mundane bureaucratic form. The concepts of "vernacularization" and "practical norms" jointly elicit this "inertiatic" pull toward institutional reproduction and the concurrent aspirational push toward "development" and the good life. It is this point that gives the particular case—gleaned from the peculiar institutional environment of an African prison—a wider purchase power. The analysis of state-crafting, bureaucratic governance, reform, and the more or less legitimate forms of meting out state violence in other contexts may call for similar attention to agentive processes of appropriation as global programs of green growth, participation, austerity, anti-radicalization, etc. seek to take effect in local institutional landscapes.

The mid-level concepts applied here are edified in social theory— "vernacularization" grows out of the literature on legal pluralism (cf Moore 2000) and the notion "practical norms" has developed within a body of research on everyday governance (cf Blundo and Le Meur 2009). Yet, these concepts enable an analytical move "from a Holy Grail of grand Theory to a softer theoreticism—more integrally related to ethnographic, historical and personal representations" (Knauft 2006, 413). Consequently, they are apt at openly exploring and empirically documenting local configurations of how people actually solicit and embrace external influences while also resisting or opposing them. And from this empirical ground, they help us elicit and frame new abstract questions about problems and potentials of being human in contemporary relations of power, precarity, and promise. This, I suggest, is one of the important contributions that anthropology brings to the study of internationalized politics.

NOTES

1. This article is based on seven months of fieldwork in Ugandan prisons in 2009, 2010, and 2012. Data was mainly gleaned from fieldwork in one large urban prison in Kampala and a small local prison in a rural setting in eastern Uganda—that is, the types of institutions populated by that the majority of Ugandan prisoners and staff populate. Issues pertaining specifically to other settings like women's prisons or prisons in conflict-affected areas are not considered here. Observations of everyday

prison practices and open-ended interviews with prisoners, staff, and other prison stakeholders were conducted freely and extensively. Informants were selected based on their role and functions in the prison system and their involvement in specific cases that unfolded during fieldwork. All informants verbally consented to be quoted, but all names are pseudonyms and ranks and places and dates of interviews and observations are not disclosed in order to protect the informants' anonymity.

2. Other examples of mid-level concepts of similar nature and potential could be Tsing's notion of "friction" (Tsing 2005), Moore's "regularization" and "situational adjustment" (Moore 2000), Candea's "arbitrary locations" (Candea 2009), or Star and Griesemar's "boundary objects" (Star and Griesemer 1989).

3. This point is also raised by Van Maanen—that is, that gaps between the formal and the real in organizational practice are not simply deviance, but patterned and potent ways to divert away from official organizational goals, but also, importantly, to support these goals (Van Maanen 2001, 241).

4. *Katikiro* is a Bugandan word for "prime minister." The katikiro was traditionally the most powerful administrative and judicial adviser to the Bugandan kings, who acted as both prime minister and chief justice. A katikiro also heads the present day Bugandan government. In some prisons, the katikiro is similarly a specific title given to the appointed head of a larger prisoner leadership structure, but katikiro is commonly used as a generic term for all the prisoner leaders.

5. Apart from the basic classification of prisoners as women, juveniles, remands, and convicts, the official classificatory system of prisoners is called the "stage system." As convicts progress in stages, they are entitled to privileges in terms of mobility in the prison, communication with the outside world, and access to a private cell (UPS n.d.:II, chap 48). However, in practice the stage system is eroded or unimplemented. To my knowledge, it only functions in Uganda's largest prison, Luzira Upper Prison in Kampala.

6. See Tanner for a description of similar court setups in Kenya in the 1960s (Tanner 1970, 198).

7. Critics argue that dynamic security also has a more regressive aspect as an attempt to expand administrative control by intelligence networks and relations (Chantraine 2008; Drake 2008; Scott 2009).

8. The concept of dynamic security is, for example, written directly into European Prison Rules 2006, Article 51.2.

9. See, for instance, the emphasis on rights-based prison management and dynamic security in the work of the most prominent international prison reform NGO, Penal Reform International, in Africa (URL http://www.penalreform.org/worldwide/cen tral-east-and-southern-africa).

BIBLIOGRAPHY

Amit, Vered, Sally Anderson, Virginia Caputo, John Postill, Deborah Reed-Danahay, and Gabriela Vargas-Cetina. "Introduction Thinking Through Sociality: The

Importance of Mid-level Concepts. In *Thinking Through Sociality*, edited by Vered Amit, 1–20. New York: Berghahn Books, 2015.

Bandyopadhyay, Mahuya. *Everyday Life in a Prison: Confinement, Surveillance, Resistance*. New Delhi: Orient Black Swan, 2010.

Bierschenk, Thomas, and Jean-Pierre Olivier de Sardan. *States at Work: Dynamics of African Bureaucracies*. Boston: Brill, 2014.

Blundo, Giorgio, and Pierre-Yves Le Meur. "An Anthropology of Everyday Governance: Collective Service Delivery and Subject-Making." In *The Governance of Daily Life in Africa*, edited by Giorgio Blundo, and Pierre-Yves Le Meur. Leiden: Brill, 2009.

Blundo, Giorgio, and Jean-Pierre Olivier de Sardan. *Everyday Corruption and the State*. London: Zed Books, 2006.

Candea, Matei. "Arbitrary Locations: In Defence of the Bounded Field-Site." In *Multi-sited Ethnography: Theory, Praxis and Locality in Contemporary Research*, edited by Mark-Anthony Falzon. Farnham: Ashgate, 2009.

Chantraine, Gilles."The Post-Disciplinary Prison" *Carceral Notebooks: Discipline, Security and Beyond* 4 (2000): 55–76.

Clifford, James, and George E. Marcus. *Writing Culture: The Poetics and Politics of Ethnography*. Berkeley: Univ of California Press, 1986.

de Certeau, Michel. *The Practice of Everyday Life*. Berkeley: University of California Press, 1984.

de Herdt, Tom, and Jean-Pierre Olivier de Sardan. "Introduction: The Game of the Rules" In *Real Governance and Practical Norms in Sub-Saharan Africa*, edited by Tom de Herdt, and Jean-Pierre Olivier de Sardan. Abingdon: Routledge, 2015.

Dembour, Marie-Benedicte. "Human Rights Talk and Anthropological Ambivalence." In *Inside and Outside the Law: Anthropological Studies of Authority and Ambiguity*, edited by Olivia Harris, 19–40. Oxford: Routledge, 1996.

Donnelly, Jack, and Rhoda Howard. *International Handbook of Human Rights*. New York: Greenwood, 1987.

Drake, Deborah. "Staff and Order in Prisons." In *Understanding Prison Staff*, edited by Jamie Bennet, Ben Crewe, and Azrini Wahidin. Devon: Wilan, 2008.

Dunbar, Ian. *A Sense of Direction*. London: Home Office, 1985.

Garces, Chris, and Sacha Darke. "Surviving in the New Mass Carceral Zone." *Prison Service Journal* 229 (2017): 2–9.

Gear, S. *In Our Boots: Discretion Tensions and Locks in Socks—A View on Correctional Officers' Negotiations of Violence, Strategies and Challenges at Section Level*. Johannesburg: The Centre for the Study of Violence and Reconciliation, 2012.

Goodale, Mark. "Toward a Critical Anthropology of Human Rights." *Current Anthropology* 47 (2006): 485–511.

Henriques, Ursula R. Q. "The Rise and Decline of the Separate System of Prison Discipline." *Past & Present* 54 (1972): 61–93.

Hornberger, Julia C. "Don't Push This Constitution Down My Throat! Ph. D. dissertation, Department of Anthropology, Universiteit Utrecht, 2007.

————. "Human Rights and Policing: Exigency or Incongruence?" *Annual Review of Law and Social Science* 6 (2010): 259–83.

HRW. *Even Dead Bodies Must Work: Health, Hard Labor and Abuse in Ugandan Prisons*. New York: Human Rights Watch, 2011.

Jefferson, Andrew M, and Steffen Jensen (eds). *State Violence and Human Rights: The Role of State Officials in the South*. Abingdon: Routledge-Cavendish, 2009.

Kapferer, Bruce. *Legends of People. Myths of State*. Oxford: Berghahn, 2012.

————. How Anthropologists Think: Configurations of the Exotic." *Journal of the Royal Anthropological Institute* 19 (2013): 813–36.

Keck, Margaret E., and Kathryn Sikkink. *Activists Beyond Borders: Advocacy Networks in International Politics*. Ittaca, NY and London: Cornell University Press, 1998.

Knauft, Bruce M. "Anthropology in the Middle." *Anthropological Theory* 6 (2006): 407–30.

Latour, Bruno. *Reassembling the Social: An Introduction to Actor-Network-Theory*. Oxford, New York: Oxford University Press, 2005.

Lawrence, Benjamin N., Emily L. Osborn, and Richard L. Roberts. *Intermediaries, Interpreters, and Clerks: African Employees in the Making of Colonial Africa*. Madison: University of Wisconsin Press, 2006.

Li, Tania M. *The Will to Improve: Governmentality, Development, and the Practice of Politics*. Durham: Duke University Press, 2007.

Lindegaard, Marie, and Sasha Gear. "Surviving South African Prisons: Negotiating Gang Practices in Order to be Safe." *Focaal* 68 (2014): 35–54.

Lund, Christian. "Twilight Institutions: Public Authority and Local Politics in Africa." *Development and Change* 37 (2006): 685–705.

————. "Approaching Development: An Opinionated Review." *Progress in Development Studies* 10 (2010): 19–34.

————. "Of What is This a Case?: Analytical Movements in Qualitative Social Science Research." *Human Organization*, 73 (2014): 224–34.

MacClancy, Jeremy. *Exotic No More: Anthropology on the Front Lines*. Chicago: University of Chicago Press, 2002.

Martin, Tomas M. "The Importation of Human Rights by Ugandan Prison Staff." *Prison Service Journal* 212 (2014a): 45–51.

————. "Reasonable Caning and the Embrace of Human Rights in Ugandan Prisons." *Focaal* 68 (2014b): 68–82.

————. "Managing with Escapes—Human Rights and the Practical Norms of Prison Governance in Uganda." In *Real Governance and Practical Norms in Sub-Saharan Africa: The Game of the Rules*, edited by Jean-Pierre Olivier-de-Sardan, and Tom de Herdt. London: Routledge, 2015.

————. "Scrutinizing the Embrace of Human Rights in Ugandan Prisons: An Ethnographic Analysis of the Equivocal Responses to Human Rights Watch Reporting." *Journal of Human Rights Practice* 9 (2017): 247–67.

McGovern, Randall. "The Well-Ordered Prison. England 1780–1865." In *The Oxford History of the Prison*, edited by Norval Morris, and David J. Rothman. Oxford: Oxford University Press, 1995.

Merry, Sally E. "Transnational Human Rights and Local Activism: Mapping the Middle." *American Anthropologist* 108 (2006): 38–51.

———. "The Potential of Ethnographic Methods for Human Rights Research." In *Human Rights Research Methods*, edited by Bard A. Andreassen, Hans-Otto Sano, and Siobhán McInerney-Lankford. Cheltenham: Edward Elgar.

Moore, Sally F. *Law as Process.* Oxford: James Currey Publishers, 2000.

Mosse, David. "Is Good Policy Unimplementable? Reflections on the Ethnography of Aid Policy and Practice." *Development and Change* 35 (2004): 639–71.

Moyn, Samuel. *The Last Utopia: Human Rights in History.* Cambridge: Harvard University Press, 2010.

Olivier de Sardan, Jean-Pierre. "Researching the Practical Norms of Real Governance in Africa." Africa, Power & Politics; Discussion Paper No.5, Dec. 2008.

———. "Development, Governance and Reforms." In *Ethnographic Practice and Public Aid*, edited by Sten Hagberg, and Charlotta Widmark. Uppsala: Acta Universitatis Upsaliensis, 2009a.

———. "State Bureaucracy and Governance in Francophone West Africa." In *The Governance of Daily Life in Africa*, edited by Giorgio Blundo, and Pierre Le Meur. Leiden: Brill, 2009b.

———. 2011: 'The Eight Modes of Local Governance in West Africa', *IDS Bulletin*, 42:2, 22–31.

Mufumba, Isaac. "A taste of hell in Uganda Prisons." *The Independent*, April 13, 2010

Risse-Kappen, Thomas, Stephen C. Ropp, and Kathryn Sikkink (eds). *The Power of Human Rights: International Norms and Domestic Change.* Cambridge: Cambridge University Press, 1999.

Schatz, Edward. "Ethnographic Immersion and the Study of Politics." In *Political Ethnography. What Immersion Contributes to the Study of Power*, edited by Edward Schatz. Chicago: University of Chicago Press, 2009.

Scott, David G. *Ghosts Beyond Our Realm: A Neo-Abolitionist Analysis of Prisoner Human Rights and Prison Officer Occupational Culture.* Saarbrücken, Germany: VDM Verlag Dr. Müller, 2009.

Sherman, Taylor C. "Tensions of Colonial Punishment: Perspectives on Recent Developments in the Study of Coercive Networks in Asia, Africa and the Caribbean." *History Compass* 7 (2009): 659–77.

Skarbek, David B. "Self-Governance in San Pedro Prison." *The Independent Review* 14 (2010): 569–85.

Smit, Dirk v. Z., and Sonja Snacken. *Principles of European Prison Law and Policy: Penology and Human Rights.* Oxford: Oxford University Press, 2009.

Star, Susan L., and James R. Griesemer. "Institutional Ecology, 'Translations and Boundary Objects: Amateurs and Professionals in Berkeley's Museum of Vertebrate Zoology, 1907–39." *Social Studies of Science* 19 (1989): 387–420.

Steinberg, Jonny. *The Number: One Man's Search for Identity in the Cape Underworld and Prison Gangs.* Cape Town: Jonathan Ball Publishers, 2005.

Tanner, Ralph E. S. *An East African Prison*. Uppsala: The Scandinavian Institute for African Studies, 1970.

Taussig, Michael. *The Magic of the State*. New York: Routledge, 1997.

Tsing, Anna L. *Friction: An Ethnography of Global Connection*. Princeton: Princeton Univ Press, 2005.

UN. *Standard Minimum Rule for the Treatment of Prisoners*. United Nations, 1955.

UNODC. *Handbook on Dynamic Security and Prison Intelligence*, Criminal Justice Handbook Series. Vienna: United Nations Office on Drugs and Crime, 2015.

UPS. *The Prisons Act*. U. P. Service, 2006.

UPS. *Standing Orders Part 1–3*. (U. P. Service, n.d.

Van Maanen, John. "Afterword: Natives "R" Us: Some Notes on the Ethnography of Organizations." In *Inside Organisations. Anthropologists at Work*, edited by David N. H. Gellner, and Eric Hirch, 231–262. Oxford: Berg, 2001.

Wilson, Richard A. "Afterword to Anthropology and Human Rights in a New Key': The Social Life of Human Rights." *American Anthropologist* 108 (2006): 77–83.

———. "Tyrannosaurus Lex: The Anthropology of Human Rights and Transnational Law." In *The Practice of Human Rights*, edited by Mark Goodale, and Sally E. Merry, 342–69. Cambridge: Cambridge University Press, 2007.

Wilson, Richard A. and Jon P. Mitchell. *Human Rights in Global Perspective: Anthropological Studies of Rights, Claims and Entitlements*. London: Routledge, 2003.

Wilson, William J., and Anmol Chaddha. "The Role of Theory in Ethnographic Research." *Ethnography* 10 (2009): 549–64.

Wimba, F., and Adure, J. "Prison staff accused of hanging inmate." *The Monitor*, March 9, 2010.

Chapter 7

The Value of "Staying Put" for the Study of International Peacebuilding

Insights from Somaliland

Jessica L. Anderson

International Relations (IR) scholarship very often neglects the "second-image-reversed"; the ways in which the international system impacts domestic politics. And yet international organizations are a perennial, powerful site of the collision between local and international politics. This chapter looks at how power is expressed in the everyday interactions between local actors and international organizations. Political anthropology can offer the tools needed to answer this question. Prolonged access to a single field site, where the local and the international collide, offers an especially crucial window into how power works in a given place.

My own work on international aid in Somaliland reveals how diffuse forms of power work when international aid agencies become enmeshed in domestic politics. Globally, these organizations have adapted their funding and hiring criteria for local actors over time to emphasize professional expertise above all else. With this newfound valorization of professional expertise, local actors in Somaliland must compete against each other to satisfy these new criteria. I call this new structural environment the *knowledge market*: international agencies and local actors carry out a series of transactions over the exchange of aid programs while professional expertise is commoditized in a new and commanding way. In the hustle of seeking and spending aid resources in the knowledge market, I find that diffuse (i.e., institutional and productive) forms of power operate in very interesting ways. International aid agencies shape policies and standards, and in turn, local incentives and subjectivities. Meanwhile, local actors adapt and resist these new standards with their own goals and appropriations.

"Staying put" can offer a crucial window into how power works when international and local forces collide in a given place. International agencies have field offices around the world where they fund and engage with domestic actors and politics. These sites are where institutional and productive forms of power play out on the ground and they are best and perhaps only analyzed through immersive, ethnographic scrutiny. I argue that prolonged access to a single field site is enormously helpful for unveiling diffuse (institutional and productive) forms of power.

In this chapter I first briefly review the role of ethnography in political science and IR. Then I discuss how ethnographic tools enhance a weakness of contemporary IR: its knowledge about the second-image-reversed impacts of global actors like international organizations. I focus on answering the question, how is power expressed in the everyday interactions between local actors and international organizations? I do so by describing my ethnographic fieldwork on international aid organizations in Somaliland.[1] Through this fieldwork I highlight how "staying put" in ethnographic work can usefully reveal diffuse (institutional and productive) forms of power.

ETHNOGRAPHY AND IR

Across disciplines, global ethnographies have become an increasingly popular way to understand international politics (e.g., Tsing 2006; Weaver 2008; Pouliot 2008; Autesserre 2010, 2014)). From the role of audits and documents to NGO advertising, they "provide windows onto larger processes of governance, power and social change that are shaping the world today" (Shore and Wright 2001, 1 in Stepputat and Larsen 2015).

I rely on Schatz's (2009) understanding of ethnography as a research method that consists of immersion through participation. The general ethnographic ethos emphasizes "the meanings that the people under study attribute to their social and political reality" (in Stepputat and Larsen 2015). The tools of ethnography can be many, but they often center on participant observation, in-depth interviewing, and document and other textual analysis. Through these tools ethnography can generate data from contexts about which empirical data might not otherwise exist. And even if data along comparable themes does exist, ethnography generates more intimate, in-depth knowledge of these social practices and relationships (Stepputat and Larsen 2015). Ethnography is particularly well suited to locate the informal processes through which power is expressed. These informal processes typically demand the proximity, trust, and intimacy of ethnographic study (Coppedge 2002: 11; George and Bennett 2005; King et al. 1994). Despite the advantages and insights of ethnography, and compared to other nearby disciplines like comparative politics, IR has only recently started to lose its allergy to ethnography (see Sande Lie 2013; Autesserre 2010, 2014).

This is a particular shame because IR has been chided for its limited understanding of how power operates in global governance. Academic scholarship (and political science in particular) on global governance is said to have "a strikingly thin concept of politics and of power" (Neumann and Sending 2010: 55). Meanwhile, Joseph and Auyero (2007) describe how "politics and its main protagonists (politicians, activists and official, among others) remain largely unstudied by ethnography's mainstream" (in Stepputat and Larsen 2015). There is a mismatch here: the power-holders in international politics are rarely the focus of ethnography. And yet, traditional studies of these power-holders likely only skim the surface of how they operate, spread power, and cause effects. Subjective leading actors in international politics to the ethnographic gaze can reveal the "inner logic" (Schatz 2009: 306) that governs behavior in International Relations" (Schatz 2013). Ethnography allows quieter or more subtle forms of power to be granted the attention they warrant. As a method it can uncover processes, discourses, and behaviors that remain, to date, invisible (Scott 1990; Schatz 2013).

I suggest that "staying put" allows for access to data and answers to research questions that otherwise would not be possible in traditional political science scholarship. Ethnography allows for a more intimate form of analysis that captures the complexity of international institutions in a way that other research methods cannot. These ethnographic insights are particularly valuable in light of how IR theory only rarely addresses the second-image-reversed. It seldom theorizes around the domestic effects of international actors, and, in particular, how behavior at the international level impacts local populations. IR theory also knows little about how international actors and local actors interact with each other and how local actors resist international rules and systems. I suggest that this is in large part because IR scholars tend not to stick around long enough in the second-image to capture these effects.

"Staying put" can enable IR scholars to better understand the domestic effects of global actors, as well as the interaction between domestic and global actors. Staying put through ethnographic methods also unveils subtle forms of power and the "inner logic that governs behavior in International Relations." It can reveal entirely new processes—formal or informal—or provide more intimate, in-depth knowledge of well-known practices and relationships. Trust-based, proximate research is especially valuable when power is diffuse, social processes are informal, and the actors of interest are at a distance.

THE KNOWLEDGE MARKET

My research suggests that a glaring way in which global governors and particularly International Nongovernmental Organizations (INGOs) impact local populations is through the evaluation criteria[2] they establish for local actors: the standards by which INGOs judge the competence of a local actor to then receive power and resources. Professional expertise is now the modern evaluation criteria, the latest in a long line of evaluation criteria for international activities, such as religion, ethnicity, and color. Evaluation criteria become the standard by which resources and influence are doled out. It comes to define everyday life through the value of people, incentives for labor, and yardsticks for success. Evaluation criteria in turn shed light on how power operates in global governance. It demonstrates how today's international NGOs promote a model for success that has significant, life-changing effects on the local populations they work for.

This research begins by describing how INGO evaluation criteria have changed over time so that professional expertise is the evaluation criteria du jour. It develops a theory of how professional expertise as the basis for evaluation criteria impacts local populations. When professional expertise becomes the basis for evaluation criteria, a new environment is created that I call the *knowledge market*. The *knowledge market* is the structural and cultural environment in which the value of services is built on professional expertise and international and local actors engage in the exchange of services and resources.

I discuss the kinds of institutional and productive power that the knowledge market generates, as well as the strategies of local actors, given their expertise resources. INGOs—through their evaluation criteria—wield institutional power that in turn leads to a variety of effects for local populations. Local actors comply with, resist and strategize against this institutional power. The structure of the knowledge market also produces a range of productive effects that dramatically affect local populations. The market ultimately determines who receives funding and resources, how local actors behave, and what local institutions aspire for. Ethnographic methods reveal the power of evaluation criteria to not only determine who receives resources but rewire everyday lives.

DIFFUSE KINDS OF POWER

In this chapter I focus on how ethnographic methods are particularly well suited for identifying institutional and productive forms of power. Coercive power, the favored darling of IR scholarship, refers to situations in which

"A has power over B to the extent that [s]he can get B to do something that B would not do otherwise" (Dahl 1957). Coercive power is both direct and interactive, and most easy to observe. Meanwhile, institutional power and productive power are indirect. They are "diffuse in their relational specificity" (Barnett and Duvall 2005). This means that there is a greater distance between those exercising power and those experiencing that power (or two subjects experiencing power). The distance between those experiencing and exercising power is why existing IR scholarship struggles to account for it, and why long-term ethnographic methods are particularly valuable.

Barnett and Duvall (2005) define institutional power as the "formal and informal Institutions that mediate between A and B, as A, working through the rules and procedures that define those institutions, guides, steers, and constrains the actions (or non-actions) and conditions of existence of others" (Barnett and Duvall 2005: 43). Institutional power is interactive—a relationship between two sets of agents—but it is social indirect. It is mediated by institutional arrangements like decision-making, lines of responsibility, divisions of labor, and other institutional rules and procedures. Examples of institutional power are when institutional rules unevenly distribute rewards across actors, or otherwise cement privilege and bias into institutional arrangements. Institutional power also includes the agenda-setting process or other situations in which an actor's future or current opportunities and choices are restricted. Institutional rules, procedures, and decision-making processes indirectly influence actor's access to rewards and other resources and the choices available to them over time.

Barnett and Duvall define productive power as the "socially diffuse production of subjectivity in systems of meaning and signification" (Barnett and Duvall 2005: 43). It refers to how subjects are discursively produced, meanings fixed, and the terms of action determined in social life (Barnett and Duvall 2005: 56). Drawing on Foucault's original work, this kind of power "operates through distant social relations to set up standards for what is appropriate, effective, and legitimate for groups or individuals to do—a power that works to structure the possible field of action of others" (Foucault 2000: 341). In this way productive power is particularly well suited to locate and analyze asymmetries in social life. It boils down to, what is a person capable of? Similar to institutional power, productive power can frame ideas and categories, and expand or limit the opportunities available to actors. They both refer to "power to" act rather than "power over" others. In contrast to institutional power however, productive power is not interactive. It is socially constitutive and emphasizes how a structural and cultural environment—rather than institutional arrangements—creates systems of meaning for agents.

INSIGHTS FROM "STAYING PUT" IN SOMALILAND

This chapter draws on twelve months of ethnographic fieldwork in the Horn of Arica. Over these months I conducted in-depth and iterative interviews with local and international NGO field staff, participant and field observations, and document analysis. I also spent my time embedded with one prominent civil society organization, which I routinely assisted with grant-writing and proposal development. I steadily assisted several other local institutions with editing and grant-writing over my time in Somaliland. I both wrote proposals and attended and participated in meetings on the direction of proposal efforts. While some of my work focused on proofreading reports and other documents for English mistakes, most focused on how to reflect the professional expertise of the aid world in a way that would appeal to donors. I welcomed these requests since they allowed me to familiarize myself with the ideas and priorities of these organizations. Embedding myself in the proposal development process with local organizations was a unique and essential access to data that ethnographic methods afforded me. The following glimpses into institutional and productive power depended on proximity, prolonged access, and trust.

Institutional Power and Local Strategies

> I see the problems of my people every day. My counterpart, they don't understand. They don't have any idea. For them it's a program, for us it's our land and our people and our country.
>
> —Mohamed

Institutional power[3] is interactive and can be reflected in the adoption of expert-driven rules, decisions, and agenda-setting abilities within institutions. While it is most often examined for its influence on agents within an institution, it can similarly influence actors under institutional rules like evaluation criteria. The institutional power of evaluation criteria becomes richly apparent in Somaliland, as do local actors' strategies of manipulation to best meet these criteria.

In order to gain funding, local actors must fulfill the evaluation criteria of aid INGOs one way or another. They either need to possess the evaluation criteria (e.g., PhD in nutrition and five years aid work experience) or need to mimic these requirements. For instance, a successful domestic NGO might reflect the professional expertise that INGOs require. But they can also write an effective proposal that demonstrates their professional expertise. They can strive to mimic the behavior of international experts, and prove that they can engage with the kinds of knowledge that evaluation criteria are intended to confirm.

The concept of an "aid language" has often been discussed in critical and ethnographic examinations of international aid. Autesserre discusses how international aid actors recruit urban elites who "speak the international language" (Autesserre 2014: 88). This language entails a knowledge of technical concepts, the logic of aid programs, and a range of knowledge along thematic categories in the aid world. Local actors disadvantaged by their level of professional expertise find ways to learn the aid language, mimicking it to their international counterparts in order to gain funding.

Abdi,[4] the director of a local research institute, learned to master the "aid language" and leverage the expertise resources around him. He talked me through the grueling process through which his institution won a major bid from an international fund after missing out on several key grants. The institute must clearly detail the social objective of their program and have a strong command of the thematic issue area on which a call for proposals was selected. They also must demonstrate that the staff is highly credentialed and competent, and that the writers of the proposal will also be implementing the program. The proposal is intended for a local actor, but in order to win, the local actors must also have an international partner—a misstep Abdi made in prior grant-seeking.

Abdi explained to me that his institute would not have been selected without applying alongside a prominent international organization that "the donors think highly of." Mohamed admitted to me, "If we applied by ourselves, I don't think we'd get it." When I pressed for what else determined their selection, Abdi said, "The language is most important. The most important thing is the consistency of the objective, the impact, the logical framework." Abdi then leaps up, and pulls several thick binders from a nearby bookcase. "See?" He says. "The proposal, the level of requirements is outrageous." He then walked me through what was a standard cocktail of requirements and component parts to the proposal process. "They want us to be a local actor but we have to look like an international actor." Mohamed admitted that he needed significant help from their international partner in order to complete the winning grant. "The requirements are absurd. We developed these big documents with [the international partner's] help. It's very good to do it with an expert but we'd like to learn these things. The jargon. Inside the expertise. We needed to learn how to play" (Somaliland Research Institute Director, June 9, 2015).

To win funding, Abdi leverages the professional expertise of his social networks, seeks partnerships with those that have professional expertise, and gains editing assistance with proposal documents from those with the necessary professional expertise. Abdi effectively reflects the necessary requirements to meet aid INGO's evaluation criteria and gains resources by doing so.

Local organizations routinely relied on people like myself—their social networks, and specifically those better versed in the "aid language" in those networks—in order to win grants. They also quickly absorbed the jargon around them and found ways to supplement their existing knowledge. They develop relationships with partner organizations abroad in order to assist them, as Abdi did, or they informally find people to help them develop grant proposals and meet expertise requirements. For these actors, the aid language offers a way to negotiate their position in the aid world when their ability to meet evaluation criteria has hit its ceiling. They seek out partners, mentors, colleagues, and informal assistants to round out their expertise. Outside the grant-writing process, they also mimic and reflect the aid language in all meetings, workshops, events, and dealing with potential donors or international partners. They master how to look best to potential funders even when they have gaps in their professional expertise.

Nonetheless, the process of either outright having or mimicking professional expertise creates winners and losers in the quest for aid funding. It reduces the opportunities of those who either do not have sufficient professional expertise or cannot find ways to mimic it. The opportunity to mimic the "aid language" provides opportunities to some local actors but further marginalizes others. In this way participant observation sheds further light on *how* institutional power manages to reduce what local institutions can access, and how they can gain support. Observable implications for other forms of institutional power—donor funding guidelines or job descriptions—are more readily available but can only reveal so much. Participant observation offers a more nuanced picture of how institutional power is exerted and resisted and what it takes to be a beneficiary of these institutional rules and arrangements.

Productive Power

> "Oh wonderful! So you can tell us if they're killing us or not" [upon describing my research topic]
>
> —Saeed, civil society leader

Fardus invites me into her home on a Saturday morning. I ask for details about her upbringing, and how she ended up as the executive director of her prominent local institution. I asked her why her institution is so successful, and how has she reached the point where she is now.

> When people know I know what I'm talking about, you can tell. When you have a discussion, they can see my background and my skills. When they see I have

that background, they respect me. When they see that they listen. The normal local organization, they can't even communicate. They lack knowledge. They don't have that aid language. (Somaliland NGO Executive Director, May 12, 2015)

Successful local actors like Fardus are not just beneficiaries in the knowledge market. They also act as brokers between the communities they work in and the international agencies. They know the aid language and find ways to leverage their expertise to address inefficiencies in the system. As one informant told me, "Knowing the aid language transforms the landscape of options. The local actor has to know the contrast space, know how to get leverage" (Moses February 2015). The leverage can be very useful in the face of donor-driven demands and programming. As Fardus told me, "The donor always has an idea behind their proposal. They want us to do A, B, C, and D. One year they focus on governance, then resilience, then GBV. Something like that. But then, you can always talk to them. At least in some organizations. What do you want us to do? They say: Governance, Resilience, GBV. But then you can manipulate. Yes, you can manipulate. You can discuss" (Somaliland NGO Executive Director, June 2015).

Last year, Fardus's organization was asked to carry out a female genital mutilation program in an area experiencing heavy drought and food security. But as the program officer explained to me, "The people trust you. Can't say that yet. The people cannot be upset. There's a severe drought, but these international groups want to do FGM [female genital mutilation] work" (Somaliland NGO Program Officer, July 12, 2015). When their NGO arrived at the community, they realized they simply could not implement the FGM program the way their donors wanted. The community members said, "Why don't you bring us something else, they'll say. They don't want help in their way."

From there, the NGO staff went to their donors and convinced them that while helping with basic needs they could address FGM too. Fardus explains how "communities are experiencing climate change, they cannot care about FGM. They cannot stand for it. So we exploit it, explain why it is a better program." Fardus found ways to leverage the aid language, to use her professional expertise in order to recast international aid programs. As she put it, "The middle of the international approach and the community needs is what we do. Their values and the international arena; we combine them. We're a language translator basically."

While some institutions find ways to use their expertise resources to redefine aid efforts and push back against international actors, Somaliland institutions often shared that they were carrying out interventions along categories of thematic expertise that were not relevant for the communities they worked in. And this ultimately had consequences for the legitimacy and prestige of Somaliland institutions. One Somaliland director of a local organization described this dynamic in the language of risk to me:

> You hear a lot about risks, risk assessment. You don't find them talking about risks to us. They're worried about risks to themselves, not risks to local people. These programs they have us do, don't work, don't fit here. They're just worried about financial risks—what about our risks? Donor, implementers, are so worried about if their money is going to be spent well, but we're talking about people who are spending millions and millions of dollars into a country and their idea of risk is still whether or not they lose 5%. (Somaliland NGO Director, June 26, 2015)

Local actors' activities have become detached from their stated goals in the name of being better professionals (and keeping their doors open). They are likely better than ever at attracting funding but perhaps worse at advocating for Somalilanders.

Many Somalilanders agreed with a version of the statement that "civil society is crippled." Abdifatah explained how he tried to teach the people he works with to act differently: "As for advocacy—I think you are right. The other civil society organizations have just become about delivering aid. I had to work hard and tell the guys—you need a strategy, you need to go to parliament, to the Guurti." Abdifatah felt strongly that Somalilanders needed more long-term funding if they were going to become better advocates. But in the short-term? "It is complicated," he said. "It's true, they don't know how to advocate." Many of the strongest local organizations were created in the aftermath of war, and they advocated strongly for local and community needs. As Somaliland has developed into a full-functioning state, donors have encouraged a civil society that carries out their affairs and better hones its professional expertise. They have often encouraged the creation of umbrella bodies that ultimately structure the field of action in society along these thematic, expert-driven categories. Although Somalilanders "own" these umbrella bodies, international ideas and knowledge are sent from above and regulate NGO activity on these topics. They now regulate and reflect international knowledge and ideas, leaving a legacy of how civil society should behave.

CONCLUSION

Internationalized politics—space where local and international politics collide—are rarely examined as a site of both power and contestation. And international organizations are a perennial, powerful site of this collision. Ethnography offers key insights into how power works in and outside international organizations. In particular, prolonged access to a single field site offers a crucial window into how power (specifically institutional and productive) "really works" when the local and the international collide. In my work, international aid agencies shape policies and standards, and in turn, local incentives and subjectivities. Meanwhile, local actors adapt and resist these new standards with their own goals and appropriations. Identifying these demonstrations of power hinged on prolonged access to a single field site.

Political anthropology has much to offer in identifying these moments of power. Ethnography simply allows for the ability to access data, opinions, and dynamics that other forms of research cannot achieve. Structural factors and diffuse forms of power are especially challenging to capture without an ethnographic gaze. These effects are politically important, and through ethnography, can become more central to studies of global politics. In particular, single-sited ethnography can capture data related to diffuse forms of power and structural factors that other methods and approaches cannot. Ethnography makes a meaningful difference in how we understand international politics. It allows us to access moments, experiences, and worldviews that otherwise would not be available.

NOTES

1. Related research for this project, conducted in Kenya and Ethiopia, was funded by the Social Science Research Council as well as the David L. Boren Fellowship. Field research in Somaliland was funded by the Cosmos Club.

2. This project focuses on international and local (domestic) aid actors in Somaliland. However, I examine domestic actors who received funding from international actors. I examine international NGOs that directly recruit a Somalilander organization on the ground to fund.

3. See Barnet and Duvall (2005) for their complete taxonomy of power. Institutional power includes instances of institutions setting the rules for selection, decision-making, and participation. Productive power includes issues like how experts frame options, classes of people, responsibility, new hierarchies.

4. Names have been changed or omitted and replaced with a general description of the participant.

BIBLIOGRAPHY

Autesserre, Séverine. *The Trouble with the Congo: Local Violence and the Failure of International Peacebuilding.* NY: Cambridge University Press, 2010.

Autesserre, Séverine. *Peaceland: Conflict Resolution and the Everyday Politics of International Intervention.* NY: Cambridge University Press. 2014.

Bennett, Andy. *Culture and everyday life.* London: Routledge, 2005.

Barnett, Michael, and Raymond Duvall (eds.). *Power in Global Governance.* NY: Cambridge University Press, 2005.

Coppedge, Michael. "Democracy and Dimensions: Comments on Munck and Verkuilen." *Comparative Political Studies* 35 (2002): 35–9.

Dahl, Robert, A. "The concept of power." *Journal of the Society for General System Research* 2 (1957): 201–15.

Duvall, Raymond, and Arjun Chowdhury. "The Practices of Theory." In *International Practices* edited by Emanuel Adler, and Vincent Pouliot, 335–54. Cambridge: Cambridge University Press, 2011.

Foucault, Michel. *Power. Essential Works vol. 3.* New York: New Press, 2000.

Joseph, Lauren, and Javier Auyero. *Introduction: Politics under the Ethnographic Microscope.* New York: Springer, 2007.

King, Gary, Robert Keohane, and Sidney Verba. *Designing Social Inquiry: Scientific Inference in Qualitative Research.* Princeton: Princeton University Press, 1994.

Lie, Jon H.S. "Challenging Anthropology: Anthropological Reflections on the Ethnographic Turn in International Relations." *Millennium,* 41 (2013): 201–20.

Neumann, Iver, and Ole J. Sending. *Governing the Global Polity: Practice, Mentality, Rationality.* Ann Arbor: University of Michigan Press, 2010.

Pouliot, Vincent. "The Logic of Practicality: A Theory of Practice of Security Communities." *International Organization* 62((2008): 257–88.

Schatz, Edward ed. *Political ethnography: What immersion contributes to the study of power.* Chicago: University of Chicago Press, 2013.

Scott, Stephen. "Measuring Oppositional and Aggressive Behaviour." *Child Psychology and Psychiatry Review* 1(1996): 104–9.

Shore, Cris, and Wright, Susan. "Moving Beyond Pronouncements: The Critique of Neoliberalism in Higher Education." *Journal of the Royal Anthropological Institute* 7 (2001): 521–6.

Stepputat, Finn, and Jessica Larsen. Global political ethnography: A methodological approach to studying global policy regimes. Danish Institute for International Studies Working papers, 2015.

Tsing, Anna. L. *Friction: An Ethnography of Global Connection.* Princeton, New Jersey: Princeton University Press, 2004.

Part III

CATCHING HOW THE WORLD IS RULED

Chapter 8

Depending on Money

Money as a Forceful Relation among Everyday Kenyans and in Kenya's International Relations

Kai Koddenbrock and Mario Schmidt

Contemporary Kenya is at the heart of new developments around capitalist money and finance. The country currently undergoes processes of financial integration into crisis-prone capital markets and promotes financial inclusion of unbanked citizens through innovative instruments like its mobile money service M-Pesa. This "financialization" of Kenya's political economy through novel forms of capitalist money combines local, national, and global monetary relations. It allows for a productive investigation of the workings of capitalist money from both an anthropological and a political economy perspective. As a relation of dependency with shifting and ambivalent effects on both creditor and debtor, money is a promising object of analysis for an anthropology of internationalized politics.

In this chapter, we focus on what money does to the state of Kenya in global competition and to members of Kenyan society and how Kenyans themselves interpret money's effects on their lives. We believe that such an analysis is central for an understanding of Kenya because many Kenyans complain about the clientelist practices of their political and economic decision-makers leading to unjust allocation of money. What is more, Kenya is at the forefront of the mobile money revolution of making money usable to the "unbanked" through mobile phones (Morawczynski 2009; Ouma et al. 2017). Yet, not only ordinary people obsess with money. Government officials have been embroiled in corruption scandals. Not long ago, in 2016, former finance minister and now president Uhuru Kenyatta capped the bank interest rates amid much media fanfare—and uncapped them in 2019 (Smith 2019). Moreover, the finance ministry and central bank have decided to integrate Kenya further into global capital markets by issuing government bonds in USD for the first time. Kenya today is indeed an ongoing monetary and financial project.

Capitalist money, formal credit, and debt relations permeate Kenyan society, politics, and economy from start to finish on a scale unforeseen fifty years before (for a historical overview on Western Kenya, Shipton 2010). Our chapter attempts to highlight the virtues of a micro-macro, anthro-IR perspective to make sense of the ambiguity of money and its ability to (re)produce inequality. Money is an ambivalent force, not simply destructive and unjust. To account for money's ambivalent character, we consider capitalist money and its role as a relation of dependency and opportunity that can be beneficial to those who use it but tends to become lopsided and can increase inequality easily unless properly checked and distributed. Money, in other words, is very often an opportunity only because its owner has become dependent on someone else—for example, by acquiring debt or another binding contract such as a labor agreement.

With this argument on the ambivalent character of money, we do not simply seek to recover what previous theories, such as world systems or dependency theory, have argued. By zooming in on money as one of the core relations at the heart of modern capitalist societies we rather invite readers to take a fresh look at how money mediates and nourishes the global structure of competition between capitalists, corporations, nation-states, social groups, and individuals. This entails breaking away from some of the dominant debates of the previous generation which have left us with partial and limited theories of global relations, which struggle to theorize larger and more-encompassing global structures. This has been partly a result of neglecting the voices of those who are, while being very much aware of it, oppressed and exploited by means of unjust national and global systems.

We thus argue that simplistic, morally neutral and globally resonating statistics of GDP and economic growth tend to lose sight of specific local distinctions such as an unequal distribution of monetary purchasing power or an overly large debt burden placed upon the shoulders of the recently "financialized" rural population. On the other hand, we accuse ethnography, by way of being "immersive" and attuned to local complexities, to bear the risk of being too sensitive, that is, the risk of losing sight of underlying formal structures (Schmidt 2017b) and the discernible logics of global capitalism and forms of monetary dependency (Koddenbrock 2015; Koddenbrock and Sylla 2019). In contrast, we have a clear empirical and theoretical focus: money. Because of its relational and ubiquitous, that is, both local and global, instantiations it seems uniquely relevant to both anthropology and international relations. Combining a political economy perspective on global money relations and dependency with a nuanced understanding of how Kenyans deal with economic pressure in their daily lives allows us to see that both states and citizens are pushed into positions of dependency by the same structural power: capitalist money.

We proceed in three steps to substantiate our argument on the power of money in capitalist social relations both at the human and the interstate level. We first provide a brief review of the international relations and anthropology literature and how it has (not) dealt with capitalism in recent years, in part because of a fetishization of complexity. In the second section, the immersive description of two Kenyans ways of thinking about and earning money underlines that the politics of money are not at all hard to understand. In the third part, we move to the state and global level of Kenyan money relations and show how money as public-private deal installs a relation of dependency which easily becomes unequal.

COMPLEXITY AND THE STUDY OF CAPITALIST MONEY IN ANTHROPOLOGY AND IR: AN OVERVIEW

Complexity has become one of the most influential concepts in the social sciences. There seems to exist an imperative for phenomena to be complex with the consequence that for humans there is little left but to react and adapt to the overwhelming complexity of their surroundings (Chandler 2014). Yet, discussions about complexity do not distinguish between complexity as a diagnosis of how the world is perceived and as a diagnosis of how the world is (cf Dan-Cohen 2017) (Figure 8.1).

What had been a difference in degree and perspective has been turned into a difference of kind. In other words, what was considered an epistemological problem in Marx and a primary goal of enlightenment philosophy and natural sciences ever since, namely how to abstract from an overly complex world the latter's simple laws, has been turned into a methodological dead end: the reality and each part of it is really complex, that is, simple laws do not exist and any attempt to find them therefore has to remain futile by default.

If one bites into the pragmatist bullet and believes that the world is complex and uncertain by default (cf. Cooper and Pratten 2014), people's sense of uncertainty as something that bothers and troubles them and that they believe can be overcome is put aside for the ethnographer and political economist. In contrast to such a pragmatist understanding of a reality allegedly characterized by insurmountable complexity that shows deep structural affinities to Hayek's form of neoliberalism (Schmidt 2014; Schmidt and Koddenbrock 2019), we, taking inspiration from Marx' methodology of "concretization" (Koddenbrock 2015), suggest to revive the epistemological distinction between what is real and what appears to be real in order to show how specific forms of action are not at all complex or uncertain but more or less calculable

Complexity Social Science Citation Index

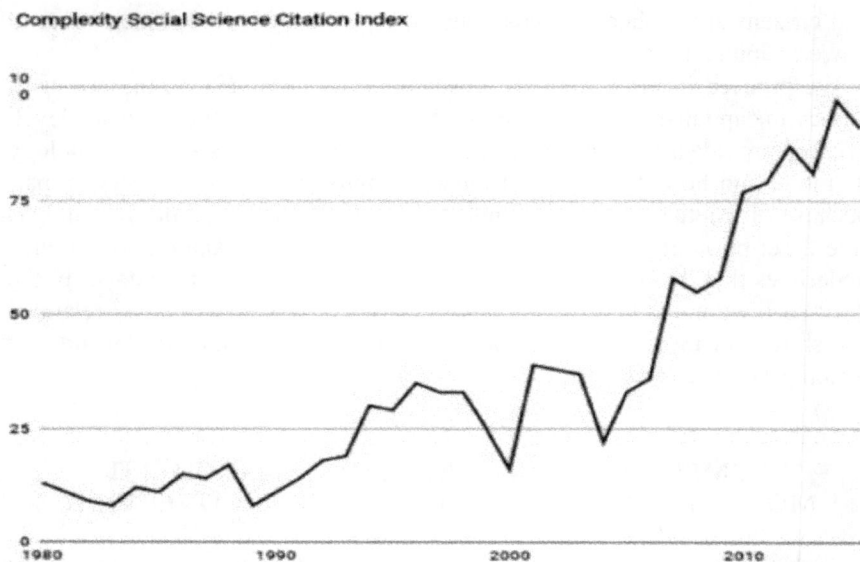

Figure 8.1 **Publications in the Social Sciences with "Complexity" in Title, Based on Data in the Social Science Citation Index (SSCI 2017).**

consequences of the strains a politico-economic constellation called capitalism puts upon average people as well as politicians.

The study of the global reality of money-mediated capitalism suffered in both anthropology and IR because its relevance had been delegitimized in various "turns," the cultural and constructivist ones in particular. While realism and the theory of imperialism had always shared a focus on the importance of power relations, the growing focus on international institutions such as the UN, global governance, and the diffusion of norms served to neglect the capitalist world market and its crucial importance for the study of international politics. How reductionist and thoroughly wrong this focus has been, has become obvious, once again, in the face of the global and economically interdependent "Corona crisis."

In anthropology, a desire to celebrate the otherness and difference of ethnographers' objects of study served to downplay the importance of capitalism and one of its central pillars: money. In this article, we will argue against influential attempts of highlighting the multifaceted tentacles of contemporary capitalism that risk overseeing the simplicity of power relations in contemporary capitalism. In contrast we suggest to capture capitalism as a solid and basic structure of politico-economic domination that emerges in different forms depending on the sociocultural and economic context while the cause, unequal power relations between social groups mediated and constituted by money, and the effect, a deterioration of the living standards of some, remain the same. In other words, sometimes opening the black box risks losing sight of the simple relations between cause (money and capitalism) and effect (injustice).

Such a focus on an underlying capitalist relation that appears in different mutations is acknowledged in Marx's *Kapital*, for example. But it is often neglected in anthropologists' attempts to formulate a critique of noncapitalist societies, rather influenced by Marx's political agenda and less so by his analysis of capitalist power relations. The 1980s and 1990s brought forth anthropological studies that—while increasingly acknowledging cultural diversity—missed doing justice to the fact of socioeconomic injustice caused by changes in the economic structure (Ferguson 2006). Instead of analyzing, for instance, the impact of money and capitalist wage labor on traditional family arrangements as had been done by implicitly or explicitly Marxist anthropologists such as Paul Bohannan (1959), Claude Meillassoux (1972), and Pierre-Philippe Rey (1971), anthropologists either argued against the "essentialization" of capitalism's and money's nature by demanding an increased attention for ethnographic details and complexity or moralized what remains, in our opinion, a politico-economic problem. This led, on the one hand, to studies focusing upon the ways in which people all over the world "symbolically" deal with socioeconomic injustice. These studies took an interest in, for instance, revitalized "occult practices" such as witchcraft beliefs (Geschiere 1997), the creative appropriation of capitalist goods (Appadurai 1986) or the semiotic "taming" of money (Bloch and Parry 1989; Shipton 1989). On the other hand, this shift away from a Marxist analysis of production, circulation, and consumption of capital is mirrored in studies pointing out the resilience of vulnerable members of society or simply raise awareness for their suffering (Robbins 2013).

This trend of studying symbolic reactions to global inequality or to merely point it out[1] misses out on two points: First, global monetary relations create relations of dependency that often lead to inequality, which becomes, for instance, manifest in the dependence on the dollar as world money which makes long-term planning for governments in the Global South difficult (Powell 2013). Second, people studied by anthropologists often know that they are systemically disadvantaged economically and attempt to criticize their marginalization quite "rationally" and without engaging in cosmological or symbolical defense strategies that lose sight of the actual causes of their marginalization (Schmidt 2017a). Faced with, for instance, an incredible amount of debt threatening one's own and one's family's bare existence, it comes as no surprise that actors develop a pragmatic approach to reality that is too often celebrated by anthropologists as creative. Instead of attempting to change the causes of economic inequality, anthropologists implicitly applaud inequality's effects by, for example, foregrounding the creative aspects of "hustling" or "navigating" (for an overview, Thieme 2017). Many disadvantaged actors, however, do know very well that it is not the world as such, but unequal power relations that inhibit them to plan their life and force them to become creative.

The recent study of international relations, by contrast, has had little interest in capitalism although it was a major object of analysis of the first IR theory avant la lettre: the theory of imperialism (Hobson 1902). In the United States, there has existed a particular brand of IR concerned with American hegemony and the structures of the international system that has taken structure (Waltz 1979) and even money and finance seriously (Keohane 1984; Gilpin 1987). However, in recent decades neither the European nor American variants of the Eurocentric discipline of IR have continued to do so. The recent conceptual foci of the dominant "isms" of realism, liberalism, institutionalism, and constructivism, for example, have been interstate behavior, democratic peace, the authority of international organizations, and the power of ideas or norms (cf. Biecker and Schlichte in this book; for a sustained analysis see Koddenbrock 2015, 2017). If global systems came into view, they were mostly studied from a formal and heuristic point of view (see for anthropological discussions of global systems Mintz 1985; Tsing 2005, Wolf 1982). When realists, whose focus on competition and war acknowledges most clearly that the international system is not a place of harmony, discuss state behavior they take states for granted and consider the state system as anarchic without making any substantive claim on what the global order consists of beyond the multiplicity of states and the distribution of power between them. The reemerging scholarship on hierarchy and domination (Mattern and Zarakol 2016) is only starting to overcome this lacuna.

The genesis and structure of the state system and global inequality have been, for several decades now, only debated in the rather marginal circles of Marxist IR, for example, under the rubric of "uneven and combined development" (Rosenberg 2013; Callinicos 2016; Anievas and Nisancioglu 2015) or "political Marxism" (Teschke 2003). Although Robert Cox's works (1987), much inspired by Gramsci's approach placing equal weight on material, cultural, and ideological phenomena for the constitution of hegemony, have been widely quoted, few substantive works on the intersection between economic structures, ideas, and the behavior of states have been published in the core of IR in recent decades. Instead, scholars interested in the nature of the global political economy have had to migrate to the sister field of International Political Economy (IPE) that continues to be oddly disjointed from the study of international politics as practiced in IR. IR has thus focused in concert with peace and conflict studies on conflict and security only (Mastanduno

1999). IPE and development studies, by contrast, have continued to try to come to terms with what constitutes global capitalism.[2] Following their lead, we discuss the promises and pitfalls of theorizing capitalism in anthropology and IR from a money perspective. Although there are many other ways of trying to come to terms with historical and contemporary capitalism like its tendency toward "imperialism" (Hobson 1902; Narayan 2017), its reliance on "monopolies" (Baran and Sweezy 1967; Nitzan and Bichler 2009), reconfiguration of social spaces (Harvey 2007) or destruction of nature (Moore 2015), analyzing capitalism without making sense of the intricacies of money and finance is bound to be incomplete in a post–2007 financial crisis and "post"–Corona world.

Our article is based on fourteen months of fieldwork conducted in Kenya since 2009, interviews with activists and policy makers in Nairobi, and an analysis of how global monetary relations impact the autonomy and leeway of many African governments and societies and Kenya's in particular. We will argue against the tendency in anthropology to stress and praise the cunningness and agency of the disadvantaged. We also aim to counteract the neglect of unequal economic and power structures in contemporary international relations. By refocusing on the relation of dependency expressed and reinforced through money we attempt to recover a more realist analysis—in the sense of being "attuned" to reality. This analysis, we posit, can make sense of economically exploited actors' behavior and analysis of their position in the world at the individual level and at the level of governmental high politics. Our analysis thereby builds upon the assumption that the current theoretical bias in favor of complexity leads scholars to neglect the simplicity of capitalist relations which may bring forth economic output but also comes with devastating effects on many people around the globe.

Our next section will, as an entrance into the everyday experiences of Kenyans, introduce Edward Ochieng, a roughly thirty-year-old unemployed father of two girls who lives in Kaleko, a small market place between the provincial towns Kisumu and Kisii, and Jack Ocholla, a twenty-five-year-old Nairobian who studies business administration, but spends most of his time in casinos and betting shops. It will become clear that Edward's and Jack's everyday "struggles" to acquire money in order to, for instance, pay school or university fees can be conceived of as a sign of their creativity. This, however, discards the way they see the situation themselves: as a consequence of an unjust political and economic situation. After thus introducing Kenya as our main empirical field, we shed light upon the ways in which money as a relation of dependency and opportunity operates in Kenya's fiscal and economic politics and its international relations. A discussion of recent trends in financial inclusion and global capital markets broadens our vista toward the substantial changes brought onto Kenyan society through the use of mobile money and the decision of the Kenyan government to go beyond aid and taxation and run into debt with global capital markets through government bonds.

THE EVERYDAY IN KENYA:
KNOWINGLY DISADVANTAGED

Whenever Mario had spent time in Kaleko, he stumbled upon Edward Ochieng, mostly by accident. Although Edward is a close member of the family in whose homestead Mario generally lives in since he first visited Kaleko in 2009, it was difficult to contact Edward, who most of the time was walking around with an uncharged mobile phone. Sometimes he met Edward on funerals where he was busy fostering his relations with local "big men," sometimes Edward just showed up at the door of Mario's house to ask him out for a stroll or was seen planting on his own or the fields of family members and friends. At other times, Mario saw Edward standing around the local minibus stand where he was discussing with local politicians, hoping to be given some money or a soft drink. Mario also often heard news about Edward being away in Nairobi where he paid a visit to the local member of Parliament or was sent by the latter to participate in seminars on topics of which he had no proper knowledge, for example, the future of Kenya's water supply. Edward, in short, lives the typical life of a male rural Western Kenyan, which could be summed up as the one of a "jack of all trades and master of none." He was unemployed and lived in an area that was agriculturally not productive, which forced him to constantly "struggle" (*chandre*) to "find" money for his wife and two daughters (cf Schmidt 2017a).

In contrast to Edward, Jack was easy to find if one had the time to pound the pavements of Nairobi's city center and search for him in one of the local casinos and betting shops. Mario first met him in a casino on Nairobi's Kaunda Street where Jack approached him to offer some bites of the meal he was eating. While eating his meal, Jack was waiting for one of his "sponsors," rich Nairobians who give out money to gamblers such as Jack, to bet on European football games. In case Jack loses, nothing happens, in case Jack wins, he cashes in a provision of 10–25 percent that is often transferred to his mobile money bank account. The typical day of Jack starts with making sure that he has no important appointments at the university after which he visits one of the cybercafes adjacent to or located inside the casinos in order to check statistical data on the upcoming games. After he picked several potential bets, he starts his journey through Nairobi and looks out for sponsors or friends in order to "find" some money that he would then send to the mother of his four-year-old daughter. He has made friends with people from all over Kenya, expats as well as tourists who he has found while walking and strolling around in the streets of Nairobi (cf on gambling as work, Schmidt 2019).

Despite the differences between the lives of Edward and Jack, their daily routine is remarkably similar. They are both males in their early thirties, one has two daughters and the other one daughter, and they do not have a regular income despite increasing pressure to buy things, pay school fees, and settle debts. They, however, show an exceptionally inventive and at the same time ironic way of dealing with their miserable situation and furthermore consider themselves wronged by people higher up the Kenyan food chain: politicians and businessmen who steal their rightful share in the country's wealth. Despite being unemployed, both also share the similar feeling of working seven hours per day—as Jack often said when Mario was late for a meeting, "I work on time." Work, for them, is what you do to acquire money (cf Ferguson 2015). For both Edward as well as Jack, it is not the "complexity" of current global and economic relations that is difficult to understand. What rather puzzles them is that their ongoing marginalization takes place despite the obviousness of the politico-economic system's actual ability to supply them with the money they would need. This is proven, for them, by the immense wealth some Kenyans are eager to show off and the enormous amounts of money spent on what many Kenyans perceive of as unnecessary infrastructural projects (the recently built Standard Gauge Railway between Nairobi and Mombasa being a prime example).

These Kenyans do not need sophisticated explanations in forms of a detour to witchcraft allegations or another kind of symbolic taming of capitalism. Edward and Jack are, in fact, aware of their poverty's actual cause, namely global political power structures that inhibit the development of Kenya as a sovereign nation-state and a Kenyan political as well as economic elite that continuously exploits or, worse, neglects Jack's and Edward's (re)productive potentials. Furthermore, they are very much aware of what they need in order to participate and reclaim membership in their local, national, and global communities: money. Kenyans have long understood that "money is money," as one unemployed neighbor of Edward told Mario after he asked him about the concept of "bitter money" (Shipton 1989; cf Schmidt 2017a), that is, money acquired through selling ancestral land which thereby acquires the ability to make people sick and eventually kill them. In contrast to such attempts to "tame" money, it appears that Kenyans have realized money to be the primary means to participate in the economy and to live a life worth living, no matter how one retrieves it, that is, by begging, gambling, wage labor, or selling vegetables. Or, to quote another friend, the average Kenyan has realized not only that "money is money" but also that "money is life" (Schmidt 2017b).

One way to find an explanation for the similarity between Edward's and Jack's lives is to assert that the world itself is constituted in a way so that Edward and Jack qua humans are forced to live similar lives. By inhabiting the same complex world, Jack and Edward are coerced to develop and maintain an ongoing creativity to shape their lives and continuously find new solutions to unforeseen situations. Such an explanation is put forward by what could be called the "ontology of complexity" that takes inspiration from John Dewey's pragmatist philosophy. The alternative is to understand Edward and Jack as inhabiting structurally similar positions in a political economy. This is what we suggest here.

GLOBAL MONETARY RELATIONS AND FINANCIAL INCLUSION IN KENYA

Capitalism's systemic force operates on the dependence on money and capital to mediate and perpetuate the bifurcated social world of haves and have-nots. Without delving into the complexities of Marx's writings on money here (de Brunhoff 1976; Heinrich 1999; Lapavitsas 2013; Stützle 2015; Soederberg 2015), we take from Marx that it is only thanks to money that capitalism is able to exist. Capitalism is a money-based social system, as many scholars after him such as Schumpeter concurred, who wrote that the "Money market is always [...] the headquarters of thecapitalist system" (Schumpeter 1934, 136).

In contrast to anthropological and other histories of money that have stressed that money as currency has existed for thousands of years in the form of shells, sticks, and as entries in books of credit (Graeber 2011), our money view of capitalism assumes, inspired by the state-focused (neo-chartalist) theory of money developed by the sociologist Geoffrey Ingham (2004), that capitalist money is based on a unique public-private "deal" (Koddenbrock 2019) linking (1) the private sector's ability to extend credit, (2) the willingness of the state to run into debts with both the private sector and wealthy individuals, and (3) the disposition or predictability of the population to pay the taxes needed to repay these public debts with interest to the creditors—be they literal taxes or other burdens imposed upon them. In short, capitalist money is a three-way public-private deal aiming to generate profit and existing between "the state, rentiers and taxpayers, which is mediated by a public bank, [. . .] bureaucratic administration and [. . .] Parliament" (Ingham 2004, 131). Who profits from this three-way relationship and how much depends on the constellation of forces in a specific locale and era. Whether money is a relation of dependency or opportunity depends on the balance in this partnership.

One of the launching pads for this three-way partnership was the founding of the Bank of England in 1694.[3] England had been at war with Louis XIV for quite some time and ran into problems generating enough tax revenue. The idea hatched by a group of London merchants was to set up a private bank, initially not much more than an "investment trust," and to loan 1.2 million pounds to the crown at 8 percent interest (McNally 2014, 12–13). This setup of the Bank of England allowed for a mutually beneficial deal: the king promised to tax enough in the future to pay interest every year, which was in the interest of the creditors. The promise to tax was further backed up by installing well-connected "Receiver Generals" in the royal tax office (Knafo 2013, 96). The government, in turn, received a handsome sum for war financing on the spot and only had to pay back a fraction because the loan came as a "permanent loan," an innovation of the day (Davies 2002, 259).

It is obvious from this process of granting a monopoly based on a mutually beneficial public-private deal that the Bank of England was not initially devised for the people but for the crown and for investors' monopoly rents. It was also a catalyst for the British colonial subjugation of many parts of the world (McNally 2014) and came with a substantial degree of internal violence because sanctions on forging money were draconic (Wennerlind 2011, 123–160). Most relevant for today's time of exploding state debt, the public-private partnership of the Bank of England for the first time installed a bond of "national" debt. No longer was the debt "personal" and only tied to the king and his erratic decisions (Davies 2002, 265; McNally 2014, 14; Peebles 2008). This "national" debt was designed to be permanent. Once this "partnership" has been permanently installed, the benefits and dangers of capitalist money can come to full fruition because the three-way deal multiplies the possibilities to play the capitalist blame game. It allows for the emergence of an alliance between a financially powerful creditor and a politically powerful debtor to put pressure upon a third, such as in the case of the European banking crisis, smaller states like Greece and their populations or subprime debtors. Instead of individual adventurers who stake their own fortune or entrepreneurs who understand their companies as extensions of a patriarchal family, such a three-way partnership allows the financially powerful creditor as well as the politically powerful debtor to count on future profits relatively risk-free.

How does this three-way relationship look in Kenya? In order to grasp the specificity of Kenyan money-mediated capitalism and the importance of its historic transformation, we suggest formalizing Ingham's three-way money-mediated relation into a creditor, a debtor, and a third party used as collateral. Such a formalization of the money-mediated form of capitalism allows us to understand recent shifts in Kenyan capitalism that can be summarized as a deepening of a coalition between financial actors from the private sector— both international banks and companies engaging in mobile money such as Safaricom—and the Kenyan state. This new coalition between the private sector and the Kenyan state has an ambivalent impact on the average life of Kenyans and the accompanying financialization and monetization of Kenyan society makes more Kenyans dependent on the money relation, for better or worse.

Money, Debt, and Financial Inclusion in Kenya

The Kenyan government organizes state funding through various channels from taxation to aid and debt. For its wherewithal it depends on a successful money generation and borrowing strategy at the national and international level. Since 2002, Kenyan growth rates have been high, and the government and corporate sector have pursued a strategy of integration into global capital markets and one of financial inclusion of the unbanked population. As one of our interviewees put it, the Kenyan elite has since taken great care to present Kenya as an economic and political example of a "capitalist democracy" to attract investors.[4]

Two recent developments are representative of this: the rise of mobile money (cf. Kusimba et al. 2013; Morawczynski 2009; Ouma et al. 2017) and the decision to issue government bonds and to run into debt with large commercial banks. Since the decision of Vodafone and its subsidiary Vodacom in South Africa to invest in Safaricom and take over a 40 percent share in the previously state-owned corporation in 2000, Kenya has accounted for half of mobile money transaction worldwide (Suárez 2016). Proponents have lauded this inclusion of people who had neither much access to cash nor to credit into the circuits of money. Critics argue that with fee rates of up to 43 percent this is hardly pro-poor growth (Mader 2016). So, while extending the reach of money and credit through M-Pesa, M-Shwari (a bank account and loan service offered through a partnership with NCBA Bank), and Fuliza (an overdraft facility for M-Pesa accounts) has increased opportunities for some, it has also landed more than 400,000 Kenyans on blacklists for overindebted people who will have a hard time getting rid of their debt through new credit in the future, at least until they redeem themselves at the infamous CRBs (Credit Reference Bureaus, cf, e.g., https://www.metropol.co.ke/).

Mobile money in Kenya illustrates the mutually beneficial ways the public-private partnership of capitalist money creation comes into existence. Safaricom, a 60 percent-state and 25 percent-Vodafone-owned corporation (Madise 2019, 233), played a major role in the so-called mobile money revolution. M-Pesa, founded in 2007, was allowed to spread its services far and wide across the country (Natile 2020; Malala 2017). Without implying banks at first, Safaricom thus became the main supplier of purchasing power through providing ways of withdrawing money in remote areas.

The Kenyan government only regulated that process lightly and considered the benefits of this massive extension of capitalist money toward broader parts of the population useful. Neither publicly minted cash nor credit issued by banks alone was at the core of this novelty but digits on phones. This innovation indicates the ever-creative ways money forms come into existence. The exact actors involved are shifting but they always form a delicate public-private balance. Because of Safaricom's UK-Kenyan, Corporate-State composition it came as no surprise that former opposition head Raila Odinga decried Safaricom's role and proximity to the government.

Extending the reach of money through phones to the not-yet fully monetized areas resulted in healthy profits for Vodafone and the government in terms of dividends. Half-year reported profits for 2017 were roughly 260 million USD, and 470 million in 2016 (BBC 2017).[5] The benefits for the broader population, the generator of profit in this arrangement, remain to be assessed. The World Bank as one of the supporters of the infrastructure of money transfers is highly optimistic.[6] In contrast, a member from the Kenyan justice NGO Fahamu suggested that a form of unbalanced and unjust public-private "deal" exists between Vodafone, Safaricom, the Kenyan government, and the Kenyan public which can be illustrated as given in figure 8.2.

It is obvious from this graph that the money-mediated relation between the Kenyan public, the Kenyan government, Safaricom, and Vodafone is economically unbalanced and politically corrupt. Our interviewee from Fahamu, for instance, suggested that the Kenyan government offers Safaricom deals and contracts such as managing the electoral process or installing cameras in Nairobi's streets only because the government possesses shares in the company. What the general public conceives of as "taxes" would rather be corruption, that is, the purchase of benefits by means of money. The Kenyan public, furthermore and in the eyes of our interviewee, is still partly controlled by shareholders residing

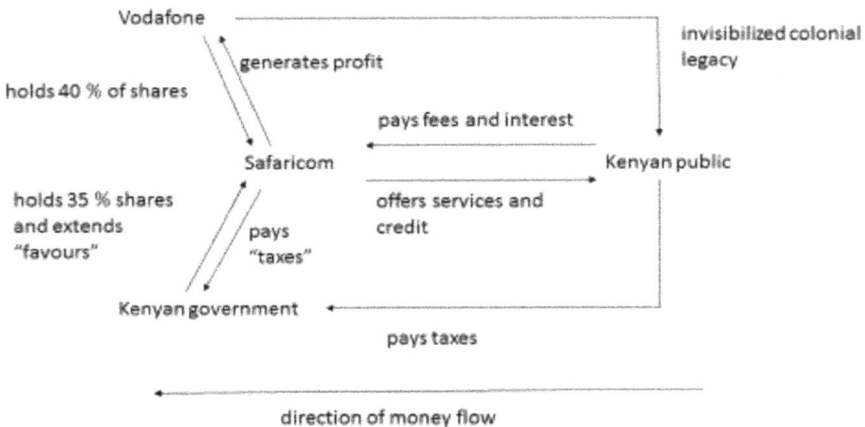

Figure 8.2   The Money "Deal" in Kenya.

in the UK, Kenya's former colonial power, and forced to pay taxes for financial services that are deemed to be necessary and—in the opinion of our interviewee — should be offered more or less for free by the state.

A similar process of broadening the reach of capitalist money into the Kenyan political economy takes the form of a public-private deal between the Kenyan government, large globally operating banks, and the IMF in the process of issuing Kenyan government bonds on global capital markets for the first time. For our analysis of how money is a relation of dependency and opportunity with a tendency to being lopsided, the exact processes leading to higher debt and the money instruments used to incur it need to be better understood.[7]

Building on our understanding of money as a public-private deal, the sovereign bond becomes the quintessential money instrument at the heart of this relationship. Sovereign bond issuance has been on the rise among "frontier markets" (Aberdeen Capital 2015) like Kenya, Ivory Coast, Senegal, and other Latin American and Asian countries since around 2007 (Hou et al. 2014; Masetti 2015). Kenya followed with its first sovereign bonds denominated in dollars at the value of two billion USD in 2014. A confluence of developments has made this possible. On the one hand, US Treasuries or German Bunds have since 2008 earned very little due to low or even negative interest rates. The Kenyan bond, by contrast, comes with more than 6 percent interest rate over ten years. In the face of the reliably austere approach recent Kenyan governments have adopted, investing into Kenyan public debt has become attractive for key money makers like JP Morgan, Barclays, and the Qatar National Bank among others (Ayaga 2016).

In the process of issuing government bonds, at first sight, the ambivalence of capitalist money as both relation of dependency and opportunity seems to be in balance. The implied parties sign the bond contract freely. Yet this balance turns into lopsidedness fast. One important inequality at the heart of the sale and issuing of government bonds is that in order to be attractive to global investors, the bonds need to be denominated in USD. Any appreciation of the US Dollar—be it because of a Fed decision to increase interest rates or because of another flight to safety (Helleiner 2014), as visible in the current Corona crisis—will necessarily entail an increased need for dollar currency for the Kenyan government. The USD as the lead currency thus creates a big policy challenge for debtors. The exchange rate risks associated with these bonds are indeed substantial. Over the last few years, warnings about the coming African debt crisis have increased and will get another boost in the wake of the ongoing economic and financial Corona crisis.

Such a lack of monetary sovereignty and the need to run into debt in a foreign currency has been termed "original sin" in macroeconomics long ago (Eichengreen and Haussmann 1999). After the financial crisis in Asia in the late 1990s, many governments in the Global South decided to manage their exposure to these currency risks by accumulating vast amounts of USD reserves. Among what Ilias Alami calls the "developing and emerging capitalist countries" such as China, Brazil, Mexico, Turkey, India, South Africa, Indonesia, Malaysia, Poland, Thailand, and Russia reserve holding "grew from about 5 per cent of their GDP in the 1980s to about 25 per cent by 2010" (Alami 2017, 3). In Kenya, foreign reserves have grown from under one billion USD in 1995 to around eight billion USD in 2017. More poignantly, the relative amount of reserve holdings against external debt has moved from under 5 percent in the 1990s to 50 percent in 2010 to decline again to 35 percent in 2017 (World Bank Database). These reserves serve as tools to, if necessary, stabilize the Kenyan shilling and therefore cannot be invested for other productive purposes. Their opportunity costs are thus very high (Rodrik 2006).

As in the case of Safaricom, the creation and management of money and debt through government bonds entails opportunities for mutual enrichment and ambivalent profits for the broader populace acting as "collateral" for the deal. Banks earn interests and fees and members of government are able to rake in a few million dollars as "fees." Fittingly, and here, Edward's and Jack's complaints about the political class and the political economy are pertinent, the Kenyan government bonds sale created an ongoing scandal because the former opposition under Odinga claimed that about one-third of the funds are stashed away in some overseas accounts of senior government figures involved in the deal (Elderkin 2016). On a more charitable reading, in terms of policy, the Kenyan government is in a tight spot between the need to roll over existing debt, invest with a long-term, and little immediate gain perspective into infrastructure, or to finance current expenditure. All this takes place with the aim of being able to tax enough in the future to repay the debt in mind. If higher tax returns are hard to generate, new debt and a growing stock of debt will follow.

The ambiguity of monetizing more realms of social and political life through mobile money and state debt with banks from the Global North and other centers of finance is obvious. The public-private deal of money creation and borrowing works if the benefits for all the actor groups involved remain in balance. Yet this balance can never be taken for granted. Giving too much weight and control to the profit interests of private corporations without the constraining effects of stiff competition or of popular power will lead to highly unequal effects and a breakdown of the partnership. Similarly, control and opportunities for enrichment for government representatives will lead to arrangements that will ultimately be to the disadvantage of the broader populace. While everyone is dependent on money to make more money in capitalist competition, who profits and who suffers is ultimately a distributive struggle.

CONCLUSION: MONEY AS A FORCEFUL RELATION OF DEPENDENCY

Money permeates most parts of social life. Yet it is wrong to take it for granted and to consider money a mere background condition to our interactions. Under capitalism, money is a forceful relation of dependency. It brings corporations, public actors, and the people together as part of a process of amassing capital. As we hope to have shown, making the dependence on money explicit allows for a better understanding of the "heavy environment" ethnographic interlocutors bemoan compared with a perspective that reverts mostly to what we have called "ontology of complexity." It is not the world's complexity that forces Edward and Jack to acquire cash constantly, but the increasing need to be "financialized" and to earn and hold money, which, in their case, more often than not means to become debtors of companies such as Safaricom. The Kenyan government takes similar risks of being unable to raise enough cash on its own by issuing government bonds in USD. In both cases, the actors bet upon a future despite rather bleak odds. That they are forced to do so in order to live is a consequence of money's central place in a capitalist economy.

Trying to come to terms with capitalist social relations that are always local, national, and global such as capitalist money, however, underlines particularly well how valuable an encounter between anthropology and IR can be. Furthermore, we hope to have shown that ethnography risks to obscure obvious inequalities for the sake of complexity. This risk, however, is also a potential: as shown by the ethnographic data from Western Kenya, participant observation can also lead to the opposite conclusion, namely to a realization that actors on the ground interpret things in a much simpler way than the anthropologist assumed before.

NOTES

1. There are, of course, many great anthropological studies on capitalism such as, to mention only a few, Bear (2015), Carrier and Kalb (2015), Kar (2018), Sahlins (1994), and Weiss (2019).

2. It should be noted though that this article originates from Germany. In Germany, IPE is much more marginal than in Britain and the United States. This means the study of global capitalism is even more absent here than in the heartlands of "the discipline of Western supremacy" (van der Pijl 2014).

3. The next two paragraphs are adapted from Koddenbrock (2019).

4. Interview with director of Fahamu, Nairobi, via Skype, November 12, 2017. Fahamu is a Kenyan social justice NGO.

5. Interview with director of Fahamu, Nairobi, November 12, 2017.

6. Interview World Bank, Nairobi, November 6, 2017.

7. Deals between banks, arms corporations, and defense ministries have been a constant feature of Europe-Africa relations since the end of colonialism. Despite many a protests and organized social movements mobilizing against it, the opportunities of collaboration between these three actor groups have remained plentiful. This collaboration has recently created another scandal in Mozambique. Credit Suisse, which earned handsomely on the arms deal, is feeling the heat and fears damage to their image. Mozambique's public debt, in turn, rose by 35 percent in 2014, the year of the deal (Hamby 2016).

BIBLIOGRAPHY

Aberdeen Asset Management. *Frontier Market Bonds. The Next Chapter*, 2015, www .institutionalinvestor.com/images/FrontierMarketsTheNextChapter.pdf.

Alami, Ilias. "Money Power of Capital and Production of 'New State Spaces'. A View from the Global South." *New Political Economy* 22 (2017): 1–18.

Anievas, Alexander, and Kerem Nisancioglu. *How the West Came to Rule. The Geopolitical Origins of Capitalism*. London: Pluto Press, 2015.

Appadurai, Arjun. *The Social Life of Things. Commodities in Cultural Perspective*. Cambridge: Cambridge University Press, 1986.

Ayaga, Wilfed. "Kenyan Auditors Now to Fly out over Eurobond Billions." May 19, 2016, http://www.standardmedia.co.ke/article/2000202309/kenyan-auditors-now-to-fly-out-over-eurobond-billions.

Baran, Paul A., and Paul Sweezey. *Monopoly Capital: An Essay on the American Economic and Social Order*. Harmondsworth: Pelican Books, 1967.

BBC. "South Africa's Vodacom Buys into Kenya's Safarcom." May 15, 2017, www .bbc.com/news/amp/business-39922634.

Bear, Laura. *Navigating Austerity. Currents of Debt Along a South Asian River*. Palo Alto: Stanford University Press, 2015.

Bloch, Maurice, and Jonathan Parry. *Money and the Morality of Exchange*. Cambridge: Cambridge University Press, 1989.

Bohannan, Paul. "The Impact of Money on an African Subsistence Economy." *The Journal of Economic History* 19:4 (1959): 491–503.

Brunhoff, Suzanne de. *Marx on Money*. London: Urizon Books, 1976.

Callinicos, Alex. "Marxism and the Very Idea of IPE." in *The Palgrave Handbook of Critical International Political Economy*, edited by Alan Cafruny, Leila Simona Talani and Gonzalo Pozo Martin, 49–65. London: Palgrave Macmillan, 2016.

Carrier, James G., and Don Kalb (eds.). *Anthropologies of Class. Power, Practice and Inequality*. Cambridge: Cambridge University Press, 2015.

Chandler, David. *Resilience: The Governance of Complexity*. London: Routledge, 2014.

Cooper, Elizabeth, and David Pratten. (eds). *Ethnographies of Uncertainty in Africa*. London: Palgrave, 2014.

Cox, Robert W. *Production, Power, and World Order. Social Forces in the Making of History*. New York: Columbia University Press, 1987.

Dan-Cohen, Talia. "Epistemic Artefacts: On the Uses of Complexity in Anthropology." *Journal of the Royal Anthropological Institute* 23:2 (2017): 285–301.

Davies, Glyn. *A History of Money. From Ancient Times to the Present Day*. Cardiff: University of Wales Press, 2002.

Eichengreen, Barry, and Ricardo Haussmann. *Exchange Rates and Financial Instability*. NBER Working Paper No. 7418, 1999.

Elderkin, Sarah. "Eurobond: Is IMF Playing Games after Kenyan Government Cooked its Books?" May 9, 2016, http://www.standardmedia.co.ke/article/200020 1117/eurobond-is-imf-playing-games-after-kenyan-government-cooked-its-books /?pageNo=3.

Ferguson, James. *Global Shadows: Africa in the Neoliberal World Order*. Durham: Duke University Press, 2006.

———. *Give a Man a Fish. Reflections on the New Politics of Distribution*. Durham: Duke University Press, 2015.

Geschiere, Peter. *The Modernity of Witchcraft: Politics and the Occult in Postcolonial Africa*. Charlottesville: University of Virginia Press, 1997.

Gilpin, Robert. *The Political Economy of International Relations*. Princeton: Princeton University Press, 1987.

Graeber, David. *Debt: The First 5,000 Years*. Brooklyn, NY: Melville House, 2011.

Hamby, Chris. "Let's Make Them Poorer and We'll Get Rich." August 31, 2016, www.buzzfeed.com/chrishamby/not-just-a-court-system-its-a-goldmine?utm_term =.kePp1PVnK#.ouQAE7D9G.

Harvey, David. *Limits to Capital*, updated edition, London: Verso, 2007.

Heinrich, Michael. *Die Wissenschaft vom Wert. Die Marxsche Kritik der politischen Ökonomie zwischen wissenschaftlicher Revolution und klassischer Tradition*. Münster: Westfälisches Dampfboot, 1999.

Helleiner, Eric. *The Status Quo Crisis. Global Financial Governance after the 2007– 08 Financial Meltdown*. Oxford: Oxford University Press, 2014.

Hobson, John A. *Imperialism—A Study*. New York: Pott, 1902.

Hou, Zhenbo, Jodie Keane, Jane Kennan, Isabella Massa, and Dirk Willem te Velde. *Shockwatch Bulletin. Global Monetary Shocks: Impacts and Policy Responses in Sub-Saharan Africa*. London: Overseas Development Institute (ODI), Working Paper, 2014.

Ingham, Geoffrey K. *The Nature of Money*. Malden, Mass.: Polity Press, 2004.

Kar, Sohini. *Financializing Poverty. Labor and Risk in Indian Microfinance*. Palo Alto: Stanford University Press, 2018.

Keohane, Robert. *After Hegemony: Cooperation and Discord in the World Political Economy*. Princeton: Princeton University Press, 1984.

Knafo, Samuel. *The Making of Modern Finance: Liberal Governance and the Gold Standard*. New York: Routledge, 2013.

Koddenbrock, Kai. "Strategies of Critique in International Relations: From Foucault and Latour towards Marx." *European Journal of International Relations* 21 (2015): 243–66.

———. "Mehr Kapitalismus wagen: Herrschaftsanalyse "jenseits der Anarchie" und die Rolle des Geldes." *Politische Vierteljahresschrift* 58 (2017): 259–84.

———. "Money and Moneyness: Thoughts on the Nature and Distributional Power of the 'Backbone' of Capitalist Political Economy." *Journal of Cultural Economy* 12 (2019): 101–18.

Koddenbrock, Kai and Ndongo Samba Sylla "Towards a Political Economy of Monetary Dependency: The Case of the CFA Franc." *MaxPo Discussion Paper*, SciencesPo Paris, 2019.

Kusimba, Sibel, Harpieth Chaggar, Elizabeth Gross and Gabriel Kunyu. *Social Networks of Mobile Money in Kenya*. Institute for Money, Technology & Financial Inclusion, Working Paper 2013–1, 2013.

Lapavitsas, Costas. *Profiting Without Producing: How Finance Exploits Us All*. London; New York: Verso, 2013.

Mader, Philip. "Card Crusaders, Cash Infidels and the Holy Grails of Digital Financial Inclusion." *Behemoth* 9 (2016): 59–81.

Madise, Sunduzwayo. *The Regulation of Mobile Money. Law and Practice in Sub-Saharan Africa*. London: Palgrave Macmillan, 2019.

Malala, Joy. *Law and Regulation of Mobile Payment Systems. Issues Arising Post-Financial Inclusion*. London: Routledge, 2017.

Mattern, Janice Bially, and Ayse Zarakol. "Hierarchies in World Politics." *International Organization* 70 (2016): 623–654.

Masetti, Oliver. *African Bonds: Will the Boom Continue?* Deutsche Bank Research Paper, 2015.

Mastanduno, Michael. "Economics and Security in Statecraft and Scholarship." *International Organization* 52 (1998): 825–854.

Meillassoux, Claude. "From Reproduction to Production. A Marxist Approach to Economic Anthropology." *Economy and Society* 1 (1972): 93–105.

Mintz, Sidney. *Sweetness and Power. The Place of Sugar in Modern History*. New York: Penguin, 1985.

Morawczynski, Olga. "Exploring the Usage and Impact of 'Transformational' Mobile Financial Services: The Case of M-PESA in Kenya." *Journal of Eastern African Studies* 3 (2009): 509–525.

Moore, Jason W. *Capitalism in the Web of Life: Ecology and the Accumulation of Capital*. London: Verso, 2015.

McNally, David. "The Blood of the Commonwealth." *Historical Materialism* 22 (2014): 3–32.

Narayan, John. "The Wages of Whiteness in the Absence of Wages. Racial Capitalism, Reactionary Intercommunalism and the Rise of Trumpism." *Third World Quarterly* 38 (2017): 2482–2500.

Natile, Serena. *The Exclusionary Politics of Digital Financial Inclusion: Mobile Money, Gendered Walls*. London: Routledge, 2020.

Nitzan, Jonathan, and Shimshon Bichler. *Capital as Power. A Study of Order and Creorder*. New York: Routledge, 2009.

Ouma, Shem Alfred, Teresa Maureen Odongo, and Maureen Were. "Mobile Financial Services and Financial Inclusion: Is it a Boon for Savings Mobilization?" *Review of Development Finance* 7 (2017): 29–35.

Peebles, Gustav. "Inverting the Panopticon: Money and the Nationalization of the Future." *Public Culture* 20 (2008): 233–265.

Pijl, Kees. *The Discipline of Western Supremacy: Modes of Foreign Relations and Political Economy, Vol III.* London: Pluto Books, 2014.

Powell, Jeff. *Subordinate Financialisation: A Study of Mexico and its Non Financial Corporations.* PhD-Thesis, London: SOAS, 2013, https://core.ac.uk/download/pd f/19090664.pdf.

Rey, Pierre Philippe. *Colonialisme, néo-colonialisme et transition au capitalisme. Exemple de la "Comilog" au Congo-Brazzaville.* Paris: Maspero, 1971.

Robbins, Joel. "Beyond the Suffering Subject: Toward an Anthropology of the Good." *Journal of the Royal Anthropological Institute* 19 (2013): 447–62.

Rodrik, Dani. "The Social Cost of Foreign Exchange Reserves." *International Economic Journal* 20 (2006): 253–66.

Rosenberg, Justin. "The 'Philosophical Premises' of Uneven and Combined Development." *Review of International Studies* 39 (2013): 569–97.

Sahlins, Marshall. "Cosmologies of Capitalism: The Trans-Pacific Sector of 'The World System.'" In *Culture/Power/History: A Reader in Contemporary Social Theory,* edited by Nicholas B. Dirks, Geoff Eley, and Sherry B. Ortner, 412–56. Princeton, N.J.: Princeton University Press 1994.

Schmidt, Jessica. "Intuitively Neoliberal? Towards a Critical Understanding of Resilience Governance." *European Journal of International Relations* 21 (2014): 402–26.

Schmidt, Mario. "'Almost Everybody Does It . . .' Gambling as Future-Making in Western Kenya." *Journal of Eastern African Studies* 13 (2019): 739–57.

———. "'Disordered Surroundings' and Socio-Economic Exclusion in Western Kenya." *Africa: Journal of the International African Institute* 87 (2017a): 278–99.

———. "'Money is Life'—On Quantity, Social Freedom and Combinatory Practices in Western Kenya." *Social Analysis* 61 (2017b): 66–80.

Schmidt Mario, and Kai Koddenbrock. "Against Understanding: The Techniques of Shock and Awe in Jesuit Theology, Neoliberal Thought and Timothy Morton's Philosophy of Hyperobjects". *Global Society,* 33 (2019): 66–81

Schumpeter, Joseph. *The Theory of Economic Development. An Inquiry into Profits, Capital, Credit, Interest, and the Business Cycle.* Cambridge, Mass.: Harvard University Press, 1934.

Shipton, Parker. *Bitter Money. Cultural Economy and Some African Meanings of Forbidden Commodities.* Washington, D.C: American Anthropological Association, 1989.

———. *Credit Between Cultures. Farmers, Financiers, and Misunderstanding in Africa.* New Haven: Yale University Press, 2010.

Smith, Elliot. "Kenya Scraps its Bank Lending Cap and Grants the IMF its Wish." November 13, 2019, https://www.cnbc.com/2019/11/12/kenya-scraps-its-bank-l ending-cap-and-grants-the-imf-its-wish.html.

Soederberg, Susanne. *Debtfare States and the Poverty Industry: Money, Discipline and the Surplus Population.* Hoboken, US: Routledge, 2014.

Stützle, Ingo. "Der Gott der Waren: Die ökonomische Theorie und ihr Geld." *PROKLA, Zeitschrift für kritische Sozialwissenschaft* 45(2015): 177–98.

Suárez, Sandra L. "Poor People's Money. The Politics of Mobile Money in Mexico and Kenya." *Telecommunications Policy* 40 (2016): 945–55.

Teschke Benno. *The Myth of 1648: Class, Geopolitics, and the Making of Modern International Relations*. London: Verso, 2003.

Thieme, Tatiana A. "The Hustle Economy: Informality, Uncertainty and the Geographies of Getting By." *Progress in Human Geography* 44 (2017): 529–48.

Tsing, Anna Lowenhaupt. *The Mushroom at the End of the World: On the Possibility of Life in Capitalist Ruins*. Princeton: Princeton University Press, 2015.

Waltz, Kenneth. *Theory of International Politics*. New York: Mc Graw Gill, 1979.

Weiss, Hadas. *We Have Never Been Middle Class. How Social Mobility Misleads Us*. London: Verso, 2019.

Wennerlind, Carl. *Casualties of Credit: The English Financial Revolution, 1620–1720*. Cambridge, MA: Harvard University Press, 2011.

Wolf, Eric. *Europe and the People Without History*. Berkeley: University of California Press, 1982.

Chapter 9

A State of Numbers

Bureaucratic Technologies of Government and the Study of Internationalized Politics

Sarah Biecker and Klaus Schlichte

International politics are often discussed in Northern Atlantic mainstream IR as a game between states and international organizations. One of the discipline's questions that have gained most attention, in particular within the "global governance" frame, has been whether states or IOs hold "authority" or states over each other (cf. Hurd 1999; Lake 2009; Zürn 2018). As we want to argue in this chapter, this discussion might cover that power and domination work in quite different ways than a reifying understanding of political institutions suggests. Instead of thinking of international politics as a power game between different states or between states and IOs, we argue that a combination of classic sociology of domination and new theoretical elements from the transdisciplinary field of Science and Technology Studies (STS) allows us to understand better and empirically more grounded how the world is ruled.

In this chapter, we want to suggest "technologies of government" as a particularly fruitful concept to study internationalized politics. By this we mean combinations of trained actors, practices, devices, and "programs" that aim both at constituting and maintaining social and political orders—and this is what government, national, and international is finally about. Fully in line with the deeply constructivist understanding that authors like Michel Foucault, Max Weber, and Niklas Luhmann developed, states and IOs are nothing else than semantic artifacts of such technologies of government. The usage of terms like "state" and "IO" is then just part of the program, of the governmentality, the *imaginaire* (Castoriadis 1975) that is a result of the successful imposition of those technologies of government that revolve around the idea of the state. But the sociology of such technologies has to address that their "programs," their personnel and their devices, as we argue, can no longer be separated as belonging either to the state's realm or to the international. Technologies of government crosscut the boundaries that constitute mainstream understandings of international politics.

In this chapter, we combine ideas and concepts of the sociology of domination with more recent products of other fields. In several disciplines of social sciences, we observe a new interest in the role of devices and material objects. This applies to lists, files, and archives in legal studies (Vismann 2008); to plans in social anthropology (Rottenburg 2009); but also to housing architecture (Akcan 2012); to airports in international relations (Schouten 2014); buildings of financial administration (Schlichte 2017); or to long-distance roads (Ferguson 1990; Beck and Klaeger and Stasik 2017) in political anthropology. Statistics and mathematical tools have also attracted renewed attention in sociology (cf. Heintz 2010; Leese 2014) with the rise of rankings and endless comparisons in a neoliberal *mise en compétition* of basically everything, from zoos to songs, to cities, states, universities, theaters, books, and, of course, human beings.

The argument of this chapter is an outcome of a theoretically informed immersion into the bureaucratic technologies of Uganda. With the analysis of numbers in a broader sense, ranging from statistics to budgets to files we attempt to meet the demands for ethnography of statecraft and the idea of stategraphy (Thelen and Vetters and von Benda-Beckmann 2014). The paper ties together state practices and images, representations, numbers and statistics in order to immerse into the realm of the Ugandan budget politics and get an understanding of the "relational setting" (Thelen and Vetters and von Benda-Beckmann 2014, 2) of the state. Such relational settings "demonstrate the fluidity and transformation of state structures, while simultaneously insisting on the particular historicity of each case" (Thelen and Vetters and von Benda-Beckmann 2014, 2).

We use ethnographic material from a long-term study on state agencies, especially police force and the Ministry of Finance in Uganda, to develop our argument in a "studying up"-manner: we try to make sense of many observations that we gained through participatory observation, the reading of collected files and publications of institutions, of inspections of buildings and spatial arrangements, by listening to everyday life conversations of state agents and from interview material.[1] As discussed in the introduction to this volume, an ethnographic approach allows us to combine data from the state of above and below. We define ethnography "first of all [as] an attempt to understand" (Cerwonka and Malkki 2007, 57) and follow Dvora Yanow's specification, which underlines our methodological claim. According to her, ethnography is

a hermeneutic-phenomenological orientation toward social life: seeing it as being meaning-filled, where these meanings are embodied in and communicated through what might be called the "underlife" . . . of human acts, language (including written, oral, and nonverbal), and objects—their situationally common-sensical, unwritten, unspoken, everyday, tacitly know textures. (Yanow 2009, 34)

With this orientation, we aim to contribute to discussions that go beyond the theme of technologies of government as such, since we think that this perspective can also contribute to our understanding of our own discipline. The issue of technology has also led to new questions of methodology: IR and its methods themselves seen as performative and producing social and political realities, so that methods of governments are not only the object of a critical investigation of international politics but renewed attention or methodological questions also helps to shed light on the effects of academic research itself. Methods are not just "tools," but technologies and uses of devices that are performative and create a world that they allegedly only describe or represent (cf. Aradauand Huysmans 2014).

Our study also sheds new light on the role of statistics in the field of internationalized politics. Statistics have accompanied the history of the modern state since in late renaissance, city-states like Venice started to count their population (van Dülmen 1992, 19). In this paper, we will look at the current state of affairs from a marginal angle. While the use of numbers and quantification of politics has been studied for Western states, NGOs und IOs for quite a while already (e.g., Porter 1995; Boltansky and Thévenot 1991; Rottenburg and Merry 2015), we use material on the state of Uganda in order to identify main technologies and practices by which the state is evoked, produced, objectified as an image, while it is at the same time a field of power (cf. Migdal and Schlichte 2005).

In the following section we will briefly outline what our theoretical idea about technologies of government consists of. For that end, we will also take recourse to selected ideas from STS and Actor-Network-Theory (ANT), in particular the concept of technology. The notion of technology will help us think about the production of the state in a new manner. This is the main content of our contribution that will be presented in the two consecutive sections. We derive from our material insights in the practices of how the state or other forms of political organization are produced by the usage of numbers (budget politics) and material artifacts (police files). In a final reflection we will discuss our observations again with regard to future encounters of international relations and political anthropology.

TECHNOLOGIES OF GOVERNMENT

For the term "technology" different understandings have been suggested: it can refer to "physical objects or artifacts" as well as "activities or processes," or the term could also refer "to what people *know* as well as what they do" (Bijker and Hughes and Pinch 1993, 4 emphasis in original). While it is in many cases difficult to separate all three meanings from each other, we want to concentrate here on an understanding of technology that combines artifacts and practices with other categories from social theory that are usually not part of STS or ANT.

The concept of technologies of government, as we want to promote it here, combines Weberian and Foucauldian ideas and refers thus to four core elements: (1) social carrier groups, (2) artifacts and devices, (3) practices that glue things and actors together, and (4) programs, symbolic representations that translate an overall political goal, the respective idea of government, into manageable practical exercises. Inherent to technologies of government is the idea of steering. Technologies of government are thus connected ensembles of personnel, practices, artifacts, and discourses that aim at the production of a particular political order. Such technologies can be very diverse, depending on what programs, what devices, and what practices are parts of it. Policing, for example, can be done in very different ways. Accounting too appears historically in very different forms, each of them having different presuppositions and effects.

In the case of the budget support, this technology is clearly bureaucratic in character. Its main devices are documents, representations that have the tendency to develop a life of their own. "The budget" as a representation of monetary flows thus becomes a representation with a life of its own. It is then no longer the practical life, the real lifeworld, but a life that is allegedly represented by numerical expressions that matter for political decisions. Numerical scales become the yardstick with which relations are measured and in whose measurements everything is judged.

In the field we have looked at, budget policy, artifacts are statistics and numbers, files, figures, and budget reports that result out of practices of counting, writing, registering, listing, or negotiating. Our STS-inspired approach intends to follow the idea that "the study of technology itself can be transformed into a sociological tool of analysis" (Callon 2012, 77). We try to do this by conceiving technologies of government as combinations of actors, understood as social carriers of imaginaries, the practices they employ in order to structure the world along such imaginaries, and the devices they use in order to reach these goals. There is intentionality involved in such technologies, and we do not need to restrict our analysis to either practices, or actors, or narratives, or materiality, but we think that our study shows that these four elements can be combined in a theoretically fruitful manner. Let us summarize what we see in our empirical observations regarding these four categories of technologies of government for our study beforehand:

Carrier groups of the technologies of government that we see at work here are both state agents, international personnel of IOs and aid agencies (the so-called expats), and Ugandan citizens, which have already incorporated state structures and symbolic orders in their daily action. These carrier groups cannot be divided along categories in which IR theories usually differentiate the world. They neither really belong to a "ruling class" nor are all of them independent "experts." Nor is it just evil Western agents in collaboration with "corrupt elites" that suppress an innocent civil society. Instead, the personnel involved in the technologies of government we looked at stems from many countries. There is an Anglo-Saxon bias in the upper echelons, but we find, for example, Ghanaians, Germans, and many Ugandans among them as well. Some of them work as independent consultants, but the majority is employed in IOs or state agencies, which share very similar bureaucratic features.

The *devices* we see being used here are different kinds of artifacts. Most visible are reports, written documents that list things and tell stories, which shall give an order to the world, at least in the way it is presented in these documents. The second sort of artifacts is files. In earlier work we have shown how files are produced and constitute something like the lifeblood of the Ugandan police force (Biecker and Schlichte 2015), and similar claims are plausible for other state agencies, in Uganda and elsewhere. Such artifacts are products of the state, they are created with a purpose, but they develop a life of their own. Typically, in modern bureaucratic organizations, the handling of files, the establishment of registers and reports, becomes the actual organizational goal while the original purpose of why all these activities are undertaken is often of secondary importance or has become folklore.

The *practices* we see performed in our observations are very diverse. We think we can distinguish practices that are connected with ideas of order from those that have other "intentions" or ideational contents, and from finally those that seem to be unconnected or void of any governmental implication. Writing, documenting, listing, recording, counting, negotiating, translating— all these are core practices in a technology of government, and it is perhaps no coincidence that all of them appear in social sciences again. As it seems, it is often hard to distinguish academic practices from practices of government. Rancière's (2004) point that parts of social sciences are actually acts of policing becomes quite acute here.

Imaginaries form the fourth element of our understanding of technologies of government. Staff is trained to think of societies or certain segments of the society in terms of problems that need treatment of some form, and the work of designing, implementing, evaluating, and revising this treatment is the work of government. All such imaginaries of government share this feature: they project a state of things into the future, measure current states of affairs against it, and problematize the divergence. Not only bureaucrats and policy practitioners take part in the production of this discourse, but social sciences too are highly active in that regard. In fact, quite some parts of social sciences can be counted as outright parts of such imaginaries. "Policy cycles" or "good governance" are abstract models or normative concepts that are part of such imaginaries of government.

In the following section, we will summarize our observations on a particular technology of government: the budget. We see in budgets a formidable example of how in the political sphere government decisions become visible, including the conflict around the legitimacy of claims, and how problems are diagnosed, how treatment is conceived, and how a technology that circulates around numbers and numerical codes operates. As we will see, our observations also show how limited the effects of such technologies often are.

We will start with a section that deals with "budget support," a policy that had emerged in "development" at the beginning of the new millennium and became a favored approach for a while. We combine our observations on this field of internationalized rule with a closer look on the budget further down, within the same state, Uganda, though. We will then look at files and their role within Uganda's police force. What our ethnographic approach reveals is that files are both a product of technologies of government and a tool, a device that is part of the technology of policing.

BUDGET POLITICS—INSIDE THE STATE

It is not really a new observation that states and statistics are closely related. Numbers are one language to speak and write about the state. Statistics are tools in the construction of meaning. Numbers are references, which come from the Latin word *referre* and means "to produce" (*herbeischaffen* in German) (Latour 2002, 45). They are references, productions respectively in a double meaning: they are produced and they produce. Numbers are produced by actors and hence results of practices, for example, practices of counting, collecting, and negotiating. At the same time, numbers represent and produce something. They are attempts of objectification and officialization (Bourdieu 2011, 2006), and they are thus part of the long-term process by which the state as the official order has acquired universal meaning.

Files (in German: *Akten*) seem to share this foundational role: "The very term *Akten* emphasizes the quality of action (*Handlung*)" (Vismann 2008, 10 emphasis in original). Like numbers files are references and derive from the Latin term *agere* (to act) (Vismann 2008, 10). Both numbers and files are the products of collections and negotiations and result as representations of something. Police files, for example, are produced as results of the writing acts of criminal cases. Within "chains of translations" (Latour 1999, 40) files transform stories into paper materiality.

Both numerical statistics and files are core features of the idea of modern statehood that has become universal through the process of European expansion. While many other instances of political organization have known forms of written documentation and information storage, the systematic claim and the transcontinental communication of knowledge in numbers and tables, in a universalized language about a population, an economy, a state, is quite obviously connected to the history of colonialism and the work of international organizations, in particular after 1945. The spread of these forms, it seems, is part of the spread of the idea of government. That the world needs to be governed, that such steering is not only desirable but necessary, is a rather modern idea. In its current epitomization, it includes "developmentality" (Sande Lie 2013, 2015), the understanding shared by African government officials, Western aid agency personnel, and IO staff that planning is needed and that it is to be carried out with the help of numbers and files.

Uganda has a quite long history of planning. It stretches from the schemes of economic development during the British Protectorate Buganda at the beginning of the twentieth century (cf. Thompson 2003) to the first fifteen years of independence following 1962. Under the rule of Idi Amin (1971–1979) an informalization of Uganda set in that endured over the years of civil war that ended in 1985 for the southern half of the country and continued in the north for some more years. With the takeover of the current regime in 1986 "development" again became the shibboleth for far-reaching activities aiming to prepare a better future, with the joined forces of the new regime and international financial institutions and, soon, NGOs. Uganda under its new president Yoweri Museveni became a "donor darling" in the 1990s, in particular of international financial institutions.

Over the last thirty years, one scheme has followed the other. The *Structural Adjustment Programs* (SAP) of the 1980s overlapped with the *Economy Recovery Program* (ERP), which the new government negotiated with the World Bank. Out of the latter came a *Poverty Eradication Plan* (1997–2008) (PEAP), a new model of developmental planning, for which Uganda should become a showcase. On this followed in 2010 a series of five-year plans. Each of them anticipates as *National Development Plan* the next step for the realization of the *Vision 2040*, which according to the newly created *National Planning Authority* will turn Uganda by that time into "middle income country."[2] This plan, the *Primary National Strategic Plan*," is unlike the PEAP less oriented in increased social services but more toward economic growth (NPA 2010: 3). The current and five consecutive five-year plans shall help to reach the goals of the *Vision 2040* in the twenty-five years left after 2015. These six *National Development Plans* are supplemented by *Sector Investment Plans* (SIP) and *Local Government Development Plans*

(LGDP), *Annual Work Plans*, and a further downscaled hierarchy of plans, reports, and assessments in the local administration.

The renaissance of planning Uganda is, however, not a national idiosyncrasy to return to socialist technologies of government. Like in other "developing" countries, it has been developed in full agreement and with open support if not on initiative of powerful external actors since the late 1980s. While the plans and visions indicate the general direction to which Uganda should be governed, the government itself has become a showcase of another political technology. This is the new instrument of development aid called *General Budget Support* (GBS). It has been applied in Uganda and in at least twenty-three other countries like Mozambique or Nicaragua in order to avoid the weakening of state institutions, itself a result of bypassing the state through donors, which had preferred for a long time to run projects with NGOs instead.[3]

Its main purpose, according to its inventors and current appliers, is however to make recipient states more efficient and more reliable, in short, to "improve governance" (Ministry NL 2012, 67). In practice, "GBS" as a policy revolves around numeric representations, particular genres of texts like tables, around reports, applications, and evaluations. Its core operation is to negotiate benchmarks, like sums devoted for certain budget items in order to direct public spending. Deviations are seen as a problem, but worse are cases where "accountability" lacks when sums vanish and expenses cannot be reconstructed.

As all interviewees involved in budget support, be it on the donor or the Ugandan government side, pointed out that budget support means a lot of bureaucratic activity. It involves personnel, offices and office buildings, meeting and negotiations on all levels, and coordinated action, and it involves scandals, as we will see later. A glimpse at the documents that are produced and negotiated in the time frame of one fiscal year might give an impression of what budget support amounts to.

"NDP, JAF, GAPR, MTBF, AFPR"—FORMAL RATIONALITY AND ITS FAILURES

The *Joint Assessment Framework* (JAF) stands in the center of negotiations between donor governments, in Uganda represented by their ambassadors and representatives of the World Bank on the one hand and the Ugandan government on the other hand. This framework is designed and agreed upon by all donors engaged in budget support and allows them to assess the Ugandan government's "performance" equivocally. Essentially, it contains a table with benchmarks and achieved results for sectors like education, water, or mining in the budget of Uganda's central government. Whether the list of categories is oriented toward the *National Development Plan* is contested among donor representatives. Some affirm this, and others bluntly reject this idea.[4] A leading employee of DFID, the British development agency, who had earlier worked as a "technical advisor" in the Ugandan *Office of the Prime Minister*, denied all relevance of the *Vision 2040* and the *National Development Plan* for the JAF.[5] Both documents were just created on pressure of donors and had caused considerable overlap between Ugandan agencies.

In 2014, the JAF contained twenty-seven indicators. A couple of years earlier, there were more than 100 indicators as more donor preferences had to be taken into consideration. Some donors give money only to certain sectors; others really do "GBS." In 2014, the fifth JAF was negotiated, which needed to be redone after a scandal (see below) had shattered government-donor relations.

The JAF refers to the AFPR, the *Annual Fiscal Performance Report*, which is produced twice a year by the Ugandan Ministry of Finance, Planning and Economic Development (MOFPED). But even this production that shall mirror the performance of Ugandan ministries is an international product: technical advisers of DFID and of USAID are placed within the Ministry of Finance and in the Office of the Prime Minister and assist as consultants in the production of this document.[6]

In APFR, the budgeted amounts are compared with effective expenditure. It is a detailed report of almost 700 pages, divided along the thirteen sectors agriculture, land tenure, housing, energy and mining, communication and technology, tourism and trade, education, health, water, environment, social development, security, law and order. All of the eighty-two ministries of Uganda are listed here, as well all other agencies that belong to the central government. Green underlines indicate expenditure as budgeted, red ones stand for overspendings.

The AFPR is at the same time the basic source for another report, the *Government Annual Performance Review* (GAPR), which is produced annually, after the end of each fiscal year by the Office of the Prime Minister, based on additional number that come from all ministries. Here as well, sums budgeted in advance are compared to those really spend. Before this review is published, there is a "retreat" of the entire cabinet with State House officials, the president's office.[7] It is here, as Ugandan officials point out, that objectives, overspending, and changes are discussed, often with a lot of controversy.[8] These discussions are the basis, according to Ugandan officials, for the governmental budget plans for the next fiscal year, which are negotated between MOFPED, Office of the Prime Minister and the State House. The general basis for these plans is, however, the *Medium Term Budgeting*

Framework (MTBF), which is produced in the Office of the Prime Minister and which lists an indexed annual value for all key titles.

Finally, donors do their own assessments, as they do it for the money they spend themselves directly, not channeled through the state's budget. For this end, they consult the *Technical Advisory Service Unit* of the World Bank, which, they say, is able to produce an assessment of the Ugandan fiscal numbers that does not depend on Ugandan statistics and government documents.[9]

Apart from the international surveillance of Uganda's budget, in 2014, sixteen years after the start of GBS, attempts were made to increase parliamentarian control of the budget. A *Public Finance Management Bill* was passed in 2015, taking effect the same year. The bill was co-designed by experts from Norway who claim to have a particular expertise in "energy governance."[10] Up until 2015, budgets were already checked by the budgetary commission of parliamentarians. There was also the parliamentary *Public Accounts Committee* (PAC), whose members use this institution for criticizing single government members for not documenting their expenses. But donor representatives doubted in interviews, however, that members of parliaments were having the competences and knowledge to supervise the government in the manner the European parliament could do it for example. Members of the PAC feel unable to follow all issues raised on the 700 pages of the Auditor General's annual report.[11]

External control and monitoring seem tight, though. But budget support in Uganda suffers repeatedly from setbacks when a major embezzlement is disguised, as it happened most dramatically in 2012. It is noteworthy that the scandalous deeds were uncovered not by donors or their personnel sitting in all high echelons of Ugandan ministries but by the Auditor General of Government, a Ugandan institution. This observation contradicts the general impression of Uganda as a thoroughly corrupt state, an image that also undergirds budget support as a technology of government aiming at the rationalization of the state.

In October 2012 the Auditor General revealed that 11.6 million USD had vanished from a budget established for the rehabilitation of the war-affected districts in the North of Uganda. Norway, Sweden, Denmark and Ireland had given huge grants to the program (PoU 2013; Irish Aid 2014). The budget was administered in the Office of the Prime Minister. As the Auditor General of Government revealed in reports to the parliament, representatives from the Office of the Prime Minister, in MOFPED and in the Bank of Uganda had colluded and used "scam accounts" to move sums forth and back so often that they believed the movements undetectable.[12] This was possible as "key controls were bypassed by the individuals who were responsible for implementing the controls" (Irish Aid 2014, 2).

In interviews and informal conversations it became clear that there is an overall agreement among donor personal that "corruption" is not only endemic in Uganda but is perceived as the decisive hindrance in creating more efficient state institutions. Almost all expatriates expressed that "corruption" was the "main problem" of Uganda, and numerous Ugandan interviewees share this view. It is less clear how to explain this pervasiveness. In rationalist accounts, corruption is explained by the information problem in principle-agent relations: "unruly agents" escape the control of superiors (cf. e.g., Simson and Welham 2014). Standard political science is fully in line here with donor policies. It strives to find solutions to the donor problems without even noticing this normative choice: that "efficient" institutions are desirable is a more or less tacit assumption shared by practical and theoretical institutionalists alike. Leading scholars in the field have now noticed that the blueprint approach of governmental reform does apparently not work. The most recent answer is more pragmatism, but not any questioning of the theoretical model: an "incremental reform" of institutions is now the new answer to decades of failed institutional reform that was just short-termed impression management and should be replaced by "problem driven iterative adaptation" (Andrews 2013).[13]

Political scientists, analysts and activists also share the view of donors that there is a lack of accountability and efficiency of aid given to Uganda. The lack of coordination of donors and "an alphabet soup of groups and frameworks," the overlapping between mandates and policies of donor groups are usually also mentioned (HRW 2013, 55). Aid agencies but also those carriers of state rationality within Ugandan agencies are all adherents of a technology of government that aims at rationalizing a social and political world that they perceive as misbehaving, deviating, corrupt. The in our view rather utopian idea is that the budget and its planning as a technology of government shall install rationality in a world that is unruly, illegal, and not structured (cf. Morcillo Laiz and Schlichte 2016). As we get down the ladder of the state and of official order, in the lower echelons of state agencies, this claim and attempt looks even less convincing and less real. Here, the budget turns into something even mysterious as we will show with regard to the Ugandan police force.

FORMAL FORMS AND CERTAIN UNCERTAINTIES—THE POLICE BUDGET

Like in any other state, Uganda's central government budget translates into thousands of sub-budgets in ministries, agencies, and finally of smallest units in each department. Like in many other states, such budgets are unstable, as budget planning comes late, numbers are not reliable, and personal meddling in the final distribution of money is frequent. The dislocation of funds, as police officers know, is not so much depending on prior earmarking but rather on the leverage single barons within the force.[14]

There are three main observations we take from our investigations within the Ugandan police force. First, there is constant uncertainty about disposable budgets, second, knowledge about general trends and patterns of budgeting does not seem to be widespread, and third, also on lower levels, external influence matters, also in terms of resources coming in. We thus see our argument confirmed here that budgeting as a technology of government is present on lower state levels as well, but its effects are limited here as well.

On demand, state agents can give full accounts of the formal procedures by which budgets are produced—as the following quote demonstrate—

> Before cabinet agrees on the budget, the committee on parliament has to agree, formally according to the law. The president presents the budget to the parliament. The budget depends on donor funding and government money. The police duty is to maintain law and order and to secure that we are safe.[15]

But in practice, it is generally difficult to assess what the exact budget of a state agency is. The translation of the government budget into thousands of sub-budget has very concrete consequences for the research about police budgets. Interestingly and although numbers and figures seem to be the basis for meetings, negotiations, and finally decisions, the search for police numbers is like fishing in turbid water. It was not so much the sensibility of the topic of police that made the research endeavor so challenging, but simply the observation that the numbers floated somewhere in the realm of police and and ministry bureaucracies, but nobody really know where they could be caught, or, as an officer in the Police Headquarters explained "the information are here. But I do not know where."[16] When the same officer, an accountant in the financial section of the Police Headquarters, asked a colleague in the Headquarters to help him finding the relevant figures, namely the police budget for the last ten years, including the actual one, his colleagues was happy to assist him because as he noted "this is even very good information for us."[17]

A member of an Ugandan NGO made the following observation:

> Police budget—it is very hard to get information about the police budget; even for us when we ask about. When you ask, they always say 'our budget is limited'. And it is not to reveal due to security purposes. Although I think they have enough money. But they cannot do their job. It is not that they don't have money. They have a reserve, I don't know how much it is. But you never know how much they have, you can get the numbers, the official numbers, but there is always something for emergency.[18]

What he meant by "emergency" became clear throughout the conversation: demonstrations and elections. It is exactly what the statistics of the police budget demonstrate. In preelection times and years the government faces riots and demonstrations, for example the "walk to work" protests in Uganda in 2011 and 2012, which were in 2011 brutally disrupted by the Ugandan police force. Among police officers, it is also stated that police budgets and personnel are often used for organizing campaign events of the ruling party, often demanding considerable sums.

A member of the British High Commission in Kampala supports this perception of a close link between police budget and political purposes in Uganda:

> To me it is a budgeting issue, when they have the budget, they increase, if not, they don't. The police always have to ask for money, they do that every year, they always complain they have too less, in pre-election the money was there.[19]

Interestingly and although figures are so hard to discover, every year the total police budget is listed in the annual report of the *Committee on Defence and Internal Affairs*.[20] According to these reports, the budget rose from approx. USD 66 million in the fiscal year 2011/2012 to approx. USD 90 million in the fiscal year 2013/2014. There is thus considerable growth of the internal security sector, and this is at least partly possible due to external support. While international donors usually are very reserved concerning answering questions about the range of monetary support for the Ugandan police, Ugandan police officials are open about explain how these processes work. On the level of single state agencies, in this case the police, international influence is present as well as aid agencies and single donors often tie grants to particular purposes:

> We use to provide sector budget support and so one of the institutions that has to benefit from this is the Ugandan police force. Austria, Dutch, they providing program support, but again to JLOS [Justice, Law and Order Sector]. All these development partners follow closely what happens across the 17 institutions that compose JLOS. Someone is looking on access to justice, someone is looking at juvenile issues. And then the democratic policing, accountabiliting and budgeting and all those. So we have this work plans among us.[21]

It is not only astonishing to see that external observers have doubts about the real function of police personnel, it is also interesting to note that there is general knowledge about the flexibility of funds and the underground working of how money is deployed and used. We interpret this as another instance of the internationalization of rule and the permeability of national boundaries. Budgeting as a technology of government seemingly is a tool that is used both by international and national actors, and this on more than one level.

FILES—THE PAPERY HEART OF THE STATE

As we have explicated above, technologies of governance are, among other elements, devices and artifacts. The devices we see being used here are different kinds of artifacts. Most visible are reports, written documents that list things and tell stories, which give an order to the world, at least in the way it is presented in these documents. The second sort of artifacts is files. In earlier work we have shown how files are produced and constitute something like the lifeblood of the Ugandan police force (Biecker and Schlichte 2015), and similar claims are plausible for other state agencies, in Uganda and elsewhere. Such artifacts are products of the state, they are created with a purpose, but they develop a life of their own. Typically, in modern bureaucratic organizations, the handling of files, the establishment of registers and reports, becomes the actual organizational goal while the original purpose of why all the busy activities are undertaken is often forgotten or has become folklore.

In this chapter we refer to artifacts of paperwork and take the examples of police documents in Uganda in order to demonstrate how they produce the state. Files are symbols of modern bureaucracies, they are the central technology of bureaucracy, or even more files *are* (the materialization of) bureaucracy. The Ugandan police are one of the institutions where the dominance of paper becomes very visible—not only in their daily life, but also in the much broader context of number and figure politics of the state.

Files play very different roles within the policing realm in Uganda, but at the same time they have a much more "global" meaning because they are the basis of every national crime statistic, which is then the basis for international programs and negotiations about these cooperation and programs, respectively. In this sense the link between files and budgets, although invisible at first sight, is very strong. The budget for the Justice, Law and Order Sector [JLOS], for example, is based on figures about crimes in Uganda—not exclusively of course, but partially. The Ugandan police as well as international actors in Uganda use these crime figures to prepare, negotiate, and implement cooperation and programs.

Every police station in Uganda has to report its crime numbers monthly to the Police Headquarters, and it has to document them for its own records. In the everyday bureaucratic police life, this means that officers start to translate their cases into numbers. Station books are translated into figures.[22] This translation practice is a two-officers-job: one is reading out the crime, which is already categorized, for example, in theft, housebreak, murder, the other officer keeps a tally. After finishing the tally sheet one officer translates this sheet into a huge sheet of paper, which is one of the main of more than 100 official police forms—the monthly crime incident summary. This translation act happens twice: the station keeps one sheet, the other one is sent to the Police Headquarters. Since records officers only rarely use computers or any other technical devises, except their mobile phones, every paper sheet is handwritten. After one year, all sheets are translated again—this time into police form 2—the annual crime incident summary.

Immersing into the daily life of a police bureaucracy has the potential to recover details, which would be totally invisible without participant observation. Reading only a police budget, for example, would never explain from where the numbers come and how they were produced. Numbers are simply not sufficient in order to explain the life beyond figures, police and budget bureaucracies, their relations and connections. With reference to Weber, Matthew Hull observes "writing establishes the stable relation between words and things necessary for bureaucracies" (Hull 2003, 256; see also Hull 2012). Our empirical research in Uganda totally highlights this relation. Written words create things, for example, budget plans, reports, or police files. However the relation is not limited to words and things, but writing also establishes a strong relation between words and practices as our research demonstrates.

Nevertheless, the practice of translation within the Ugandan police starts much earlier; the translation of cases into numbers is one of the last steps in this process. The starting point of all "chains of translation" (Latour 1999, 91) is at the counter where an orally told story is translated into a case and finally into a file. It is the moment when clients come to the police station, go to the counter, and tell their experiences to the counter officer. This officer makes a first translation, namely the translation of an orally told story—and often physically experienced incident—into written words, which is the entrance of the station diary. With this entrance, the officers decide whether the story becomes a "case." The counter officer then transfers the clients to her colleagues in the CID[23] or traffic offices, where further documentary takes place. The translation continues: the story now becomes a case and finally a file when the responsible officer writes down the statement and files this paper into a red folder. Against this background, the counter has a particular meaning within the policing realm in Uganda. It is a not only the first contact point for every civilian who enters a police station, but the counter is very literally a border—for people as well as stories. Not all people can cross the counter and enter the station's offices, and not all stories become cases bundled into a file. Thus, police work, as well as police research, has a lot to do with border crossing. Here again, ethnography plays a crucial and double role within police research. First, ethnography enables the researcher to understand the counter as a border and second, it is exactly this approach, which creates the necessary trust so that the police allow the researcher to cross the border and to continue research on aspects of police work that otherwise remained hidden.

The observations of and at the counter of police stations in Uganda uncover the usually hidden processes within a bureaucracy, and they uncover the relations between people and numbers; between the police, clients, and international actors; between stories, cases, figures, and numbers. It shows how files of the Ugandan police are translated into international politics by being a basis for different kinds of international programs.

While the translation of files into numbers and figures demonstrates the paperwork's journey out of the police, the documents have another life, which develops within the police and shows how bureaucratic power is much more a play and negotiations between different actors than a one-side phenomenon. Bureaucracies are powerful, but the Ugandan example shows impressively that this power is less based on the institution per se, but much more on different actors and their capabilities and possibilities to use their power. While it is the police who record the story, translate it into a case and finally a file, it is clients who decide to report their cases to the police at all. Knowing about the power of documents, some clients in Uganda use files in order to threaten others by "opening up a file at the police" (cf. Veit and Biecker forthcoming). Conflicts within families or between neighbors or business people, for example, can be "institutionalized" by decision of single persons. "Clients" of the police dispose of quite some discretion in making use of the police and are able to influence procedures by a myriad of tactics.

What this excursion into the world of files, the lifeblood of any bureaucracy shows, is how deeply internationalized and at the same time contextual core state activities can be. The creation of professional police forces has become a core feature of states in general, and police cooperation has turned this field into one of intense exchange, mutual training, joint information gathering, and planification. And yet, as the ethnography of policing in Uganda shows, there are limits to the reach of these universalized schemes of internationalized domination.

TECHNOLOGY AND (OR) SOCIETY?

Why is the ethnography of documents, statistics and numbers helpful in order to approach politics in Uganda and what do we learn here about international politics that we did not know before? Firstly, in this chapter, we have argued that such studies reveal how not only bureaucratic representations are part of technologies of government, a concept that we want to promote for the study of internationalized politics. Secondly, we may assume that the analysis of such documents, of their structure but also of their handling by carrier groups of governmental technologies, constitutes this international space at the same time. Number, statistics, "immutable mobiles" to quote Latour (1987; 2005), are tools for the production of comparisons, of measurements which as intellectual operations are integral to any attempt to rule the world.

We admit that we did not discover anything new but just applied older insights in new scales. Following Didier's interpretation of Gabriel Tarde's work on statistics, statistics do not reduce the world into simple categories (Didier 2010, 208). On the contrary, the production of figures is a creative endeavor, something is produced and added (Didier 2010, 208). Through the numerification of politics materialized in statistics and budgets, we uncover "series of similarities" (Didier 2010: 309) of internationalized actions. However, while we agree that the production of figures is a process of additions and subtractions, of negotiations even, we understand this "creative endeavor" with clear limitations. Statistics are also codifications, and, following Pierre Bourdieu, codifications are formalizations—attempts of rationalizations (Bourdieu 2011, 108)—not aiming at creativity and improvisations, but at accountability and predictability.

Long before Science and Technologies Studies emerged, Max Weber and Michel Foucault demonstrated the importance and significance of numerical codes for governmental constructions and mechanics. Statistics and power are closely linked. In our chapter, we followed this path by focusing on budget politics, numbers, and statistics. We understand this numerification as embodiment of international politics. Actions of both sides, Ugandan and international, are translated into numbers. They are the materialization of power that aspires to "dominate everything by means of calculation" (Weber 2012, 342). This process of numerification can be described in Latour's terms as "chains of translations" (Latour 2002, 40). Actions of budget support are translated into numbers. Results of attempts of domination in negotiations become literally visible in numerical state statistics.

Our ethnography of budget support and police files in Uganda has, however, also shown that there are limits to the effectiveness of such technologies of government. The deviation of government spending from the stipulated plan, the constant irritation about the "real numbers" about the budget in Uganda's police force, or the leverage that citizens have on the dealing with files by the police—all these instances show that technologies of government do not equal total domination. There is leeway for other all actors involved, and the deviation from the model is presumably the reason for the constant application and innovation of further technologies.

We see several lessons in our exemplary presentation of government technologies. First is a lesson for our understandings of states. States are not just produced internally, but also through ascriptions from outside— states are produced through practices of signification, through categories and indicators, through language games and "façon de parler." Second, this production includes the personnel, the trained staff, the carrier groups of administrators and policy implementers. "Subjects produce themselves by administrating themselves, by feed-back effects of their own action" (Vismann 2011, 235, our translation). The budget with its stipulations, and all the practices of reporting and evaluating, earmarking and correcting, planning, etc. seems to constitute a field of meanings to which the actors can relate professionally, and this field tends to be global. The spread of the form of statehood seems to be linked to the global advancement of related technologies of government.

A second lesson can be drawn concerning the applicability of this concept. It is still to be explored. Policing, administrating people, formal education and the steering of health or any other policy could be studied under that angle as well, producing new insights about global entanglements, without falling into the traps of functionalism as "governance" models do. However, not any political activity is automatically part of a technology of government, and a next step might consist of studying technologies of opposition, the art of resistance, as well. With the global spread of practices like occupying city squares and mobilization in international forums through "social" media, we have enough reason to assume that such technologies have been internationalized as well.

And finally, our contribution has hopefully shown that an ethnographic approach is not an exotic and foreign idea for creating yet another "turn" in the field of IR. Instead, what we can gain by immersion and by going new ways of gathering data and reflecting our research, is a new reading of the world we live in and in which we might need to develop even more skeptical and critical perspectives to question what is usually taken for granted.

NOTES

1. Field research on which this chapter is based was funded by Deutsche Forschungsgemeinschaft in the framework of the Priority Program "Adaptation and Creativity in Africa." It was carried out in several stays between 2011 and 2018 in Uganda.

2. Interview with an official from the *National Planning Authority*, Kampala, February 2014. Uganda is in no regard particular here. Kazakhstan has a *Strategiya 2030*, Rwanda a *Vision 2020*, and even Germany had an *Agenda 2010*.

3. Despite the image of innovation that surrounded General Budget Support, this practice is not really new. Single donors, notably France in Mali, Niger, and other countries, have often directly supplemented government budgets in Africa since the 1970s. What is new is the highly bureaucratized form in which this is done.

4. Donor ideas do not necessarily coincide with national or local government preferences. A Chief Administrative Officer from a Ugandan district describes his view in these words: "for them they say we are financing education, primary health

care, agriculture, water. So then the government will be forced to go by what these people have dictated on us to do and then they also pass over the same dictatorship to LG [Local Government, KS] and tell them these are the priorities that we want you to implement. Moreover, they also say, we are sending you a technical expert" (Chief Administrative Officer, July 25, 2012, quoted after Ayeko-Kümmeth 2014,163). Presumptuous attitudes of donors are resented by the head of state, Yoweri Museveni, as well: "donors should not tie development assistance to demands for better governance and democracy. Donor aid should come in areas where Uganda needs development, not in governance. I am already an expert in governance. Who can again lecture me on governance?" (quoted after Kobusingye 2010, 84). On the occasion of the opening of a five-level underground parking for Members of Parliament, President Museveni was applauded for saying "the mentality of 'donorism' which some Ugandans have been suffering from—'nothing can be done before the donors give us the money'—will soon be no more," (New Vision, November 8, 2013). After being declared the winner of the 2016 presidential elections he declared, "I love those foreigners. But I never accept foreigners to give me orders about Uganda—all about anything in the world. They have their own countries to run, let them go and run them" (https://www.youtube.com/watch?v=d5wikGU4jgs). Meanwhile, Ugandan journalists also report about poverty and human rights issues in the United States (cf. Mwenda 2019).

5. Interview February 27, 2014, Kampala, KS.

6. Interview with head of a European governmental aid agency, February 26, 2014, Kampala, KS.

7. Interview with official from MOFPED Planning Unit, February 19, 2014, Kampala, KS.

8. Interview with DFID official, February 27, 2014, Kampala, KS.

9. Interview with European "Head of Coordination," February 13, 2014, Kampala, KS.

10. Interview with Scandinavian diplomat, October 4, 2012, Maputo. From 2006 onward several oil reserves were discovered in Western Uganda. Due to immediate regulatory disputes between the Ugandan government and international oil companies, revenues are not expected before 2020.

11. "They overwhelm us." Interview with former chairman of the committee, March 11, 2016, KS.

12. For details see the report of *Public Accounts Committee* of the Ugandan parliament (PoU 2013).

13. The criticism, however, exists since more than twenty years, cf. Hibou (1996).

14. Interview with two high-ranking police officers, Kampala, March 20, 2016, KS.

15. First Secretary Ministry of Internal Affairs, Kampala, January 22, 2013, SB.

16. Interview Assistant Commissioner Accounts, Police Headquarters, Kampala, November, 27, 2012, SB.

17. Interview Police Headquarters, Kampala, November 27, 2012, SB.

18. Interview with member of a Ugandan Human Rights NGO, Kampala, January 22, 2013, SB.

19. Interview British High Commission, Kampala, January 17, 2013, SB.

20. Figures from the Annual reports of the Committee of Defence and Internal Affairs from the years 2011 to 2014.

21. Interview Irish Embassy, Kampala, December 11, 2012, SB.

22. The following is based on field observations between 2012 and 2014 in different police stations in Uganda, due to the topic's sensitivity, all places and names are withheld (SB).

23. CID is the Criminal Investigation Directorate of the Ugandan police.

BIBLIOGRAPHY

Akcan, Esra. *Architecture in Translation: Germany, Turkey and the Modern House.* Durham, London: Duke University Press, 2012.

Andrews, Matt. *The Limits of Institutional Reform in Development. Changing Rules for Realistic Solutions.* Cambridge, Mass.: Cambridge University Press, 2013.

Aradau, Claudia, and Jef Huysmans. "Critical Methods in International Relations: The Politics of Techniques, Devices and Acts." *European Journal of International Relations* 20(2014): 596–619.

Ayeko-Kümmeth, Jane. The Politics of Public Decisions in Local Government in Uganda. PhD Dissertation, Bayreuth: University of Bayreuth, 2014.

Beck, Kurt, Gabriel Klaeger, and Michael Stasik. *The Making of the African Road.* Leiden: Brill, 2017.

Biecker, Sarah, and Klaus Schlichte. "Between Governance and Domination—The Everyday Life of Uganda's Police Forces." In *The Politics of Governance: The State in Africa Reconsidered* edited by Lucy Koechlin, and Till Förster, 93–114. New York: Routledge, 2015.

Bijker, Wiebe E., Thomas P. Hughes, and Trevor J. Pinch. *The Social Construction of Technological Systems. New Directions in the Sociology and History of Technology.* Cambridge, Mass.: MIT Press, 1993.

Boltanski, Luc, and Laurent Thévenot. *De la justification. Les economies de la grandeur.* Paris: Gallimard, 1991.

Bourdieu, Pierre. *Rede und Antwort*, 3rd ed. Frankfurt am Main: Suhrkamp, 2011.

Callon, Michel. "Society in the Making: The Study of Technology as a Tool for Sociological Analysis." In *The Social Construction of Technological Systems. New Directions in the Sociology and History of Technology,* edited by Wiebe E. Bijker, Thomas P. Hughes, and Trevor J. Pinch, 77–97. Cambridge, Mass.: MIT Press, 2012.

Castoriadis, Cornelius. *The Imaginary Institution of Society.* Harvard, Mass.: MIT Press, 1975.

Cerwonka, Allaine, and Liisa H. Malkki. *Improvising Theory. Process and Temporality in Ethnographic Fieldwork,* Chicago and London: University of Chicago Press, 2007.

Didier, Emmanuel. *Gabriel Tarde and Statistical Movement. Social After Gabriel Tarde.* London: Routledge, 2010.

Ferguson, James. *The Anti-Politics Machine. 'Development', Depoliticization and Bureaucratic Power in Lesotho.* Cambridge, Mass.: Cambridge University Press, 1990.

Heintz, Bettina. "Numerische Differenz. Überlegungen zu einer Soziologie des (quantitativen) Vergleichs." *Zeitschrift für Soziologie* 39 (2010): 162–81.

Hibou, Béatrice. *L'Afrique est-elle protectionniste? Les chemins boussoniers de la liberalisation extérieure.* Paris: Karthala, 1996.

HRW (Human Rights Watch). "Letting the Big Fish Swim". Failures to Prosecute High Level Corruption in Uganda, Washington, DC: Human Rights Watch and Allard K. Loewenstein International Human Rights Clinique at Yale Law School, 2013. (http://www.hrw.org/sites/default/files/reports/uganda1013_ForUpload_1. pdf, accessed January 10, 2018).

Hull, Matthew S. "The File: Agency, Authority, and Autography in an Islamabad Bureaucracy." *Language & Communication* 23(2003): 287–314.

Hull, Matthew S. "Documents and Bureaucracy."*Annual Review of Anthropology* 41(2012): 251–67.

Hurd, Ian. "Legitimacy and Authority in International Relations." *International Organization* 53 (1999): 379–408.

Kobusingye, Olive. *The Correct Line? Uganda under Museven.* Milton Keynes: AuthorHouse, 2010.

Lake, David. *Hierarchy in International Relations.* Ithaca, NY: Cornell UP, 2009.

Latour, Bruno. *Science in Action: How to Follow Scientist and Engineers through Society.* Cambridge: Harvard University Press, 1987.

Latour, Bruno. *Pandora's Hope. Essays on the Reality of Science Studies.* Cambridge, Mass.: Harvard University Press, 1999.

Latour, Bruno. "Zirkulierende Referenz. Bodenstichproben aus dem Urwald am Amazonas." In *Die Hoffnung der Pandora,* edited by *Bruno Latour, 36-95.* Frankfurt am Main: Suhrkamp, 2002.

Latour, Bruno. *Reassembling the Social. An Introduction to Actor-Network-Theory.* Oxford: UP, 2005.

Leese, Matthias. "The New Profiling: Algorithms, Black Boxes, and the Failure of Anti-discriminatory Safeguards in the European Union." *Security Dialogue*45 (2014): 494–511.

Ministry NL (Ministery of Foreign Affairs of the Netherlands). "Budget Support: Conditional results." IOB Evaluation no. 369, The Hague, 2012.

Morcillo Laiz, Álvaro, and Klaus Schlichte. "Rationality and International Domination: Revisiting Max Weber." *International Political Sociology* 10 (2016): 168–84.

Mwenda, Andrew. "America's Human Rights imperialism." *The Independent (Kampala)* September 23, 2019.

NPA, National Planning Autority. 2010: *National Development Plan (2010/11-2014/15).* Kampala: NPA, 2010.

Parliament of the Republic of Uganda. Report of the Committee on Defence and Internal Affairs on the Ministerial Policy Statements and Budget Estimates for the Fiscal Year 2012/2013, Kampala, 2012.

Parliament of the Republic of Uganda. Report of the Committee on Defence and Internal Affairs on the Ministerial Policy Statements and Budget Estimates for the Fiscal Year 2013/2014, Kampala, 2013.

Porter, Theodor M. *Trust in Numbers. The Pursuit of Objectivity in Science and Public Life.* Princeton, NJ: Princeton University Press, 1995.

PoU, Parliament of Uganda, Public Accounts Committee. Special Audit Investigation into Allegation of Financial Impropriety in the Office of the Prime Minister OPM, Kampala, 2013.

Rancière, Jacques. *Disagreement. Politics and Philosophy.* Minneapolis, Mn.: University of Minnesota Press, 2004.

Rottenburg, Richard. *Far-Fetched Facts. A Parable of Development Aid.* Cambridge, Mass.: MIT Press, 2009.

Rottenburg, Richard, and Sally M. Engle. "Introduction: Why another contribution to metrology?" In *The World of Indicators: The Making of Governmental Knowledge Through Quantification*, edited by Richard Rottenburg and Sally M. Engle, 1–33. Cambridge: Cambridge University Press, 2015.

Sande Lie, Jon Harald. "Challenging Anthropology: Anthropological reflections on the ethnographic turn in international relations." *Millenium* 41 (2013): 201–20.

Sande Lie, Jon Harald. *Developmentality. An Ethnography of the World-Bank-Uganda Partnership.* New York: Berghahn, 2015.

Schlichte, Klaus. Uganda's Budget and Kampala's Houses. On architecture as a sign of internationalized rule.2017. >http://trafo.hypotheses.org/6753< (accessed January 21, 2018).

Schouten, Peer. "Security as Controversy: Reassembling Security at Amsterdam Airport." *Security Dialogue* 45 (2014): 23–45.

Simson, Rebecca, and Bryn Welham. "Incredible Budgets. Budget Credibility in Theory and Practice." 400. *Working and Discussion Papers*, London: Overseas Development Institute, 2014.

Thelen, Tatjana, Larissa Vetters, and Kebet von Benda-Beckmann, "Introduction to Stategraphy. Toward a Relational Anthropology of the State." *Social Analysis* 59 (2014): 1–19.

Thompson, Gardner. *Governing Uganda. British Colonial Rule and Its Legacy.* Kampala: Fountain Publisher, 2003.

van Dülmen, Richard. *Entstehung der frühneuzeitlichen Europa 1550–1648, Fischer Weltgeschichte*, vol. 24. Frankfurt a.M.: Fischer, 1992.

Veit, Alex, and Sarah Biecker. forthcoming: *Love or Crime? Law-making and the policing of teenage sexuality in Uganda and the Democratic Republic of Congo.*

Vismann, Cornelia. *Files. Law and Media Technology.* California: Stanford: Stanford University Press, 2008.

Vismann, Cornelia. *Akten. Medientechnik und Recht.* Frankfurt am Main: Fischer, 2011.

Weber Max. "Science as a Profession and Vocation.", in: Sam Whimster and Hans Henrik Bruun (eds.), Hans Henrik Bruun (trans.), *Max Weber. Collected Methodological Writings*, London and New York: Routledge, 335–353.

Yanow, Dvora 2009: What's Political About Political Ethnography? Abducting Our Way Toward Reason and Meaning, in: *Qualitative & Multi-Method Research. Newsletter of the American Political Science Association Organized Section for Qualitative and Multi-Method Research*, 7(2), 33–37.

Zürn, Michael 2018: A *Theory of Global Governance. Authority, Legitimacy, and Contestation*, Cambridge, Mass.: Cambridge University Press.

Afterword

Jean-Pierre Oliver de Sardan

ANTHROPOLOGY AND POLITICAL SCIENCE: LOVE MARRIAGE, MARRIAGE OF CONVENIENCE, OR *MÉNAGE À QUATRE*?

The long history of the relationship between political science and anthropology is woven with misunderstandings and missed appointments. It is a matter of "I love you, neither do I." In addition to mutual ignorance, fostered by academic boundaries and career management, the interference between these two disciplines has not always been happy. The introduction of culturalism in political science is an example of this: it is a scientific ideology typical of anthropology, which favors unanimity, homogeneity, shared values, collective identity, forgetting that in any social group, contradictions, mistrust, struggles for influence, discordances, and rivalry also prevail. In the other direction, anthropology has sometimes borrowed from political science and political philosophy an abstract and all-embracing focus on power and domination that has brought it closer to rhetoric and further away from empirical investigations.

But this book finally offers us a happy ending: "They were happy and had many doctoral students." In the wedding basket, political science brings its privileged themes (state, public policies, international organizations), anthropology brings its methods (immersion, free interviews, observation).

This combination constitutes what can be called a "winning formula." Schlichte, Biecker, and their colleagues demonstrate in a particularly convincing and sometimes even enthusiastic way how the study of international relations (but this applies to political science as a whole) has everything to gain from benefiting from anthropology's methodological contributions. The main characteristics of this methodology are known: an approach that is attentive to everyday life, aimed at understanding the "actor's point of view" (thinking like a native), quick to unveil the informal behind the formal, the effective practices behind the prescribed practices, the private discourse behind the public words, the routines behind the facades, or, as Goffman would have said, the backstage behind the front stage. Contrary to widespread opinion, intensive field research (often called "ethnography") is subject to strong methodological constraints that guarantee its empirical validity: there is a "rigor of the qualitative" (Olivier de Sardan 2015). One aspect of this rigor is based on methodological eclecticism: anthropology combines several modes of data production; it intersects and "triangulates" discursive, bio-graphical, observational, and documentary information.

Intensive field research also has a major advantage specific to the study of international public policies (and in particular development policies): it makes it possible to document the "test of the contexts" (the confrontation with the contexts, which often turns into the "revenge of contexts"), in other words how a standardized public policy, when implemented in various con-texts, is circumvented, dismembered, or bypassed by multiple stakeholders and various actors in the field (Olivier de Sardan 2019). Ethnography is typi-cally context-oriented; as Schlichte and Biecker put it in their introduction to this volume, it allows "to get into the hermeneutics of a context."

But anthropology also benefits from the winning formula: it is a win-win exchange. Indeed, political science helps it to get out of its primitivist, and traditionalist drifts. It enables it to renew its research objects (less kinship, rituals, myths, segmental societies, and more organizations, bureaucracies, governance, development, power relations, mobility).

There were precursors, of course. We can't list them all, and we will limit ourselves to mentioning the anthropology of organizations (see Bate 1997) on the one hand, and George Bailey (1969) on the other, both being fre-quently forgotten. But it is relatively recently that a phenomenon of positive convergence between political science and anthropology has taken shape, which this book reflects and helps to develop. Africa has been the privileged (but not exclusive) terrain for this. For anthropologists, it is the interest of Africanist researchers in development that has been the triggering factor (see, for instance, Bierschenk 1988; Olivier de Sardan 2005). Development anthropology has become an "arena-centered anthropology" rather than a "group-centered anthropology," which it was for a long time, and is still to a large extent. In other words, the heroes of the research have become mul-tiple, diverse, often contradictory, belonging to different strategic groups: developers and "developees," field actors and international experts, senior civil servants and street-level bureaucrats. Similarly, development anthro-pology has become interested in the "drifts" between development projects on paper and their implementation in the field, thus joining implementation studies by bringing them the added value of its method. An anthropology centered on arenas and an anthropology of implementation gaps are a demonstration (among many others) that the ethnographic method can perfectly well leave the exotic terrains and the monographic perspective to function on very different objects, at the price of certain adjustments ("How to Study Bureaucracies Ethnographically," Bierschenk & Olivier de Sardan 2019).

On the side of political scientists, it is the conversion to intensive field investigation that has been the major innovation, particularly visible over the last ten years or so in many PhD theses devoted to Africa written by political science students, whose quality sometimes makes their fellow anthropologists admire or envy them. This book is another example.

But this honeymoon, like all honeymoons, takes place in an uncertain, sometimes hostile, sometimes ambiguous environment. The winning formula is such only for a minority of political scientists and a minority of anthropologists. The dominant currents in each discipline do not want it: either because obsession with quantitative comparativism in political science or because anthropologists wanting to keep a monopoly on ethnography and to preserve the ineffable character of personal diving into exotic lands.

Another threat is counterfeits and cheap copies. Thus, from the point of view of method, the ethnographic approach has sometimes been reduced to quick and superficial techniques, fast-food type surveys. This is what Schlichte and Biecker reproach the so-called "ethnographic turn" in political science: immersion has been forgotten in favor of few quick interviews and focus groups. The same could be said of the approach which, in development studies, refers to itself by the ambitious and somewhat misleading name of "political economy": under this label, consultants trained in political science intend to draw up a general picture of a problem on the basis of qualitative data collected in an expeditious manner by subcontracting the data collection to local assistants. But everyone has to sweep in front of their door: anthropologists themselves sometimes abandon prolonged insertion into the field in favor of anecdotal investigations. Methodological vigilance is never acquired and knows no disciplinary boundaries.

The metaphor of a happy marriage between anthropology and political science (or its subset of international relations studies) also comes up against a limit, that of the profound unity of the social sciences. History and sociology in particular must also be included. All inquiry-based social sciences (as opposed to hermeneutic sciences on the one hand and experimental sciences on the other) share the same epistemology, which is very clearly defined by Jean-Claude Passeron's (2006) "neo-Weberian" analysis: they all have in common that they are plunged throughout history, that they have a regime of evidence based on plausibility (and not falsifiability), that they are not nomological, that they use empirically indexed concepts, that they adopt approaches that are as little normative as possible, that they reason in natural language.

Therefore, beyond the winning formula between anthropologists and politicians, we must also make room for our fellow historians and sociologists (and if possible economists, but many of the latter have locked themselves up in fortifications that are inaccessible to us). Each particular discipline (a relatively artificial product of academic vagaries and academic power relations) is only one element of a vast and unique social science based on inquiry (a relatively coherent producer of argumentative knowledge investigating small bits of social space-time). Of course, each discipline has its preferred themes, references, and methods, inherited from the past. But all of them have an interest in borrowing as much as possible from their neighbors.

But then one realizes that it is data production techniques that constitute the main internal dividing line in the social sciences (rather than disciplinary boundaries), with a relatively constant division between quantitative and qualitative methods that in fact cuts across all disciplines. These two methodological registers imply different modes of data production, different techniques, different regimes of evidence. Within qualitative methods, ethnographic-type investigation occupies a central place, and works mainly on interactions and cases, and, more generally, on the study of pragmatic contexts (focused on actors, their arrangement, their logics, their repertoires of norms). The qualitative side of history does the same, as, for instance, micro-history (Lévi 1991). Within quantitative methods, statistics and questionnaires dominate, and function mainly on variables, which make it possible to describe structural contexts, in a language of representativeness and occurrences.

Obviously, mixed methods should make it possible to combine the respective advantages of the two registers, and undoubtedly constitute the future of social sciences. But the road to achieving this, although paved with good intentions, is not as easy as it seems, and the current hegemony of quantitative methods in the world of economics, management, public policy, international relations, and the media is not the least obstacle. Any progress in qualitative methods (and this book is a significant step in that direction) should therefore be seen not as a revenge of the small against the big, but as a step toward a finally egalitarian collaboration between quantitative and qualitative methods.

If this transdisciplinary cleavage between methods is unquestionable, what about concepts? Don't disciplines still have strong conceptual identities that can serve as boundaries? This may have been true in the past (anthropology had the potlatch when sociology had the norms and political science had the state), but everyone can see the extent to which concepts circulate today, regardless of the discipline from which they originate or the cultural area that gave birth to them. Nevertheless, certain de facto cleavages remain, especially two of them, "empirically rooted concept" versus "general and abstract concept," "concepts referring to the North" versus "concepts referring to the South." The most abstract concepts enjoy more favor and reputation than concepts "close to experience" (Geertz 1986: 73), "medium-range" theories (Merton 1968), or "grounded theories" (Glaser & Strauss 1973), and that is a pity. As a result, philosophy, whose concepts are the most general/abstract and least empirically weighted, has often served as favored references for many social scientists, particularly through the mediation of political science. But anthropology, despite its more empirical vocation, has not always escaped such a philosophical seduction, far from that. Similarly, concepts produced from the North are clearly more popular among researchers than concepts produced from the South, and this too is a pity. For both can be productive outside their preferred area (Comaroff & Comaroff 2012), especially when considering states and public policies (Bierschenk & Olivier de Sardan 2014).

In other words, if the study of international relations now benefits from anthropology's methodological contribution, it can also benefit from its conceptual contribution just as anthropology can benefit from political science (cf. Bierschenk & Olivier de Sardan 1997). Concepts emanating from anthropology of development and public policies, such as strategic groups (Bierschenk 1988), practical norms (Olivier de Sardan 2015), sedimentation (Bierschenk 2014), multi-accountability (Blundo 2015), can fruitfully be combined with concepts emanating from political sciences, such as politics from below (Bayart 1981), street-level bureaucrats (Lipsky 1980), limited statehood (Risse 2017), technology of governments (Biecker & Schlichte 2020). The same applies to history and sociology.

We therefore need to change the formulation of the winning formula. It is the combination of the objects of political science and the methods of anthropology, but within a framework extended to history and sociology, the long-term perspective of a development of mixed methods, and a mutual circulation of medium-range concepts and grounded theories coming from all cultural areas.

REFERENCES

Bailey, Frederick. *Stratagems and Spoils*. London: Basil Blackwell, 1969.

Bate, Paul S. "Whatever Happened to Organizational Anthropology? A Review of the Field of Organizational Ethnography and Anthropological Studies." *Human Relations* 50 (1997): 1147–75.

Bayart, Jean-Francois. "Le Politique par le Bas en Afrique Noire." *Politique Africaine* 1 (1981): 53–83.

Bierschenk, Thomas. "Development Projects as anAarena of Negotiation for Strategic Groups. A Case Study from Bénin." *Sociologia Ruralis* 28(1988): 146–60.

Bierschenk, Thomas. "Sedimentation, Fragmentation and Normative Double-Binds in (West) African Public Services." In Bierschenk, *States at Work. The Dynamics of African Bureaucracies*, edited by Thomas Birschenk, and Jean-Pierre Olivier de Sardan. Leyden: Brill, 2014.

Bierschenk, Thomas, and Jean-Pierre Olivier de Sardan. "ECRIS: Rapid Collective Inquiry for the Identification of Conflicts and Strategic Groups." *Human Organization* 56(1997): 238–44.

Bierschenk, Thomas, and Jean-Pierre Olivier de Sardan. "Studying the Dynamics of African Bureaucracies. An Introduction to States at Work." In *States at Work. The Dynamics of African Bureaucracies*, edited by Thomas Bierschenk, and Jean-Pierre Olivier de Sardan. Leyden: Brill, 2014.

Bierschenk, Thomas, and Jean-Pierre Olivier de Sardan. "How to Study Bureaucracies Ethnographically." *Critique of Anthropology* 39(2019): 243–57.

Blundo, Giorgio. "The King is not a Kinsman. Multiple Accountabilities and Practical Norms in West African Bureaucracies." In *Real Governance and Practical Norms in Sub-Saharan Africa. The Game of the Rules*, edited by Tom De Herdt, and Jean-Pierre Olivier de Sardan. London: Routledge, 2015.

Comaroff, Jean, and John Comaroff. *Theory from the South, or How Euro-America is Evolving Toward Africa*. Boulder: Paradigm Press, 2012.

Geertz, Clifford. *Savoir Local, Savoir Global. Les Lieux du Savoir*. Paris: PUF, 1986.

Glaser, Barney, & Anselm L. Strauss . *The Discovery of Grounded Theory. Strategies for Qualitative Research*. Chicago: Eldin, 1973.

Levi, Giovanni. "On Micro-history." In *New Perspectives on Historical Writings*, edited by Peter Burke. Cambridge: Cambridge University Press, 1991.

Lipsky, Michael. *Street-Level Bureaucracy: Dilemma of the Individual in Public Services*. New-York: Russel-Sage Foundation, 1980.

Merton, Robert. *Social Theory and Social Structure*. New York: Free Press, 1968.

Olivier de Sardan, Jean.P. 2005 *Anthropology and Development. Understanding Contemporary Social Change*. London: Zed Books.

Olivier de Sardan, Jean-Pierre. *Epistemology, Fieldwork and Anthropology*. Palgrave, 2015.

Olivier de Sardan, Jean-Pierre. "Practical Norms: Informal Regulations within Public Bureaucracies (in Africa and Beyond)." In *Real Governance and Practical Norms in Sub-Saharan Africa. The Game of the Rules*, edited by Tom De Herdt, and Jean-Pierre Olivier de Sardan. London: Routledge, 2015.

Olivier de Sardan, Jean-Pierre. "Miracle Mechanisms, Travelling Models and the Revenge of the Contexts. Cash Transfer Programmes: A Textbook Case." In *Cash Transfers in Context. An Anthropological Perspective*, edited by Jean-Pierre Olivier de Sardan, and Emmanuelle Piccoli. Oxford: Berghahn Books, 2018.

Passeron, Jean. C. *Le Raisonnement Sociologique. Un Espace Non-poppÈrien de Líargumentation*. Paris: Albin Michel, 2006.

Risse, Thomas (ed). *Governance Without a State. Policies and Politics in Areas of Limited Statehood*. New York: Columbia University Press, 2011.

Index

About the Contributors

Jessica L. Anderson is an adjunct professor at the Elliot School of International Affairs, George Washington University, Washington, DC. She has carried out extensive field research in Somalia (Puntland) and is a democracy fellow in Conflict, Fragility, and Peacebuilding, USAID. She has worked at the International Organization for Migration, Oxfam, and the South African Human Rights Commission.

Sarah Biecker is a research fellow at the University of Bremen, Germany. Currently she is working on female perspectives on policing in Northern Uganda. She was guest researcher at the University of Witwatersrand in Johannesburg and worked extensively on questions of policing, bureaucracy, and power. She conducted field research in Rwanda, Uganda, and Germany.

Christian Bueger is a professor of international relations in the Department of Politics and International Relations, Cardiff University, UK. He is an honorary professor of the University of Seychelles and has held positions as visiting fellow at the University College London, at the National University of Singapore, and at the University of Copenhagen. He is a coeditor of the *European Journal of International Security*. He coauthored with Frank Gadinger *International Practice Theory* (2nd edition 2018 [2014]).

Tessa Diphoorn is an assistant professor at the Department of Cultural Anthropology at Utrecht University, Netherlands. She is currently working on a research project on police reform and oversight in Kenya. She previously conducted research on security and policing in South Africa and Kenya and published *Twilight Policing: Private Security and Violence in Urban South Africa* (2016). She is also the coeditor of *Security Blurs: The Politics* *of Pluralized Security Provision* (2019) and her work was also published by *Journal of Contemporary Ethnography, Policing and Society, Theoretical Criminology, Medical Anthropology,* and *British Journal of Criminology.*

Julian Eckl is a research fellow at the Department for Political Science of the University of Hamburg, Germany. He has won the Teaching Award of his university for a seminar on "Ethnography in International Relations." His research has been published in *Global Health Governance, Medical Anthropology, Global Social Policy, Third World Quarterly,* and *International Political Sociology.*

Sophia Hoffmann is currently leading a Young Scholar Research Group on "Learning Intelligence: the Exchange of Secret Service Knowledge between Germany and the Arab Middle East" at the "Zentrum Moderner Orient" in Berlin, Germany. Previously, she spent ten years studying migration and humanitarian aid in Syria and its neighboring states. Her book *Iraqi Migrants in Syria: The Crisis Before the Storm,* published in 2016 by Syracuse University Press, draws on several years of ethnographic research in Damascus. Her research is also published in *Refuge: Canada's Journal on Refugees, International Journal of Middle East Studies, Security Dialogue,* and *Peripherie.*

Kai Koddenbrock is a postdoctoral researcher in international relations and international political economy at Goethe-University Frankfurt. He is working on global hierarchies and Africa-EU relations with a particular focus on money and finance. He did extensive fieldwork for his book *The Practice of Humanitarian Intervention* (2016) and has published in journals such as the *European Journal of International Relations, Globalizations, Journal of Cultural Economy,* and others.

Tomas Max Martin is a researcher at Dignity: Danish Institute against Torture in Copenhagen, Denmark, where he is currently working on legacies of detention in Myanmar. He is an international leading expert on prison management and social life in detention. His work has been published in several edited volumes and in the anthropological journal *Focaal.*

Klaus Schlichte is a professor of international relations and world society at the University of Bremen, Germany. His main English publications are The Dynamics of States (ed., Aldershot 2005) and In the Shadow of Violence (2009). He has carried out research on political violence and political domination in Serbia, France, Senegal, Mali, Germany, and Uganda. His work also appeared in Revue de Synthèse, Armed Forces and Society, European

Journal of Sociology, International Political Sociology, Geopolitics, and other German and English social science journals.

Mario Schmidt is a postdoctoral fellow at the a.r.t.e.s. Graduate School for the Humanities at the University of Cologne. He has published in several journals, including Africa, Journal of Eastern African Studies, Ethnohistory, and HAU: Journal of Ethnographic Theory. Currently, he attempts to excavate the interdisciplinary potential between anthropology and behavioral economics. He is also interested in scrutinizing the economic strategies of educated but unemployed migrants living in Nairobi's tenement housing. Mario's latest book *Money Counts: Revisiting Economic Calculation*, coedited with Dr. Sandy Ross, has been published by Berghahn in 2020.

www.ingramcontent.com/pod-product-compliance
Lightning Source LLC
Chambersburg PA
CBHW030649270326
41929CB00007B/279